To: Elaine Giles,

With appreciation for all you have done for the family over the years and for being such a good friend.

Love, Jocelyn & Nevelle

CALLED TO BE A SURGEON

Not For Bread Alone

AUTOBIOGHAPHY BY NEVILLE K. CONNOLLY,

MA, MD, FRCS, FACS, FAAP

AuthorHouse™
1663 Liberty Drive
Bloomington, IN 47403
www.authorhouse.com
Phone: 1-800-839-8640

© 2009 Neville K. Connolly, M.D. All rights reserved.

No part of this book may be reproduced, stored in a retrieval system, or transmitted by any means without the written permission of the author.

First published by AuthorHouse 11/4/2009

ISBN: 978-1-4490-3429-0 (e)
ISBN: 978-1-4490-3427-6 (sc)
ISBN: 978-1-4490-3428-3 (hc)

Library of Congress Control Number: 2009910196

Printed in the United States of America
Bloomington, Indiana

This book is printed on acid-free paper.

This book is dedicated to the three ladies who have most influenced my life:

My Mother, Kathleen Maud (Kitty), who taught me Christian principles and values, was always there to help and support me with nonjudgmental love.

My first wife, Agnes, gave me unstinted love, and through her brave, uncomplaining and overcoming attitude toward her disabilities taught me real "empathy".

My second wife, Jocelyn whose love and outstanding capabilities, amongst other things, have enabled me to have a farm where we can take care of horses and I can live in the country which I have always wished to do.

Trust in the LORD, and do good; so shalt thou dwell in the land, and verily thou shalt be fed. Delight thyself also in the LORD; and he shall give thee the desires of thine heart.

Psalm 37 3-4

PREFACE

This book details the upbringing which led me to want to become a physician with the primary objective of caring for people in need of help. It details the somewhat unusual path down which this ambition led me. The influence of World War II and its sequelae on the whole practice of medicine has been remarkable. The sixty odd years that I have been able to observe this have been years of continuous change with great historical importance.

Having started in England without any intention of working anywhere else, various circumstances led me to an international training and ultimately to emigration to the United States. I was started in English Boarding schools. By the beginning of 1939, while finishing my last year at my "Public School", I won a scholarship to Kings College Cambridge where I started my training as a doctor. Life at English schools immediately prior to World War II seems historically important. As a medical student I was deferred from the draft until I graduated as a doctor. This allowed me to continue my studies at Cambridge. The University was a fascinating place to be at the start of the war. While it tried to preserve as many of its old traditions as possible it had to succumb to the inevitable changes of the altered circumstances. It was extremely interesting, particularly with hind-sight, to realize that this was a time when lasting changes in the whole atmosphere of the university were starting. What it was before and how it tried to hang onto its traditions had to be lived through to be appreciated. Many undergraduates had to leave to serve the country, as did many of the dons (faculty). There were enough left to carry on most of the traditions. War seemed to affect those who remained surprising little, though food was rationed and fuel was in short supply. We were all prepared to repel any Germans who landed with what arms we could get hold of. No one that I knew of was prepared to surrender alive.

In 1940-41 the Rockefeller Institute in the USA decided that it would bring 30 medical students a year to the USA to continue their education there. Prior to the war it had taken post graduate fellows for advanced work but, because there were none of these available, due to their being in the Armed Services, and because some of the English medical schools had been disrupted by the bombing, it decided to give these fellowships to undergraduate medical students. These were to be awarded on the basis of interview and record. I was fortunate to be elected and sent to Harvard Medical School.

Having arrived at Harvard, I was just in time to see the school go through the throes of coping with the country's entry into the war in December 1942, after 'Pearl Harbor'. It was an interesting transition because the authorities decided to speed up the medical curriculum by cutting it from four to three years. This could be accomplished by cutting most of the vacations but not the teaching. The thing that impressed me most was the contrast between the English and the American systems of education. I have tried to discuss some of these and outlined my experiences of life as a neophyte in a strange country. As soon as I graduated from medical school I was obligated, as a condition of my studentship, to return to England to finish at my English medical school. This entailed passing my final exams at Cambridge.

After I got back to England and had graduated from Cambridge, I started on my post graduate training with the hopes of becoming a pediatric surgeon. I have recounted that training in some detail and outlined some of the prospects in store for me. I had to do my national service which I did in the RAF Medical Corps and was demobilized just at the time the National Health Service was introduced. This gave me an opportunity to work in this service at its inception and to realize how good it could be. From a surgical career point of view the acquisition of a permanent appointment as a consultant was somewhat chancy. After a great deal of heart-searching I decided to return to the USA and to try my luck there. I have outlined some of the problems that I encountered while trying to obtain a license to practice and to adjust to the very different atmosphere of surgical practice which I found in Washington, DC. Professionally I encountered the problems of trying to introduce pediatric surgery as a specialty The need for such a specialty was not generally appreciated at that time in that area.

After 40 or more years in this new atmosphere I have been increasingly disillusioned both by the way circumstances have altered the distribution of medical care and by the deterioration of the ideals of medical practice. These have been forced upon doctors by outside interference, financial, political and legal. They are worth discussing and I have tried to do so. Finally I have made some suggestions as to how I think this situation could be improved. It is a very personal narrative and the opinions, judgments and recommendations are my own.

About The Author
Neville K. Connolly

The author had the unique experience of undergoing a medical education and then the practice of surgery both in England and the United States at the end of World War II, and for forty or so years thereafter. He believed that the practice of medicine was a "calling" similar to that of the priesthood.

He has advanced medical-surgical degrees. In England, MB.BChir from Cambridge University and a Fellowship from the Royal College of Surgeons. In the US, he has an MD from Harvard Medical School and a Fellowship from the American College of Srgeons and the American Academy of Pediatrics. His Residency training was in England under the National Health Service at the time of its inception. Because of the relative lack of specialties in England at that time, his experience in General and Pediatric Surgery was broad ranged and encompassing.

About The Book

This autobiography compares my medical training, both in England and the United States, and portrays the complications of trying to combine two different traditions regarding the practice of surgery on the two sides of the Atlantic. Tremendous changes have occurred with regard to medical knowledge since the end of the Second World War which has had a profound effect on the attitude of the doctors and the circumstances of their practices. How this played out in my life accounts for some interesting tensions. Yet I adhered to my original ideals throughout and still believe the practice of medicine to be a "calling". Regrettably many factors beyond the doctor's control have made the business aspects of medical practice of vital importance to too many of them.

Chapter 1

HOW IT ALL BEGAN

After the sun went down, a glow continued to be visible in the West. It had to be the first evidence of America. After sailing for 10 or more days across the Atlantic in convoy, it was a welcome relief. The convoy had sailed without lights except for the absolute minimum necessary to prevent collisions, so this glow suggested that we were nearly at our destination.

1942 was not a very safe time to cross the Atlantic Ocean as the U-boats were very active. The destroyer escorts were reassuring but in no way a guarantee. I had boarded the freighter bound for New York in Liverpool. Among the other passengers was one with whom I became quite friendly. I found myself sitting next to him at meals. He told me that he was returning across the Atlantic to pick up another ship. On his last trip the ship on which he was the First Mate had been torpedoed and had sunk under him. This was hardly a reassuring start for the crossing, though his cavalier attitude to the danger had a soothing effect. These merchant marine sailors were astonishingly brave and England owes them a tremendous debt of gratitude. Without their refusal to be cowed by the dangers and continuing hazard of sailing the Atlantic, the supplies that were so urgently needed in Britain could never have been delivered.

On the first night out the weather in the Irish Sea was sufficiently rough to spoil my appetite. My table companion assured me that it was essential to eat and that this was the best way to minimize seasickness. We were served Spotted Dick which is boiled pastry stuffed with raisins. After I had managed to eat it, I realized how right he was. The pudding was so heavy that it was impossible for me to bring it back up. By the next morning I felt fine and had no more queasiness.

Now there was land in sight at last. The glow in the western sky was reminiscent of the glow of London seen from the suburbs when it was burning as a result of the German bombs. We thought that we would be in New York early next morning. This was not the case because we were coming in from the north east and had to sail all the next day down Long Island Sound before swinging into New York Harbor late in the evening. The brightness that was visible 24 hours out to sea was the browned out lights of New York.

That night the ship anchored off the Statue of Liberty. It was a wonderful opportunity to appreciate the skyline and the lights of the city. Coming from a country that had been "blacked out" for three years, it was most impressive. A sense of awe and of excitement kept many of us on deck in the warmth of that July night. It had taken almost two weeks in convoy to cross the Atlantic and the expectation that we would be safe on dry land the next morning was a welcome relief.

I, and several of my colleagues, was traveling to accept medical studentships donated by the Rockefeller Foundation. Prior to World War II, this Foundation had awarded Fellowships to medical graduates so that they could continue their studies. Now there were no available medical graduates to whom to award these fellowships as they had all been drafted into the armed services. The Foundation decided that the medical schools in England had been disrupted by the bombing and that it would spend the fellowship money to bring twenty five medical students each year to the States to study at American medical schools. After their graduation, they were to return to England where they were expected to take (and pass) their exams at their English universities. I was lucky enough to be one of the beneficiaries of this generosity.

After that initial night in New York harbor we disembarked and called the Rockefeller Institute. We were told to take a taxi to the Hotel Iroquois where we were to be met by a Dr. Lambert. He was our official sponsor and was responsible for briefing us as to our next moves. It was a Saturday and we were not expected to move on to our final destinations until Monday. Dr. Lambert took charge of us until we were to move on to our allotted medical schools. He gave us a brief tour of parts of New York including the view from the roof of the Rockefeller Center. While at the Center we were taken to a show and appreciated the precision and other aspects of the Rockettes, a famous high-kicking chorus line. Afterwards he took us to a local restaurant where we were devastated by the variety and quantity of food available. After three years of rationing it was unbelievable. Two things with regard to that meal were particularly memorable. We all had a dessert which consisted of half a cantaloupe filled with ice-cream and raspberries, unbelievable luxury. The other was that when the time came for the bill which the Rockefeller representative picked up, one of the attractive waitresses took the opportunity to slip a note with her telephone number to the most handsome member of our group. We thought that this was the epitome of hospitality. What came of the invitation, I did not inquire. On Monday we were each given our travel instructions by Dr. Lambert as we were all going off to different Medical Schools. I was to catch the afternoon train to Boston where I was to join Harvard Medical School.

Some explanation is necessary to account for how I came to be in this situation in the first place. Having been brought up in England as a member of a very strict religious sect known as the Plymouth Brethren I had relatively little experience of worldly things. They were all taboo; no cinemas, theaters or other temptations that would lead me astray. My father had joined this sect later in his life and was much less strict than some of the other members. Consequently my upbringing was more liberal than for some of the other boys in this sect.

At the age of sixteen my father had to make his way in London after leaving his nine younger siblings in Dublin. He was adamant that I should have as good an education as he could afford. He wanted me to have the advantages that he had struggled so hard to achieve. Starting from nothing he had obtained a law degree from Gray's Inn, one of Britain's foremost legal institutions. To do this he had to work two jobs in order to make the money required for the law courses. Amongst other things he taught calculus at the Polytechnic in the evening although he had never had a course in this subject. He had to read it up the night before each class. During this period he had joined the Civil Service and was working in the Inland Revenue Department (IRS). He was assigned to the City of London where his duties included checking the taxes paid by the big businesses centered there. He told me of a very interesting experience that he had. He was sent to the House of Rothschild, the headquarters of that financial institution, to explain an error that they had made when paying their taxes. He was shown into the palatial office of Mr. Rothschild himself. My father introduced himself rather apologetically. He had to explain that the House of Rothschild had overpaid their taxes by a little over one million pounds that year, a very considerable sum in those days. The old man looked up and said, "Young man, forget it. The country needs the money". This was during World War I. It is a story that deserves to be better known.

After the war my father was transferred from the Treasury to the Air Ministry when that was first formed in 1919. This was the civil side of the newly formed Royal Air Force and was responsible for its administration and finances. In 1923 his work necessitated his serving abroad first in Baghdad, (Mesopotamia) for three years and, after a year in England, in Egypt for another five years. He had married my mother in 1918. She came from a Protestant English family who lived in Dublin where her father worked for the British Government. It was a very large and musical family with nine surviving to adult life. They had a double quartet that sang anthems and sacred music on Sunday evenings with my mother playing the piano. She had never had a musical lesson but her older sister did and my mother listened in. Mother had much more talent and learned to read music and practiced. My father had met her before he left Dublin and kept in touch with her. This was very smart of him as she was an exceptional lady and very gifted. She was utterly unselfish and was affectionately admired by everyone she met. She proved to be a devoted loving wife for the rest of his life. I was born in 1920. When my father was sent to Baghdad my mother was not permitted to go with him as the British Government did not consider it safe to allow wives there. My mother had a brother who was in the R.A.F and also stationed in Mesopotamia. His wife with her two boys joined up with my mother and spent this period at Paignton on the English south coast. One of my cousins was almost exactly my age so we became very close. During World War II he joined the R.A.F. and was sent to Singapore. When the Japanese took Singapore in 1942 there was great confusion. The British evacuated as many as they could. But what happened to many of the troops remains a mystery to this day. My cousin, Dennis, was one of those missing and we do not know what happened to him. His mother never truly recovered from his loss. The mental agony of not knowing exactly what happened to him can only be appreciated by other parents of soldiers missing in action and never accounted for. My aunt had frequent nightmares for the rest of her life though she controlled her grief remarkably so that she always appeared cheerful and ready to help others.

Naturally, after three years forcible separation from my father, my mother was anxious to join him when he was sent to Egypt. There was a conflict between my parents married life and my education. I was expected to have an English education in England. A compromise was reached. My mother stayed in London for a year and I went to a day school there, Colet Court, where I had started as soon as my father returned from Baghdad. At the end of that school year, I left the day school in London to spend three months with my parents in Cairo. A tutor was engaged to teach me French. This was a disaster as I was an unwilling and inept pupil. All I learned during those three months was how to swim and how to be a thoroughly mischievous little boy around the country club. On returning to England

I was enrolled in boarding school so that my mother could rejoin my father during the winters.

The school, Lynchmere, I went to was a very small one in Eastbourne on the South Coast. There were only thirty other boys and their ages ranged from 7 to 14. It was run by a most remarkable man, Mr. Gilbert, who taught almost all the classes himself. I was 10 years old when I went there and I found it a rude awakening. I was older than the other new boys and had to establish my position in the pecking order. This necessitated my having to "belt fight" with an older boy. Since this consisted of beating each other with the buckle end of the belt with only a light towel as a shield it was a somewhat painful experience. Since I survived this experience without breaking down or complaining I was accepted. Almost as soon as I arrived the headmaster asked me, in class, what he had just said. I had not been paying sufficient attention and could not answer him. I was dragged up and beaten on the hands with a ruler in front of the rest of the class. I am not sure whether the pain or the humiliation was the worst part. The lesson was most salutary. I do not think I missed another word he said for the next four years. Besides being a stickler for demanding attention, Mr. Gilbert demanded that everyone speak up loudly and enunciate clearly. This was a lesson that stood me in good stead thereafter. Every Sunday evening the headmaster Mr. Gilbert, used to gather us in his study and read to us from classics such as The Cloister and the

Hearth and Les Miserables, which he condensed as he went along.

He was a very original character in many ways. He was convinced that little boys would be much healthier if they were toughened up. We were allowed only two thin blankets on our beds and all the windows had to be open, even in the coldest weather. Getting into bed on cold nights was an ordeal. One solution was to go in head first and blow until the bottom of the bed had the chill off it, then turn round, curl up in a fetal position and get to sleep. One of the students was a delicate boy, according to his mother. He had always been sickly. Gilbert refused to make any compromises for him. He had to be treated as every other boy. During the time that he was there he never had a day's sickness. Gilbert may have been unconventional but his methods worked. Besides the grassy area at the side of the school where we played some games, there was a separate playing field a short distance away. Most of the care of this field devolved upon the boys. This included the mowing which was done by multiple wheel blade mowers towed behind a model T Ford. A twelve year old boy found it great fun to be detailed to drive this. This school not only provided an excellent basic education in the fundamentals, but was a real character building experience. Besides the normal games such as soccer and cricket we were taken on walks over the Downs nearby and to run with the local Harriers in the Pevensey marshes where we had to pole jump some of the streams that ran through them.

During the summer holidays my mother took me to join my father in Switzerland. We stayed either in Vevey at the eastern end of the lake of Geneva or at a chalet up in the mountains nearby. These were memorable times for me with many long walks with my parents on the mountain paths. There were wonderful teas with jam and cream cakes at chalets up in the mountains. While we were in Vevey my parents found a roller skating rink where they turned me loose. Besides the wonderful sightseeing I learned to become quite proficient on roller skates. On one occasion we were having dinner in the hotel when I noticed a fellow diner eating his peas in a most unusual way. He picked them up on his knife and ran them down the length of his knife into his mouth. I was fascinated, watching to see if he would drop any, which he never did. I was rebuked by my parents for staring but could not take my eyes off this phenomenal trick. I was sent to bed without dessert.

In England at that time the school system was complicated. There were local schools which were free, Grammar Schools where the fees were subsidized by the local government and therefore relatively cheap, and private schools. The Grammar schools varied in reputation and some were very prestigious, producing very famous graduates. Basically the private schools consisted of two units. There were those who took children from ages 7 to 14 and were known as Preparatory Schools. After the age of 14, the student moved on to a 'Public School'. It spite of the name it was 'private' in that the parents had to pay the full costs. Neither of these two groups of private institutions was coeducational. The private school system was expected to be used by most children of the upper or upper middle class. My father, as a rising Civil Servant, was expected to use this method. It was reputed to provide a better education though this assumption was not universally true.

When the time came for me to move on to the next school, the Public School, Mr. Gilbert persuaded my parents that I was bright enough to try for a scholarship. Such a scholarship would relieve my parents of some of the expenses associated with a private school. I tried for one offered by Harrow, the school in London that Winston Churchill had attended, but was unsuccessful. Gilbert then suggested that I try for one at a relatively new school, Canford, which was situated in the country near Wimborne in Dorsetshire. He drove me with another boy from a nearby Preparatory school to see the school and to be interviewed. The other boy turned out to be Christopher Milne, the Christopher of Winnie the Pooh. I was sorry for him as I thought that it must be very difficult to live with that background in a school where one is bound to be teased unmercifully. When I saw Canford School I fell in love with it immediately. Christopher Milne was much less impressed and never did apply to go there. This school was for boarders and was set in an old country house, the origins of which dated back to John of Gaunt in the 14th century. John of Gaunt was the third son of Edward the Third, and by a complicated set of circumstances, the founder of the Lancastrian claimants to the throne. His kitchen still survives amongst the school buildings. The story goes that there is a secret passage from this kitchen leading underground to an old oak tree in the grounds known as Mount-joy Oak (pronounced Mungy). Presumably it could have been used as an escape route if the house was besieged during the Wars of the Roses. Though the Kitchen is still there and so is Mount-joy Oak, with one side filled with concrete, no one has found the secret passage.

Canford School Dorsetshire, England

The school used the local village church as its chapel. It had been built right after the Norman Conquest. When seen on a moonlit night, sited as it is amongst the ancient yew bushes and the tombstones, it was a truly eerie place. It was easy to conjure up all kinds of ghosts. Most of the school buildings had been rebuilt in the late 19th century by Lord Wimborne. It was said that he and his family had acquired a fortune making nuts and bolts. His motto, carved into the stone of one of the entrance gates, was Ferro non Gladio. (By Iron not the Sword). His family, the Guests, sold the place and it was converted into the school in 1923. The grounds were superb with a river on one side and acres of playing fields on the other. The main playing field had been laid out by the Guests who were great polo players. It was absolutely flat and was regarded as one of the best cricket pitches in southern England. The cricket pitch itself was in the center of this area and was sacrosanct. None but the cricket players and the grounds men were allowed on it. It was known as 'God's Acre'. Around the cricket pitch there was enough room for two field hockey pitches. These were superb to play on but were so smooth that we found ourselves at a disadvantage when we had to play away games against other schools whose grounds were less perfect. Beyond the playing fields was a moor 12 miles square that was open for horseback rides. The school had stables and horses. Students, for an extra fee, could take riding classes. I bargained with my father that if I got a scholarship which would help to pay the expenses of the school, I would be allowed to take riding as an extra. I got the scholarship and the riding.

Canford Village Church
(Used by the School for a Chapel)

"God's Acre" Canford School Playing Field

While I was there, the school acquired a riding master. He had been in charge of an army cavalry school and was an experienced riding instructor. He arranged for the school to house Metropolitan Police horses, which were reserves, provided we kept them schooled. This meant that they had to be taken out every morning and put through their paces. Though this was really a dressage course, it did not preclude schooling them in jumping. It was excellent training for the riders as well as the horses. In the afternoons they were allowed to be taken on trails and across country. They were superb horses and we found them to be excellent jumpers.

Shortly after the Captain, the new riding master, took charge we went out onto the moors one afternoon. He had not been on the moors himself and was anxious to explore them. When we arrived for him to inspect them and explore them, he said to the group of riders with him, "You see that chimney in the distance. Go straight to it as fast as you can". This was a wonderful invitation for a bunch of young Turks. I was mounted on a beautiful young mare and off we went. There was a big solid mound ahead about five foot high and six foot wide. The correct technique is for the horse to jump on top with the forelegs, change feet on the top and leap off. This requires careful balancing on the part of the rider as it is really two jumps in one. However, Nemoins, my horse, thought that this was unnecessary so she cleared the whole obstacle cleanly; a feat which, though satisfying, was rather disconcerting. For some of the riders another privilege was granted. With the permission of the masters concerned with a student's academic accomplishments, the student was allowed one day off during the term to go fox hunting. The local hounds, the Portman Hunt, met in the neighboring parts of Dorsetshire. On one occasion they actually met at the school itself. Otherwise they usually met near enough for us to be able to hack to the meets. I managed to go once each term in my last years there. We were extremely well mounted with the horses that we were keeping in trim for the Metropolitan Police. I remember one time when the hounds ran beside a field where they were putting up jumps for a steeple chase. Some of us were unable to resist the temptation to take our horses over the course. Though we accomplished the jumps without any trouble our efforts gained us a severe rebuke. Two other episodes remain clearly in my mind. Cantering along a hedgerow my mare put her foot in a rabbit hole causing her to stumble onto her knees. I went over her head onto my head. Fortunately I was wearing a reinforced bowler hat and was not hurt. After remounting and catching up with the rest of the hunt, people started laughing at me. The cause of their amusement was the big dent in my hat where I had landed on a stone. That hat had saved me from serious injury. The other mishap occurred when we were galloping along a path in a wood and came to a wide puddle. Neither the horse nor I realized that there was a stream in the middle of the puddle. She put her forelegs into the middle of the supposed puddle only to find there was no ground under her. She recovered herself but not before I had flown over her head landing full length in the rest of the puddle, getting wet and dirty. The remainder of that day was most uncomfortable and hacking home, still wet and cold, was torture

On the occasion when the Portman Hunt met at the school there were a number of visitors who came and parked their cars in the grounds. My house-master, Mr. Tireman, owned a Rolls Royce of which he was extremely proud. The Chaplain, Mr. Penny, owned an old Austin. He had found a Rolls Royce radiator which he attached to his battered Austin. He proceeded to park this beside Mr.

T's genuine Rolls. Mr. T was not amused but the students were, and approved of the Chaplain's sense of humor. He was over six foot tall and had been a rowing blue at his university and while at the school became engaged to a rather small lady, Miss Farthing. The Penny Farthing union caused some amusement.

There was another activity available for the riders, which was quite unique to this school. It was called 'vaulting'. It consisted of riding bareback with only a girth which had handles on it. The rider could slide off the horse, bounce on the ground either from side to side or back onto the horse's back. The faster the horse went the easier it was to vault. By encouraging the horse to canter and running beside it, it was easy to catch the pommel (the handle on the girth) and swing up onto the horse's back. The normal way to mount was to stand facing the horse's rear, catch hold of the pommel and swing up. One somewhat mischievous horse soon learned what we were doing. He would wait until one's back was turned, then spin his head round and nip the rear end of the potential rider. Everyone except the rider thought that this was very amusing. We learned to stand on the horse when it was both trotting and cantering. This was easiest if one stood over the rump. The final accomplishment was to stand on the horse while going over a jump. Another activity was to stand on one's head on the horse. This was remarkably easy as one could put one's shoulder on the withers, hang onto the pommels and have a three point base. The school became known to the equestrian pundits because of these gymnastic tricks. The school was invited to send a team to the Royal Horse Show in London in 1938. To my disappointment, though a member of the team, I could not go because the Show coincided with my scholarship exam at Cambridge. Our team alternated with the Russian Cossacks who were demonstrating their trick riding prowess. We were astonished at their ability to stand on the horse while taking a jump at full gallop. We found out that they had a small wire rope attached to the front of their saddles which gave them a firm grip. Talking with them, our team found that they were equally admiring of our ability to stand without that support.

At Canford I was reasonably successful both at work and at games. There was much emphasis put on athletic activities but the work was not neglected. Having started at the bottom of the ladder, being curator or fag for the senior boys, I became the employer myself as Head of my house and a school prefect. There was almost no bullying of the junior boys by the time I arrived, contrary to what is related in many of the older books about English Public Schools. Curating for the older boys required a certain amount of menial chores such as cleaning shoes, fetching and carrying, but insufficient to be a real hardship. Discipline was quite strict and basically maintained by the boys themselves. Minor offenses were punished by penal runs but for more serious offenses the senior boys, the prefects, were allowed to beat the offenders using a tennis shoe. This shoe was frequently modified to make it a more effective implement but never enough to make it really damaging. Permission had to be obtained from the housemaster before a beating could be administered. The miscreant had the right to appeal. Serious offenses were dealt with by either the housemaster or the headmaster. There was a nearby school, Bryanston, which had abolished beating. We got to know some of the boys there through playing games against them. They confessed to being jealous of the fact that we were beaten for our offenses when they were forced to run to the entrance gates of the school and back, a matter of two miles, in a prescribed time. They seemed to think that a swift beating was preferable to a prolonged run. None of my contemporaries seem to think that their psyches were damaged by what has become considered a primitive and brutal assault.

At Canford all the boys were compelled to take formal exercise every afternoon. Usually there were games, according to the season. We had rugby in the autumn, field hockey in the spring and cricket in the summer. The school was divided into six houses and these played against each other and each had several teams according to age and ability. The games took place every afternoon after lunch and before the afternoon classes which started at 4 PM. There was considerable rivalry between the houses and various inter-house competitions. My house was not noted for its athletic prowess but it often won the prize for academic success. Besides these house teams we had school teams which played against other schools. Consequently there was almost always a team for each boy to play in. We also had squash courts, tennis courts and the river to swim in. We had one of the few 'Royal Tennis' courts in England. This is now known usually as 'court' tennis. It is an interesting and difficult game played in an enclosed court with nets on one side and one end, sloping roofs which can be played off. It is played with balls made of tightly wound twine covered with sewn cloth. These are very hard and are hit with a lopsided racket like a heavy lawn tennis racket.

If a student was not included in a formal game he had to go for a cross country run. I hated running unless there was a ball to chase. One afternoon I had no formal game to play and so was supposed to go for a run. Just before I was ready to set out, the head of riding told me that there was a spare horse to be exercised that afternoon and would I go. I jumped at the opportunity and rode instead. The next day I was sent for by the school prefect who was in charge of games and told that since I had not been on the assigned run, I would be sent on a penal run. I was incensed as I thought that the order to ride had superseded the previous 'run' order. After undergoing the punishment I appealed to the headmaster. He was very sympathetic, told me it was most unjust but that it was an excellent lesson. It showed that life was full of injustices and the sooner one appreciated that the better.

In the light of our current mores and the various things that have been written in the past about the sexual activities that take place in all male public schools, I feel it is incumbent on me to state that in the five years that I was at this school I came across no overt homosexuality; masturbation, yes, but no sodomy.

The first two years at the school consisted of a general education with standard subjects. After this term there was an exam called a School Certificate. This was a National exam which was also a qualifying exam for university entrance, though it did not entitle the candidate to entrance to any specific university. Having passed that, the student entered the lower sixth form for a year and then on to the upper sixth. The teaching in these forms (grades) was intended to qualify the student for the Higher Certificate exam. This exam was more specialized, usually concentrating on three subjects. Those who passed it were almost certain to obtain a place at a University. Because of this concentration on major subjects I had to decide on the career which I wished to pursue.

Probably because of my religious upbringing, I felt that I needed to do something to help people. Though I was interested in things mechanical and was reasonably adept with my hands I did not think that engineering would satisfy my more altruistic motives. I decided that the practice of medicine would be a better solution. This was not an easy decision as I was a rather squeamish young man and was not certain that I would be able to stomach the surgical aspect of the training. I decided that the ultimate rewards would be worth the psychological trauma and that

I would go ahead. Consequently I concentrated on science, particularly biology, in my last years at school.

After passing enough exams to get into medical school I decided, with my parent's concurrence, that I would try for a scholarship to Cambridge University although this would require an extra year at school. During my last years, the school had acquired a new biology master, Mr. Dowdeswell, who had just graduated with honors from Oxford. He was a real enthusiast and a wonderful teacher. I sat the Scholarship exam and won an Exhibition to King's College, Cambridge. Each college awarded a major scholarship, a minor scholarship and an exhibition in each subject. There is a monetary value to each of these awards but this is liberally allocated according to the needs of the winners. If the major winner does not need the money he gets the honor but the money goes to a needy, though less academically successful, applicant. The exam consisted of writing five essays with a choice out of seven possible subjects and then an interview. When I returned to school I showed the questions to the biology master. We agreed that I knew quite a lot about four of the questions, but he wanted to know which question I had chosen for the fifth. I told him that I had chosen to write on 'Parental Care in Animals'. He was horrified as he assured me that I knew nothing about the subject. I happened to have read a book during a vacation in which the author related the fact that if one excised a specific endocrine gland from the bug Rodnius, whatever that is, it neglected its offspring. On this slender basis I wrote the essay suggesting that there could be a real hormonal influence on parental behavior. Several years later while chatting with one of the deans at King's College I asked him if he could remember why they had given me an exhibition. He told me that it was because of an essay I had written on parental care in animals and the concept was sufficiently interesting to intrigue them.

The award of the exhibition to King's was in the fall of 1938 for entry to the college in the fall of 1939. As a result I had to spend the rest of the year at school with no very specific academic requirements. Though I continued with biology, I had to take Latin, English and Philosophy as well. Since this was not a very busy schedule, I went to the art studio to try my hand at oil painting. My progress was so slow that the horse chestnut tree which was in full bloom when I started to paint it, had leaves which were a wonderful autumn copper color before I finished. My art teacher was the headmaster's wife, Mrs. Canning, a charming lady. Besides being an accomplished artist, she was a classical scholar and an Oxford graduate. Though I never achieved any artistic skills, it did give me a lasting appreciation of other's work.

The English teacher assigned to us did not know what to do with barbaric scientists, so he decided that we should read plays aloud in class, each taking a part. This was infinitely more fun than studying a play and analyzing it line by line as we had done in previous English classes. I acquired a lasting taste for this entertainment however; it never did improve my ability to write well. When I had returned to school after obtaining my Exhibition at King's and reported to the headmaster, his response was "What, in spite of your English." I well remember the report sent to my parents by one of my previous English teachers. It read, "Has a certain amount of native wit, but his style is barbaric." Unfortunately it is something that has not changed very much over the years.

Chapter 2

CAMBRIDGE 1939-1942

The summer vacation in 1939 was rudely interrupted by Hitler. I was due to go up to Cambridge at the end of September. The Government decided that medical students would be exempted from the draft until they were qualified as doctors. As a result I was told to report to Cambridge at once. When I got there I found that there were in residence at King's, my College, two or three other medical students and the Choral Scholars who come up early every term to sing in the choir. One of the other medical students with whom I shared a room had been a Chorister (a member of the King's boys' school which supplied the boys' section of the college choir). He knew the Choral Scholars and the Organ Scholar and introduced me to them. Until that time my musical education was sadly lacking. My mother was very musical and an excellent pianist although too shy to play anywhere but at home. I had listened to her playing and had some knowledge of classical piano music but that was all. My new friends were all brilliant musicians, particularly David Willcocks, the organ scholar. They had little or no interest in medicine and so I had to learn about their interests. It was fascinating to discover how much fun it could be if you were a brilliant enough musician and did not take yourself too seriously. David was rather shy but a real genius. It was said that when he was about nine years old he was being examined for a musical scholarship to a school. He was asked if he had written anything that he could sing for the examiner. He produced a piece. The examiner said that he would play it for David to sing. To which David replied that he thought that he had better play it himself as it was rather tricky. He got the scholarship anyway.

At King's there was a close camaraderie between the dons (faculty) and the undergraduates. Many of the extracurricular activities were shared, particularly the parties. During that first year the Organist, Boris Ord, was co-opted into the Air Force as an intelligence officer. I believe he was co-opted to help with the Enigma deciphering project. He was replaced by Harold Darke. Boris gave a party to introduce him to the choir. At that party they played musical games with Harold Darke playing the opening chords of various pieces of music. The members of the choir were expected to guess what they were. After a number of successes one chord stumped them all. David had been sitting quietly and offering no answers. Someone asked him if he did not know what the piece was. David, rather apologetically, said that it sounded like a specific piece but it was in the wrong key. Darke was most embarrassed and admitted that he had indeed played it in the wrong key. After one year David was called up for military service. He got his music degree in that one year although it is a three-year course. There are two parts to that course and he got first class honors in both, a feat unique and unlikely ever to be repeated. In the army he refused to accept a commission as a musician. He spent his spare time playing popular music in the messes for his fellow soldiers. When he had time off he would return to college and we would repair to the Chapel for David to play the organ. Someone asked him to play a specific Bach prelude and fugue. He had not seen it before but proceeded to play it, sight reading the score. At the end he was furious with himself as he said that he had misplayed one note on the foot pedals. None of us had noticed. Another time we asked him how much volume he could get out of the instrument. It was enough to rattle the windows of the Chapel. One night we were there and the Chapel was in darkness except for the organ loft over the screen. We had not noticed that there was an air raid warning. The next thing we were aware of was the appearance of one of the college porters. He came to tell us that the local authorities said we were making too much noise during an air raid. Then there was the evening we got one of the choral scholars, Sandy Forsyth, to go into the choir with a single candle and sing a solo with David's organ accompaniment. The rest of the Chapel was in darkness. Being in the Chapel at night with the only real light being the moon shining through the stained glass windows and the organ being played by a master is an experience that one can never forget. Such an opportunity is rare indeed. David has gone on to achieve a very distinguished musical career and has been knighted. It should be mentioned that David served as an infantry officer and was awarded medals for his distinguished leadership and bravery after he went ashore on D-Day where he held a vital area though losing half his men in the process.

War time at Cambridge was different and in many ways marked the beginning of a change that no one foresaw at that time. The old traditions were still preserved as much as circumstances allowed. Dinner in Hall was required. Sleeping in College was necessary for a stipulated number of nights in order to be eligible for a degree. Caps and gowns had to be worn after dark outside ones' own College. It was not until after the war that the changes became really noticeable. Immediately after the war the University was flooded with demobilized servicemen who were trying to catch up with their education. Then the Government entered the field, trying to open up the University to a wider range of applicants. I remember talking with Professor Dean who was the Master of Trinity Hall, another College, about the Government's plan to subsidize more students from other backgrounds. He complained that it was a waste of money because the University already had more scholarships than there were people worth giving them to. His contention was that there was a difference between a university and a trade school. The object of the former was to open the mind, to enable it to think for itself on a broad range of subjects rather than just to learn a specific subject. Often it was the extracurricular activities that were more important than the specific courses being taken. The personal contact between the students and the teachers, socially as well as academically, was the key. In many ways the College system allowed this to come to the fore. There was considerable variation among the colleges with regard to the intimacy of association between the Dons, (official teacher/administrators of the college) and the undergraduates. At Kings this was particularly well developed.

Colleges seem to attract groups of students specializing in specific subjects. Gonville and Caius always had a large number of medical students. Kings tended to concentrate on those studying Classics, English, Music and the Arts. As a result the medical student at King's was forced to socialize with people who had little interest in the sciences. The extracurricular activities that were so readily available and so tempting were excellent for broadening the mind of a medical student. Because the Colleges are independent organizations within the University, they tend, within limits, to have their own rules and admission standards. They were originally founded and endowed by specific donors as places for students of the University to live. Most were so generously endowed that they were independently wealthy. It is reputed that a few centuries ago there was a student of Queens College who promised to leave it a bequest in his will. Later he quarreled with the college, but rather than renege on his promise, he left the college a large tract of swampy land. This turned out to be Southampton

Water where, later on, the harbor and docks were built. It became a vast source of money for the College. Various other endowments to colleges have developed into very substantial financial holdings. King's was founded by King Henry VI, a somewhat unbalanced religious eccentric. He also founded Eton. The association between the two foundations remains close even now. Until about one hundred and fifty years ago King's College was closed to all but old Etonians (graduates of Eton College). Furthermore, attendance for three years at King's in those days entitled one to a degree whether one passed an exam or not. Such discrimination did not last into a more enlightened age. It is an interesting example of the autonomy that the colleges had in the past.

While the University organizes the courses and is responsible for providing the teachers, it is the colleges that advise the students with regard to these courses. The vast majority of the University teachers are members of one or other of the Colleges. The University runs the examinations which occur at the end of each year. Except for the medical students who have oral exams after they have finished dissecting each part of the body, there are no exams until the end of the year. These Finals are very important as they determine the type of degree that is obtained. The lowest degree is a pass. It used to be almost impossible to fail completely. The story goes that one examiner regretted that he could not give even a pass to a candidate because that candidate could not spell his own name correctly.

More prestigious accomplishments at the exams are graded into four categories. The lowest of these is a Third; the Seconds are divided in to 2/2s and 2/1s. The top class is the First. The grading system is entirely different from that which I observed when I got to Harvard Medical School. A pass at Cambridge was obtained by achieving a 30% mark, while a First represented a mark of 70% or above. Such a mark was given to relatively few. It must be remembered that all the exams were in the form of essay questions. There was no True or False or multiple choice questions. Consequently much depended on the examiner who had to read all the essay answers. The system is open to the prejudices of the examiner and requires a great deal of time-consuming work. On the other hand, it has the potential of allowing the examiner to judge the thinking of the candidate. To get the highest mark it was necessary to write something original that would interest the examiner. It was said at one time that women obtained a very high percentage of 2/1s but very few Firsts. This was because they were very good at learning what was taught but did not do well at original thinking. Time has shown that this concept was totally misguided because nowadays, percentage wise, at least as many female undergraduates as males get Firsts.

Before World War II there was a distinctly anti-feminist attitude at Cambridge. There were two colleges for women,

Newnham and Girton. Their members could attend the University lectures though in the 19th century they had to be chaperoned. They could sit the Tripos exams (the final exams referred to above) but they could not receive an official degree. Now they have become full members of the University and the all male colleges have thrown open their doors. This has led to a number of very significant changes. In my day women were not allowed in college after 10 PM and you had to be in your own college by 10 PM or pay a fine. This necessitated devising ways of climbing in over spikes, barbed wire or walls covered with broken glass. Many of these methods were traditional, well known and winked at by the authorities. My tutor at King's, Donald Beves, explained his method when he was an undergraduate. He would hire a Hansom Cab and get the driver to stop along the wall of the college in a narrow lane between King's and St. Catherine's. After paying him off, he would climb onto the roof of the cab, throw his gown onto the top of the wall to protect him from the broken glass on the top and climb over.

The segregation of the sexes now seems to be very old fashioned but it had its merits. It certainly enhanced the value of the ladies as far as the males were concerned. There was insufficient familiarity to breed contempt. At that time the rules of the University with regard to the behavior of the undergraduates were enforced by the University itself. To do this there was a system of Proctors appointed from Fellows of the colleges. Each Proctor had two Bullers.

These Bullers were chosen from the college servants and were noted for their athletic abilities. The proctors could exercise their authority in the town but not in the colleges themselves. The rules that they enforced most frequently concerned the wearing of caps and gowns when out after dark. In an old-fashioned attempt to enforce some morality the Proctors were entitled to request an introduction to any female companion who was with an undergraduate. There are two stories, the truth of which I cannot substantiate. An undergraduate was stopped with a young lady on his arm. When the Proctor asked to be introduced, the young man said that she was his sister. The Proctor said, "Don't you know that she is one of the most notorious young ladies in town". The reply was "There is no need to advertise the family misfortunes". The other relates to a Proctor who had a somewhat unsavory reputation. When he stopped an undergraduate and asked to be introduced to the young lady he was with, he was greeted with the reply; "Never! I only introduce my sister to gentlemen." Because the Proctors authority did not extend into the colleges themselves any miscreant undergraduate who could run into a college was safe. This led to an interesting situation. Outside the main entrance of Kings College is an area about 20 ft wide with a lawn surrounded by a low wall. In the center, in front of the main gate which is closed at 10 PM, is a cobbled area between the gate and the road. This area officially belongs to Kings. Anyone in this area, known as the Cobbles of Kings, was outside the jurisdiction of the University Proctors. On one famous occasion an undergraduate ran to the cobbles hotly pursued by a Proctor and his Bullers. There he sat on the wall and waited. Since he could not get into any college but his own after 10 PM the Proctor decided to wait him out. There they sat until just before midnight when the undergraduate got up, rang the bell and went into Kings where he belonged. The University authorities were not amused and requested the Provost of Kings to allow them to exercise their authority over the Cobbles of Kings. The Provost refused this request but agreed to allow them to exercise HIS authority there. (The Provost of Kings is the equivalent of the Master or Head of any other College).

If one was out late one was fined. Between 10 PM and 11pm it was six shillings and eight pence (One third of a pound). Between 11 PM and midnight it was double that. After midnight one was required to see the tutor the next day. At Kings we did not have to pay these gate fines. The story goes that one day an undergraduate was running up the lane between Kings and the Senate House to get into Kings before the 10 PM fine would be in force. As he rounded the corner he knocked down an old lady. Being a gentleman as well as a King's man, he stopped, picked her up and dusted her off. She inquired as to why he was in such a hurry. He explained that he was trying to avoid a fine for being late. Subsequently she left in her will an endowment to pay for the gate fines at Kings so, in my day, we never had to pay any.

With a university dating back for so many centuries there remain many archaic rules which have never been rescinded. Some undergraduates have taken a delight in finding these and exercising their long forgotten rights. I believe that, as a Scholar, I was entitled to play Marbles on the Senate House steps. I never tried it. One of the more famous archaic rules concerned the right to practice archery. In the days when archery was an important aspect of English power, it was liberally encouraged. Undergraduates were allowed to have a small street called Petit Curie cleared on Saturday for archery practice. A group of undergraduates decided to exercise this privilege and informed the authorities. Times had changed and Petit Curie had become a narrow and very busy street, particularly on Saturdays. The Proctors duly cleared the street and the butts and targets were set up. The undergraduates dressed up in green and practiced. They considered their activities a major triumph until the Monday morning when they were summoned to appear before the authorities. It was noted that the statute stated that the archers were required to wear Lincoln green and it was decided that their green was not Lincoln. They were fined and the statute repealed.

Before World War II there was always a major celebration on Guy Fawkes Night, November the Fifth, to remember the attempt that was made to blow up the Houses of Parliament during the reign of James I. This celebration got very unruly at times and the Market Place was a center of activities. In the middle of the Market

Place is a stone cross over a small fountain. One year the Proctors decided that they would cordon off the Market Place and only allow two people at a time to cross it. An enterprising undergraduate got word of this plan. He went around the county and bought up all the calcium carbide that he could find. He distributed this to his friends. That evening, November the Fifth, these friends crossed the Market Place in couples and surreptitiously tossed the calcium carbide into the fountain. The last couple flicked a match in. The resulting conflagration was magnificent and its scars can still be seen today.

There is, or was, a bicycle made for four available for rent in Cambridge. On Nov 11, Armistice Day, the end of World War I, undergraduates frequently collected money for charities by selling Poppies. On one occasion four enterprising members of a College Choir, not Kings I hasten to add rented this bicycle. They dressed up in clerical collars and proceeded to cycle around the town, stopping to sing in harmony the bawdiest songs imaginable. When they passed the plate around, they are reputed to have raised a considerable sum.

To me, my three years at Cambridge were a most significant part of growing up. They were each very different. I went up from school where I had been quite successful both academically and athletically. Because of my religious upbringing, I was naive and unsophisticated. I still belonged to the Plymouth Brethren and was expected to attend their services every Sunday. Such High Church activities as went on in King's College Chapel were an anathema to the Brethren. To me the beauty of the building and the music were most appealing. Perhaps it was here that I first began to question the narrow views of the Brethren. Subsequently I came to realize that their exclusivity was far removed from truly Christian ideals and I became a member of the Church of England. But this conversion took time.

When I first went up there was not room for me to live in the college and I had to stay in a lodging house outside the college. Very soon the college started to empty as more and more of the undergraduates were called up for active duty. I applied as vigorously as I could to get one of the rooms in College which was being vacated. When Scott Maldon was taken into the RAF, to become one of our fighter pilots, I was offered his room. I bought his furniture at a knock down price and he left some of his books and china. I still have a couple of his books and two beer mugs that have survived many moves. These rooms consisted of a study on a corner of the building which overlooked the chapel from one window and the Backs (a section of the river Cam which runs behind some of the Colleges) from the other. There was a small bedroom separated from the study by a few stairs. Being in college enabled me to meet many other undergraduates in the college and not have to confine my friends to those taking medical courses. These courses were demanding as they required not only lectures but laboratory work. The most demanding was the anatomy course. Each part of the body had to be dissected and learned in detail. This dissection went on in a lab crudely known by the irreverent students as the Meaters. In spite of the fact that it contained only a number of partially dissected bodies and reeked of formalin it became a friendly rather than a sinister place. Four of us were allotted to each part and we had to work together. As one finished dissecting each part, an oral test was given. Very detailed and accurate knowledge was required. These were the only exams other than the Finals that were required.

The other subjects that the medical student was required to take were physiology and pathology. On the basis of these subjects, the successful candidate was awarded a BA (Bachelor of Arts). Passage also entitled one to move on to the clinical aspects of the medical course. This was studied at a teaching hospital of one's choice. After three years, walking the wards, one returned to Cambridge to take the final qualifying exam. If successful in passing the exam one became a doctor with a small D and could become licensed to practice medicine. The actual degree was MB, Bchir, (Bachelor of Medicine and Bachelor of Chirurgy) and was not a doctorate. The degree of Doctor of Medicine was a further degree awarded after the presentation of a thesis and the defense thereof. If one did not go to a university but went straight from school to a hospital medical school one did the first two years there studying anatomy etc. This was the more usual practice and shortened the course by one year.

I found both the pathology and the physiology fascinating, particularly the latter. Basically life was a mixture of pleasure and work and the undergraduate could determine for himself how much of each he chose. There were lectures and labs to attend but most of the afternoons were free. This enabled one to play games and to get outside. I played field hockey, rugby and squash for the college. The former was my favorite and I played for the university. These activities did not preclude my enjoying punting and canoeing on the Cam. For full enjoyment of this a girl-friend was desirable. Because of the war, two women's colleges were evacuated from London to Cambridge and they increased the availability of female companionship. Most evenings after dinner in Hall, the college dining place, I retired to my rooms with a large cup of coffee and my books. I spent the best part of four hours studying.

I was elected to the Ten Club at Kings. This was a club which met in someone's rooms every other week to read a play. The host was required to supply beer which was consumed between one of the acts of the play. The members consisted of both Dons and undergraduates. Two of the Dons were particularly distinguished and superb readers. My Tutor, Donald Beves, was an amateur actor and had been written up in a London newspaper as the finest Falstaff ever seen on the stage. The other was the College Bursar, George (Dada) Rylands, who had written a book about Shakespeare's plays and had produced The Duchess of Malfi on the New York stage. With these as leaders the standard of reading was high. The parts for the plays were assigned by another Don whose name I have conveniently forgotten as he was known as the ugliest man in Cambridge. He was a delightful character and had a wicked sense of humor which he indulged when casting. The plays that we read ran the gamut from pre Elizabethan to modern, and were well laced with Jacobean. For me, one of the most memorable meetings was held in Donald Beves' rooms. At refreshment time he apologized that he had forgotten to order the beer. However, he said that there was a case of Claret in the room and the glasses were in the glass case. Uncle Donald as we called him, was a bachelor and in charge of buying the wine for the college. He spent a considerable part of his summers driving his Bentley around the vineyards of France sampling and selecting the best wines for the college. We were happy to avail ourselves of his hospitality and took the glasses from the case. These glasses were antique twist-stem glasses. It turned out that he had one of the best collections of these in the country. I developed an appreciation not only of good wine but of the glasses as well. I have tried to collect them ever since.

This club gave me a significant insight into the interest that the Dons took in their undergraduates. The members of the club were elected by a vote of the membership. At one meeting the Tutor (Uncle Donald) suggested that we should elect an undergrad who had just come up with an engineering scholarship. He had been a miner from the North Country who, through brilliance and hard work, had won his academic success. Most members of the club felt that he would be out of place in the club. Uncle Donald said that he thought election to the club would be good for him. It would introduce him to other undergraduates and stop him from working too hard. He was elected and he turned out to be a great asset. He came right out of his shell and was a most popular member. Thus the Tutor's insight significantly changed this man's whole life. At the same time it revealed how much the Dons were concerned with all aspects of the lives of members of the college.

Normally the Natural Science Tripos was a three-year course. It was divided into two parts. Part one could be taken in two or three years. If one took Part one in two years, one could take Part two in the third year. This was a much more specialized course. During the war one was expected to take part one in two years and then, as a medical student, proceed to a hospital for clinical work. I took Part one and was awarded First Class Honors. As a result, I was promoted from an Exhibitioner to a Scholar at Kings. The only real difference this made was that I had to read some of the Lessons in Chapel and say the long Latin grace before dinner in Hall. At the same time I was awarded a Scholarship to St. Thomas's Hospital in London where I could go for my clinical work.

During the previous year the Rockefeller Foundation had started to award studentships for 25 medical students each year from the U.K. to study at American medical schools. I had come to know the Professor of Pathology, who was also Master of Trinity Hall, another College. He told me that if I stayed another year at Cambridge and read a Part two, I would have an excellent chance of winning one of the Rockefeller awards. Since he was a member of the selection committee, I took his advice. I refused the scholarship to St. Thomas's Hospital and stayed at Cambridge to study Physiology for another year. This was a most enjoyable time with far too many extracurricular activities. I moved my rooms in college to share a suite of rooms in The Gibb building with another medical student. When this building was built in the early nineteenth century plumbing was not considered essential. There is notation in the minutes from a college meeting which states that, since the term is only eight weeks long, there was no necessity to put in baths. The building stretches across the front courtyard from the Chapel. There is only one toilet in the building and this had been added to the ground floor suite nearest to the Chapel. This was done to accommodate an elderly Don who could not hold his water any further when emerging from Chapel services. Our suite was very luxurious if one overlooked the plumbing and heating. There was a tap in the hall and a single gas ring where one could boil water and, if one was enterprising, cook bacon and eggs. The suite consisted of three rooms, a living room, a study and a big bedroom. The living room overlooked the front courtyard and the other two rooms the Backs. The rooms had 16 ft ceilings, paneled from floor to ceiling, but only one small fireplace. There was no central heating but we were allowed to use a small electric heater. It was cold in winter. We had to walk across to another building for baths and the use of other plumbing facilities. This was somewhat of a trial in winter particularly when it snowed. The college supplied basic furniture which was included in the very reasonable rent we were charged. Since my roommate, Hugh Thomlinson, had some very nice furniture of his own, we were extremely well set up. The college supplied a bed maker who was responsible for cleaning our rooms. Our bed maker was a tiny lady, Mrs. Shed, whose habits left something to be desired. Besides cleaning our rooms, she had to collect our 'commons', milk mostly, from the buttery every morning. She would clean our fireplace before fetching the milk. Since she had three jugs of milk to deliver, she would put her fingers into the jugs to be able to hold them all. As a result we always had a thin layer of coal dust on the top of the milk. She was a very short lady so nothing above three feet high ever got cleaned unless we did it ourselves. Because of the lack of plumbing facilities, we were supplied with a 'vase de nuit' or chamber pot. She was responsible for emptying it every morning, though where she did this I have no idea. One day Hugh returned to our rooms unexpectedly only to find the dear lady wiping our chamber pot with his bath sponge. Since he was a rather fastidious young man he was not pleased. It is important to remember not to eat asparagus for dinner if one has to use a chamber pot (Aspartic Acid has a strong and lingering odor.)

Hugh was a very interesting person. Though rather slight of build and of a somewhat effeminate appearance, he was very much tougher than he at first seemed. His hobby was mountain climbing and was happy to practice on the buildings which surrounded us. Before the war a book had been published called the Night Climbers of Cambridge. The authors had been caught while climbing on some of the buildings and their photographs confiscated. They had been made to promise not to publish their achievements. On this basis their photographs were returned to them. They proceeded to write the book and publish it abroad. Hugh read the book and noted that they had not climbed the building in which we lived. They had looked at it and decided that it would be difficult. This was a challenge that Hugh could not resist. After considerable study he decided that there was one way it could be done. Climbing buildings is a rather dangerous occupation and more than a few have been injured attempting it. It has to be done at night as the authorities do not approve of the activity. Not only is it dangerous, but of far more concern to the authorities is the fact that climbers sometimes damage the buildings and have been known to knock off gargoyles. In order to climb Gibb building in which we had our rooms with any degree of safety it was necessary to be roped so that a fall could be controlled. In this way the chances of serious injury would be minimized. Since it required at least two people, I was co-opted as the second man. I was not an accomplished climber though Hugh had taught me some of the essential elements. In the middle of the building is an archway which goes through the building and has pillars on each side. It is known as Jumbo's Arch, supposedly because there was an undergraduate from India who was a Maharajah. He insisted on bringing an elephant with him and there was nowhere else to keep the elephant except under this arch! We chimneyed up the building between the wall and the pillars until we could wriggle around onto the top of the lower arch. This got us about half-way up. Then we had to go up beside the big window to get to the top overhanging arch. After a double pull up with no real support for the feet, the overhang of the top arch had to be negotiated. There did not seem to be any way of getting around this overhang which jutted out what seemed an impossible distance. There was no grip above it. It was necessary to use the flat of the hands to get sufficient purchase on the top to squirm over the lip. Fortunately Hugh was leading. I had the rope fixed while Hugh went up over this hazard. In this way, if he fell, he would only drop about half-way before the rope held him. He managed to get himself over the obstacle and thus achieved his objective. He belayed the rope around a chimney and I had to follow. The double pull-up was not too difficult as I was in pretty good shape, but the getting over the lip at the top was one of the scary things I have done. Without Hugh and the rope for safety, I would never have attempted it. Perhaps we cheated at the end because we did not descend the way we had come up but found a door which gave us access to the building. We came down inside.

King's Chapel and Gibb Building with Jumbo's Arch (My rooms were the two windows on the second floor to the right of Jumbo's Arch.)

On another occasion Hugh was trying to teach me to traverse on a narrow ledge. We were doing this along a ridge about three feet above the ground on the side of the building. At that moment one of the Deans came along and observed what we were doing. After rebuking us he added, "Anyway you are doing it all wrong". He proceeded to get up so show us how it should be done. He made us promise never to try to climb the Chapel as it had been damaged by previous attempts and one of the gargoyles broken. The cost of the repairs which required extensive scaffolding and stone carving had been tremendous. We were also made to promise not to climb the Porters' Lodge at the entrance to the College because the last person who attempted it had been severely injured. This was not the last of our climbing escapades. A day or two before we were to get our degrees in the Senate House we decided to place an opened umbrella on the top of the chimney of that building. It was not a very difficult climb and the next day when we went to get our degrees we were able to admire the new decoration. My parents came for the graduation ceremonies and Hugh and I pointed out the umbrella that was crowning the building. My father was vastly amused until we informed him that it was his umbrella.

The standard method of transportation was the bicycle. Though bicycles were very common, it was considered inexcusable to steal someone else's. Hugh's was stolen one day. Shortly thereafter he saw a young man riding it down a lane between colleges. He stopped him and went as if to punch the offender. His opponent took a retaliatory swing at Hugh. Hugh had some knowledge of the art of combating such an attack. He caught the swinging fist in his hand and, turning his back as he gave the arm a twist, he bent over sharply. His opponent had to sail over Hugh's head or have his arm broken at the elbow. Hugh left his opponent crumpled on the ground and reclaimed his bicycle. Since he had reported his loss to the police, he went round to report the recovery. The policeman asked how he had found it. Hugh gave a detailed account of what had happened. The policeman said; "I wish we were allowed to do that."

When I was celebrating the finish of my exams at the end of the second year, I found myself at the rear entrance to the college after the gate was shut. Rather than walk all the way round to the front of the college I decided to climb in. At that entrance there is a ditch that is difficult to jump over. This ditch is crossed by a bridge with an iron gate. Beside the gate are diagonally sloping rails with spikes on them, two on each side. These spikes are not long but rotate. It is possible to grasp the rails and swing around if one is careful. I attempted this but was not careful enough. My foot slipped as the spike I was using to put my weight on rotated. As I fell I ran a spike into my leg. It seemed rather deep, so I spoke to a junior Don who lived near my rooms. Being a doctor he looked at it and decided that the wound was both deep and dirty. It required more than a bandage. He had to take me out of the college and to the emergency room at the hospital. Since it was after 10 PM he had to get permission to take me out of the college. At the hospital I had the wound excised and sewn up. The doctor there had an extremely attractive redheaded nurse to help him. Having found out who she was, I was delighted to discover that she was not averse to having an undergraduate boyfriend. Over my last year she became a frequent companion. To leave college at the end of each term it is necessary to go to the Tutor to get an official exeat signed. After my spiking episode, when I went to see the Tutor to get my exeat signed, I was a little apprehensive as to what he might say. His only comment was; "I expect that you will be more careful next time you are climbing in". There was very little that the Dons did not know about the activities of the members of the college.

During that last year at Cambridge I had several world-renowned teachers. Prof. Adrian was a neuroscientist who was working on the function of the brain and the localization of its functions. In his lectures he had set up some machinery that could broadcast brain waves from electrodes placed on a subject's head. He had an assistant named Casey. He would ask Casey to whom he had attached electrodes, a simple question. The loudspeakers would crackle with startling intensity. Then he would ask Casey to think of nothing. Instead of the previous crackles, the speakers would become silent. Casey was the only person known who could really think of nothing. In the laboratory Prof. Adrian had an experiment where there was a cat with its head opened to expose the brain. The cat was anaesthetized and electrodes could be placed on various parts of the brain so that functional areas could be mapped. This experiment had to be conducted in a metal wire cage to prevent interference with the recordings. When the class was allowed into the room for a demonstration, the cage was removed so that all could have a better view.

This demonstration took place in 1942 at the height of the war. After the cage was removed and the machine turned on, areas of the cat were supposed to be stimulated to try to locate the sensory areas in the brain. But instead of this working, the cat acted as a radio aerial and Lord Haw-Haw, the English traitor broadcasting from Germany, came over the speakers spouting German propaganda. There was no evidence that it was a German cat.

Professor Adrian was the Master of Trinity College, a position of great honor. Besides being a great scientist he was a remarkable writer. His book, The Basis of Sensation, though a scientific treatise, is so beautifully written that it can be understood and read with pleasure by everyone. There are stories about his undergraduate days that suggest he was not averse to participating in some practical jokes. He was supposed to have been part of a group of undergraduates who put on an exhibition of Russian Paintings. They sold several of these, one of which was bought by a college to hang in the senior common room. These paintings had been painted by the undergraduates themselves; a fact that was stated in very fine print at the bottom of the flier announcing the exhibition. The money they made was given to charity. On another occasion, the story goes; there was a party in some rooms overlooking the main road. On looking out of the window Adrian noted a policeman below. He asked him if he would not like a beer. When the policeman said that he would, Adrian told him to tie his helmet onto a string that he would lower and that they would put the beer in the helmet. The policeman performed as requested and the helmet was hauled up. Unfortunately the poor man lost his helmet as it was not returned. It is not easy to verify this tale.

Another famous Professor was Feldberg who was studying the ways nerve impulses are transmitted to muscles. His was some of the original work on the chemicals which are responsible for this link up, known now as neurotransmitters. Specifically he was working with Acetylcholine which was the first neurotransmitter discovered. Feldberg was a Jew who had been the Professor of Physiology in Berlin. To avoid the pogroms, he fled via Israel to England where Cambridge University welcomed him with open arms. He was a delightful character. He lectured at 4 PM in the afternoon and this was a little inconvenient for me as I was trying to get into the university field hockey team. We had practices or games most afternoons. When Feldberg found this out he changed the lectures to 4.30. Even so, I was a little late sometimes and still in my games clothes. He would stop the lecture to ask whether we had won. He often invited me to his house and introduced me to the operas that he loved so much. He informed me, quite correctly, that as I grew older I would find increasing pleasure in the human voice as a musical instrument. In the process of his work he discovered that the shock used by Sting Rays to immobilize or kill their prey was dependent on the buildup of Acetylcholine in their stinging organs. One of the most potent of these creatures is the Torpedo Ray. Feldberg had a friend in the States who was also working on this project and they tried to communicate. However this was difficult because Feldberg's letters were censored and so arrived in the States full of blanks. The references to Torpedoes were too much for the censors!

1942 was the quincentennial of the founding of King's College. Every year the college has a Founder's Day feast to which all current members are invited, together with a rotation of previous graduates. In spite of the war the authorities decided that the Feast should properly commemorate 500 years. At these feasts sherry is served before dinner by any Don who has the light on in his room. The dinner is a full 5 or 6 course affair with the appropriate wine served with each course. Between the courses the choir sings glees from the minstrel gallery. At this time I was acting as a guinea pig for a metabolic experiment. This required me to measure everything I took in and put out. All the food was supplied in the lab where we ate. We had to eat 1 1/2 lb. of different breads each day for four three-week periods. Unfortunately King's feast fell during one of these periods. Since I had to save one fifth of everything I drank, I figured that the only thing to do was to drink five glasses and save one. I finished with a whole bottle full of a mixture of wine which represented a fifth of my consumption. It was a major disaster both for me and the experiment. I was sick as a dog and tried to take a fifth of this production back to the lab. I was not popular. It taught me that gross overindulgence has serious drawbacks. I was not the only person who overindulged that night. The Mayor of Cambridge was an invited guest. On the way home he staggered in front of a car and was knocked down. Fortunately he was not seriously injured.

Some misguided official decided to stage an emergency fire drill at the college that night. Needless to say the college had been closed to all nonmembers except for official guests. The porters who manned the gates knew where their loyalty lay. The emergency crews who arrived because of the fire drill were not allowed to enter or to disrupt the Feast. It is amazing how local circumstances can alter priorities.

Some of the courses that I had to take that year were beyond my comprehension. Whether this was because of lack of ability or the pressure of more entertaining distractions, I am not quite sure, probably a bit of both. I did not do very well in the exams at the end of that year. The Provost who was a somewhat eccentric character used to greet new scholars at the college with the advice; "Don't work too hard. Remember you are at the University now". When he saw the result of my Part 2 exams which had descended from a first in part 1 to a 2/2 he said; "Well my boy, no one can say you worked too hard".

Fortunately the selection for the Rockefeller studentships occurred before those exam results were announced. This process of selection consisted of submitting a complete resume of all the candidates' activities up to that time, both at school and at the university. After that each candidate who had made the short list was interviewed. I was selected for an interview and found myself sitting before a long table with a number of seemingly elderly gentlemen on the other side. They asked some questions about my various activities. One asked me what the Ten Club was. I explained that it was a college club that read plays. I was then asked to give some examples of the plays that we read. I was totally unprepared for this question. My mind went a blank but I did recall a couple such as The Playboy of the Western World and The Revenger's Tragedy. Then I remembered that we had read The Chaste Maiden of Cheapside. This title startled the interviewers who asked what kind of a play it was. I explained that it was a rather Rabelaisian pre Elizabethan play about the low life of commoners in Tudor London. It must have been on the basis of this reply that I was sent to Harvard.

That last year at Cambridge was considerably different from the previous two. I suppose I thought that I was very smart since I had gotten First Class Honors and been made a Scholar rather than an Exhibitioner. Being a Scholar was more than an honor since it entailed, in rotation with other scholars, reading the lesson in Chapel at the daily matins service at 8 am and on Sunday at the choral service. This latter was rather nerve-racking. The lectern, at that time, was between the massive screen which divided the antechapel from the choir and the altar. The reader's voice went over the screen and echoed back off the west end wall almost a syllable later. This made it fatal to listen to yourself as you were reading. The other duty, which also rotated, was to read the Grace before dinner in Hall. It was a long elaborate Latin grace. One of the other scholars had a severe stutter. He would get up and, after a hesitating start; rush through the whole thing in one breath. It was quite a feat.

Because of my misapprehensions about my abilities, I did considerably less studying. I found some of the subjects somewhat out of my depth, particularly those that demanded detailed understanding of molecular biochemistry or of electrical physics. One of our teachers was working out the electrocardiograph. Unfortunately I did not understand what it was all about, nor did I realize the potential. As a result I have never been able to read electrocardiographs and still have to get some else to interpret them for me. The other subject that defeated me was that of the electrical potentials across membranes which have been shown to be important in so many aspects of metabolism and fluid transfers. I now regret that I did not take the trouble to confess my inability to understand these things as I am sure there were plenty of people who would have helped me. Instead I occupied my time with sports of one sort or another.

During the winter of 1942 it was very cold from January through March and the river froze hard enough to skate on. Some brave souls skated from Cambridge to Ely, a matter of some twenty miles. They went roped together because the ice was rather thin where the river flowed under bridges and the current was swifter.

There was a deep quarry filled with water near the university and this froze solid, remaining so for a couple of months. It was a great place to skate and I went there frequently. My roller skating experience in Switzerland gave me a good start. In a very short time I was trying to do a little figure skating. There was a girl there who was obviously very competent. I asked her if she had done any dancing on skates. She said she had not, but that she thought that it would be fun. She admitted that she had a silver medal for figure skating and would be able to teach most of the necessary steps. We got a book outlining the patterns of the dances and set up a gramophone on the ice. It was a lot of fun though we never became at all expert. That next vacation we decided to meet at a skating rink in suburban London and to try our luck there. At these rinks there used to be dancing intervals between the times of general skating. We set out together to try to dance and had minimal success. It must have been obvious that we were having a lot of fun and some frustration as, at the end of that session, one of the instructors came up to us and offered to give us a professional lesson. She said that they had been watching us and that we were obviously having such a good time that she would like to help.

When the weather became warmer there were two other distractions, organized sports and the river. The river provided both pleasure and sport. It divides itself into three areas. Downstream from the town is the area for rowing. Through the area where some of the colleges back onto the river it is known as the Backs and is used by sightseers drifting in punts. Upstream above the weir the river winds through the country and is used for pleasure punting and picnicking. Downstream the colleges have their boathouses where are kept various types of boats ranging from eights (long narrow racing boats for eight rowers and a cox) to single sculls. The main event for the rowers is the May Races held in May week which occurs at the end of the Academic year. These races are the Bumps, so called because they are bumping races! The river is not wide enough for two eights to row side by side so the system of Bumps was devised. It may seem a complicated system at first glance but is really very simple. It works like a ladder competition. There are several divisions depending on the number of boats entering. Each college can enter as many boats as it can man. A division has about ten boats and these start one behind the other in the order that they finished the year before. Thereafter, during the three days of racing, they start according to their finish the day before. Along the bank is a series of posts set at equal distances. To these are attached light lines. The eights line up one behind the other with each cox holding the line attached to the post at his allotted position. A gun is fired, the cox lets go of his line and the oarsmen get to work. The object is to catch the boat in front and overlap it sufficiently to swing the bow so as to touch the stern of that boat. If this happens both boats are required to move to the bank as rapidly as possible so that the boats behind can continue the race. The lead boat in the first division is The Head of the River and tries to remain so by avoiding being bumped. At the race the next day a bumped boat starts behind the boat by which it was bumped the day before. The first boat in the second division starts as the last boat in the first division on the second day while the bottom boat in the first division becomes the first boat in the second division and so on down all the divisions. These races generate a great deal of enthusiasm even among those who do not row. The results are celebrated, or drowned in sorrow, wisely or unwisely, at Bump Suppers held in each college at the end of the series. One unfortunate Don of rather small size was waylaid by a hefty oarsman during one of these celebrations. This inebriated young man grabbed a watering can and proceeded to douse the Don saying; "Grow you silly little man. Grow" Wiser Dons, unless they were part of the rowing crowd, stayed clear on these occasions.

Because the river is winding as well as narrow, various parts of it have acquired names. The area where the oarsmen are getting their second wind and the strain is greatest is known as the Gut. This gave rise to the famous story about a young man who was taking his maiden aunt to watch the races. With great enthusiasm he was heard to shout, much to his aunt's embarrassment; "Oh look. Jesus has bumped Lady Maggie in the Gut". Jesus is one of the famous rowing colleges and Lady Margaret is the boat club of Johns' College, so named because the college was founded by Lady Margaret Beaufort.

During the war there was a shortage of students available for rowing, although so many were less qualified by weight and skill, they were co-opted into the boats. This allowed me to join the King's first boat where I rowed as bow. I am proud to say we made a bump. It also led to the first injury to my back. I was lifting weights in the boat house and had hoisted a fifty pound weight in each hand above my head. As I was letting them drop, I realized that they might damage the wooden boat house floor so I tried to catch them before they landed. I finished up bent over with a sharp pain in my lower back. It seemed to recover quite quickly and I thought no more about it until a couple of years later when I twisted my back playing squash.

I became very good friends with another medical student, Paul Beves, who was a keen oarsman and rowed stroke in our eight. During the summer that year he and I had a lot of fun, not only in the eights but in single sculls and pairs. We found the latter challenging as these craft are very unstable. Pairs are different from double sculls where each rower has two oars. In a pair each rower has only one oar and accurate cooperation is essential. Since the boat is very narrow, smooth sided and with almost no keel, the only way it can be kept upright is if each rower keeps his oar on the water so that it acts as an outrigger and then pulls synchronously and evenly. Paul, (known as Toby) and I had several unpremeditated swims before we acquired sufficient skill with the oar. During the summer we liked to continue to take the eight out but it was not easy to find enough people to man it. On one occasion we were short of a cox, so I persuaded one of my girl friends to take that place. We had assured her that all she had to do was sit still and steer the boat so that we did not hit the bank. At first all went well, but then we decided to try a rowing start. This consists of several short strokes with maximum effort to get the boat moving as fast as possible. The acceleration is quite dramatic and, if one is not expecting it, very surprising. Our cox was not expecting it, so she tipped back and found she was lying sprawled on the rear deck. She let go of the lines connected to the rudder. By this time the boat was moving rapidly and out of control. Sitting in the bow seat I realized the bank was approaching rapidly. I screamed; "Hold her hard, all" which is the signal for everyone to jam his oar into the water and hold it there. This stopped the boat as quickly as we had started it; thus we avoided hitting the bank and severely damaging the boat. Our cox managed to recover her composure and to see the humor of the situation.

Paul was a remarkable character, and though not perhaps the most studious of my friends, a man of many talents. He was very musical and a great organizer. He started a group called COI which stood for Cambridge Operas Idiotique. Needless to say it was based in Kings. This group sang operas virtually unrehearsed in someone's rooms. Because of the musical talent in the college it was always possible to find one or two people to play the piano and the choral scholars could sing the parts. The onlookers provided the chorus and young ladies who were interested in singing careers were co-opted from members of the female colleges. Paul continued this hobby for the rest of his life. He became an anesthetist in a town in the country and had a music room built onto his house. He would organize parties for informal presentations of operas and, because of his charm and enthusiasm, had no trouble persuading some very well known singers to come down from London to join the fun. The fact that both he and his wife, Topsy, were superb cooks and he had inherited his uncle's wine cellar was an added incentive. His uncle was the Tutor at Kings, Donald Beves, whose duties included buying wine for the College. His selections were always outstanding.

There is a weir upstream from the Backs dividing them from the river above. A boat house is there from which punts can be rented for use either on the Backs or, above the weir, to punt upstream. It was an activity that provided a great deal of pleasure on a lazy, warm and sunny day. Punts are flat-bottomed boats with square ends which are about three feet wide and very stable. The punter stands at one end, which is flat-decked, and pushes the boat forward with a long pole. It is easy to guide the punt if you remember that the pole on the bottom remains fixed and ones feet in the boat move relative to that fixed point. The most frequent cause of trouble is getting the pole stuck in the mud at the bottom of the river. This makes it difficult to pull it up ready to take the next push. Hanging on to a pole which is stuck in the mud is inviting disaster. The boat does not stop and the punter has to decide whether to let go of the pole or hang on and find they are suspended, momentarily, over the water. The subsequent ducking is a source of much embarrassment to the punter but great merriment to the onlookers. Those with experience know that giving the pole a slight twist as it is withdrawn will release it from the mud and avoid this situation.

Punting on the Cam

An excellent plan for a punting outing is to place an attractive young lady on the cushions in the bow, add provisions for a picnic and punt her gently upstream. When a suitable stopping place is found, there enjoy her company and the meal. I found the nurse that I had met when being repaired after my spiking injury was a very satisfactory companion. One can punt up to Grantchester, a matter of a couple of miles, where refreshment is available. In May Week, which is at the end of the academic year and perversely occurs in the first week of June, many of the colleges have May Balls. These are very formal all-night dances. They start at 9 PM and continue until dawn. Supper is served during the night and when the dancing is over some couples get together and punt up to Grantchester for breakfast. This is done in full evening dress. It is quite a strenuous routine but can be a lot of fun. My Tutor informed me that it was easier to get through the dance if a magnum of champagne a head is opened during the night.

The Backs are supposed to be a peaceful area for drifting and admiring the colleges. One Sunday afternoon a punt containing some hefty rugby players from another college and their female companions came down past a part of Kings which overlooks the river. They had a gramophone and were playing it loudly. Some residents in the rooms at Kings which overlooked the river took exception to this and, taking an air-gun, leaned out of the window. With great accuracy they shattered the record on the gramophone and silenced the machine. The occupants of the punt were incensed and, banking the punt, proceeded to the staircase of the building from whence the shot had come. Climbing the staircase they got to the room which they thought housed their attackers. They found that the Oak was sported. This is the outer of a double door to each of the rooms on a staircase and is only sported or shut when the occupant is away. Finding the Oak sported, the irate attackers figured that they were on the wrong level and so went up another flight of stairs. There they unceremoniously flung open the door with the idea of punishing their tormentors. To their utter chagrin, they found the chaplain sitting quietly reading his Bible. They never did get to those responsible for the dastardly deed. They were sitting, rather nervously, behind the sported Oak.

What I have written must give the impression that Cambridge and its students were very little affected by the war. This was not the case. Too many students had to leave early to serve in the armed services, many never to return. Those of us who remained were very conscious of the fact that our country might be invaded at any time. Hugh and I discussed what we would do in such an eventuality. We were fully determined to kill as many of the invaders as we could but always to save the last bullet for ourselves as we would never be captured alive. If Germany conquered England they might have found an almost uninhabited country as we were not alone in our determination. The women were as determined as the men. One of the foreign pilots who were flying with the Allies had to bail out over the countryside. He was nearly killed by some women with pitch forks before he could identify himself. They thought that he was a German infiltrator. Unless you had lived through that time in England, it is difficult to appreciate the intensity of the underlying refusal to give in. It broke down all social barriers in the face of a universally accepted danger. This aspect of the national character of entrenched obstinacy has persisted for hundreds of years. Though the Normans conquered England they never conquered the Anglo-Saxon spirit which eventually defeated them. It changed their language, their customs, and their laws eventually leading to the formation of a democratic constitutional monarchy.

One day Hugh and I were experimenting with a revolver. We found that if you had a revolver put at the back of your head, it was possible to spin round and knock the revolver aside before it could be fired. Even if the gun was cocked it was not possible to fire it before it was knocked aside. The only safe way to march a prisoner was to put a finger at the back of the head and to hold the pistol well back in the other hand. Fortunately we never had to put this knowledge to a practical test and I am not sure that it would apply to the modern rapid-fire, repeating pistols but it might. I do not intend to try.

During the summer vacations, when I was not attending the courses of the Long Vacation term, I either worked on a farm in Somerset or drove my father to air force stations.

My father had risen in the Air Ministry to become Deputy Permanent Undersecretary of State for Air. His job entailed being in charge of all personnel, from the senior officers to those responsible for maintaining the aircraft. He got along very well with the senior officers as he had known many of them when they were junior and stationed in Baghdad twenty years before. They would call him when they thought they needed more personnel. To achieve maximum efficiency it was imperative to repair damaged aircraft as quickly as possible so that they could fly again. The manpower problem was my father's responsibility. He liked to see the situations for himself and so would visit the stations whenever he could. He hated driving a car and rather than use an official car would ask me, when I was available, to drive him. Instead of leaving me with nothing to do while he worked he would introduce me to some of the pilots. They were kind enough to give me a ride in the planes that they were checking out. One daring pilot offered to let me fly one of the two-seater fighter training planes, a Miles Master, after he had gotten it airborne. This was a great thrill as I had no idea how sensitive and maneuverable these machines were. I had the privilege of meeting some of the ace fighter pilots, including Bader, and, when being taken up by one in a night fighter, was asked to be careful not to push the button as the guns were armed.

The extent of my father's responsibilities came home to me one evening when I was at home. That Saturday evening the phone rang and my father answered it. After some time he returned looking rather pale. My mother and I asked him what had happened. It was at a time when Malta was under siege and painfully short of supplies. A convoy was loaded in Liverpool with a highly explosive cargo and about to sail. The port authorities refused to allow it leave port unless they had a guaranteed indemnity against it exploding and destroying everything around. Since the supplies for Malta were in the province of the Air Ministry, my father had been contacted. It was Saturday evening and quite impossible to get in touch with the Government authorities at very short notice. The matter was of extreme urgency as the situation in Malta was desperate. My father authorized a two million pound guarantee for which he had actually had no authority. He figured that if the worst happened we would be ruined. On the other hand if he tried to go through the proper channels Malta might be lost because of the delay. Fortunately the convoy left safely from Liverpool and enough of the ships got through to relieve the immediate danger to the island.

The farm which I worked on was typical of a small general farm in England. It was situated in its own valley or coomb. My family had stayed there for a vacation before the war and we had gotten to know the farmer and his family. They were very happy to have my cousin and me stay there whenever we could, to help with the work. Though we were not paid, we got free board and lodging. I volunteered to help milk the cows. After the first morning, when they found that I was still working on the first cow while they had finished all the rest, it was suggested that I would be more useful if I serviced the tractor. This became my responsibility. The farm made its own clotted cream; a delicacy generically known as Devonshire cream. To make this, the milk is put through a separator and the cream poured into a vat about 8 inches deep. This is heated slowly for a few hours until it thickens on the top and forms a loose crust. This crust is skimmed off as clotted cream. It is served with buns and jam for tea, with fruit for dessert or, as the farmer himself liked it, on fresh bread sprinkled with salt. The fluid left after the cream was skimmed off is fed to the pigs.

One day the farmer sold off the lambs while the ewes were still producing milk. It was necessary to milk the ewes to relieve them. They were herded into a smallish pen where they could be thrown onto the ground. I was one of several helpers at this work. When the ewe was on the ground it had to be milked where it lay. No attempt was made to collect the milk and it was allowed to squirt where ever the teat pointed. Sometimes another worker was in the direct line of fire. We all emerged from this work covered with ewes' milk which is a rather unpleasant sticky fluid.

In the south west of England cider is a very popular drink among the locals. Many of the farms make their own cider for their own use. This is done by crushing windfall apples into a large barrel and leaving it there to ferment. The resultant fluid is drawn off from the bottom as needed.

It is a rough drink, not very sweet as most of the sugar in the fruit has fermented into alcohol. It is very thirst quenching but surprisingly intoxicating. One day, when we were harvesting wheat, I was up with the farmer helping him on the haystack he was making. I was handing him the sheaves as he was placing them neatly so as to form a stable stack. It was a hot summer's day. We had a pause in the work and the cider was handed out to all the workers. I was very thirsty and drank a couple of glassfuls as they were handed up to me. Suddenly I realized I was becoming very unsteady and had to ask to be helped down. Though the locals were amused, I was humiliated. On an occasion when the cider barrel leaked, the pigs got into the mess. Drunken pigs are quite entertaining, but it is a method of giving pork an apple flavor that is not recommended.

All was not work on the farm. It was situated at the edge of the Quantock Hills in Somerset. These hills were home for many deer which come down to forage on the neighboring farmlands. They were hunted by a pack of hounds known as the Quantock Stag Hounds. The farmer was an enthusiastic supporter and used to ride with them whenever he could. He had a pony as well as his horse and used to let me ride the pony. The pony proved to be a superb mount as it could cope with the hilly terrain better than the horses that most of the other hunters were riding. I went on several hunts with him and was in at the kill on one occasion. When the hounds cornered a stag the huntsman killed it with a humane killer pistol. This may seem a cruel sport but, with no natural predators surviving, it is necessary to control the deer population. Some farmers tend to take the law into their own hands and shoot the deer when they see them stealing their crops. Unfortunately many of these deer are not killed but only wounded. They go away and die slowly and miserably. When they are hunted with the hounds they either get away uninjured or are killed outright. There are no easy answers to the conflicts which have developed between animals and man.

The rest of that summer of 1942 was spent preparing for my transfer across the Atlantic to Harvard Medical School.

Chapter 3

HARVARD MEDICAL SCHOOL 1942

After my original weekend in New York City I got on the train to Boston and had my first look at some of the American countryside. It was a pleasant day but I was too anxious to find out what awaited me at my final destination to appreciate what I was seeing. While on the train I was approached by a total stranger who realized that I was a newcomer to his country. He was charming and invited me to his house if I was ever in his neighborhood. I fear that I neither remember his name nor where he lived but I was impressed by his generosity and obvious desire to be helpful.

When I got to Boston I found my way, as I had been instructed to do, to the dormitory of the Medical School, Vanderbilt Hall. At that time I did not realize that there was more than one medical school in Boston. When I got to Vanderbilt Hall I found arrangements had been made for me to have a room and for another medical student to meet me and to take me under his wing. He was a tall, exceedingly pleasant young man, Alex Randall. We became good friends and he was a constant companion for the rest of my stay. I can never thank him enough for all his kindness to me. He helped me in more ways than

I dare to remember. There were so many things to learn besides medicine. Being in a foreign country, even if the language was almost the same, necessitated learning many new customs. Vanderbilt Hall was a very convenient place right opposite the main medical school buildings where all the non-clinical teaching took place. Besides rooms for the students there was a dining room, a tennis court in the middle of the building and a squash court.

Before I could join the courses I had to see the Dean, Dr. Hale, and have my health checked. Besides a chest X-ray, I was given a Tuberculin test. This consisted of the intradermal injection of Tuberculin to see if I would react to it. React I did, to the extent that my whole arm swelled up. Since my chest X-ray was clear, the conclusion was that I had been exposed to tuberculosis as a child but had no active disease at that time. I decided that I must have developed a very active resistance to the disease since I reacted so dramatically to the test .This gave me an advantage over my colleagues. Sometime later several of us went for a weekend of skiing, staying at a B&B farm in New Hampshire. We were served wonderful farm food with lots of fresh butter and cream. The others found out that the dairy produce was not pasteurized so they would not touch the milk, cream or butter. I was not at all deterred and had a wonderful time.

Because of the courses that I had at Cambridge I was exempt from the first year studies and was expected to join the second of the four-year course. The first year would have been a study of anatomy and physiology. The second year consisted of pathology, bacteriology and similar basic sciences. It had already started when I arrived but this did not bother me as I had already had these subjects at Cambridge. Alex led me to the lectures and the labs. The latter took place in the afternoons, but because the weather was beautiful, I skipped some of these sessions and took the opportunity to look around a little of Boston. One afternoon, almost as soon as I arrived, I found a couple of questions written on the black-board and I was told I was expected to answer them. I thought nothing of this and scribbled a quick response. To my surprise I received my answers back at the next session with an F on them. Perplexed, I asked Alex what this meant. It was then that I got my first shock and an inkling of the difference between Harvard Medical School and Cambridge. Alex explained that an F was a fail and furthermore that the results of these tests were counted towards the final grade on the course. This was horrifying but I decided that, since I was there as a scholar, I had better show that I could do much better. Alex explained that they had these "quizzes" every two weeks and that they were concerned with the particular aspect of the course taught during those two weeks. I decided to read up in the compendious text book, Topley & Wilson, everything about the current subject, Tetanus and its toxoid. I was sure that I knew everything necessary when the questions were put up on the board. The next session I got my paper back with an E. In my ignorance I told Alex that I had really improved from 'fail' to 'excellent'. Alex rapidly disabused me of my illusions. He explained that E did not stand for excellent but was only one minor stage from the lowest. I was very upset and decided to discuss the matter with the teacher. He explained that my answers were inadequate because I had not put down how many bugs there had to be in the solution nor to how many degrees the mixture had to be heated in order to prepare the vaccine. I said that I had no idea that I was supposed to memorize those details because I would not remember them later; and I would not dream of trying to make the toxoid without referring to the book to be sure I was doing it right. I was thoroughly conversant with the theory, the basic mechanism of the process and the utility of the product. It became apparent that the whole teaching was very different from what was expected at Cambridge. There the emphasis was on the principles and the theories behind them rather than the details and mechanics of the processes. Here it seemed necessary to clutter up my mind with a mass of details which I was most unlikely ever to use. At the end of that course there was a final exam which consisted of a number of true or false questions. It was the first exam of this kind that I had seen but I had little difficulty with it. I received a B for the whole course and the teacher, after the final result, said to me that he had no idea that I knew so much. It was an interesting, though rather traumatic, introduction to what was, for me, an entirely new system.

The Rockefeller Institute paid all my medical school fees which, I was led to believe, were only $400 a year in those days. They gave me an allowance of $100 a month for all the rest of my expenses. This had to cover food, clothes, books and other necessities. Because of the British currency regulations it was illegal for my parents to subsidize me in any way. Needless to say, I was and still am, exceedingly grateful to the Rockefeller foundation for subsidizing so much of my medical education. This was the first time in my life that I had lost the security blanket of a loving and generous family. The money, the local customs and various values were all alien to me and adjustments had to be made. The first problem was how to eat as economically as possible. Cereal for breakfast in my room was a start and the local drug store provided sandwiches and other small sundries at a reasonable price. Very little money seemed to be left over for extracurricular activities. When the US entered the war it brought change to the medical students at Harvard. The students were drafted into the military services, either the Army or the Navy. The Army took over Vanderbilt Hall as a barracks for the Army students but allowed the Navy students and the few aliens to continue to live there. The Army ran the Vanderbilt Hall and its kitchens. These provided three meals a day. For a very modest sum we aliens were allowed to subscribe to the privileges of the mess. Though the food was served on tin trays, it was excellent and solved my food problems most satisfactorily. While the Army students were subject to some mild discipline, the Navy students and the aliens were treated more as if they were guests. Alex, who was in the Navy, and I had become good friends by then. We decided to share one of the double rooms when it became available.

We worked out a study system which was most advantageous. Alex was a slow starter in the morning whereas I would get up to take a cold shower. This woke me up thoroughly. When we went to the first lecture in the morning, Alex was half asleep but I was wide awake. About half way through the lecture the heat in the auditorium got to me and I started to drift off to sleep. Alex was just beginning to wake up. I would nudge him and relax. I had taken the notes for the first half of the lecture and Alex took the notes for the second half. That evening we would go over the notes together which meant that we could review the whole lecture and discuss it. This process was great for helping both to understand and to remember the contents.

Together we developed a small group of friends who seemed distinct from the rest of the students. One was a Peruvian, Don Trojevo-Bravo, who was a little older and who had spent some time in England before coming to the States to go to medical school. The second was a Yugoslavian, Bronco Zec, who claimed to have been a friend of King Peter and left there when Peter was thrown out. Between these two they covered all European languages fluently with the exception of Finnish and Romanian. This was a great advantage when we got to the clinical phase of our training. The third member, Ed Lerner, was an American who was part Canadian and who was going to medical school because his advisor at Harvard College had told him that if he wished to pursue a career in bacteriology he would be well advised to get a medical degree. Alex was a Philadelphian and seemed somewhat different from many of the others who came from all over the States. We were a curious group as we all had very different backgrounds. Don was the athletic member of the group and we played squash many evenings before going to bed. This was another learning experience for me as the game here is played with a slightly larger and harder ball and a larger racket than I had been used to in England. One day another student came to ask if I would teach him to play squash. I knew he was supposed to be a good tennis player and looked forward to teaching him the elements of the game. I was totally chagrined when we played the first game as I only managed to get three points. I continued to lose overwhelmingly. He was a naturally gifted player with superb hand to eye coordination. I found out subsequently that he had been ranked in the top ten tennis players in California. Later on he was stationed in Europe during the war and entered the World Badminton Championships. He won this championship without losing a game, a feat with had never been accomplished before.

During that October my father had to go to Montreal on business for the RAF. He flew down to Boston in an

RAF Hudson and, after looking around my set up; he flew Alex with me down to New York for the weekend. Alex was going on to his home in Philadelphia for the weekend. It was a long weekend as it was between semesters. When we got to New York my father rang up a Dr. Stollery who was a Plymouth Brother and to whom he had an introduction. We were invited to stay with him and his family at his home in New Jersey for the weekend. We met him at a hotel in New York where we had dinner before he drove to his home. During my visit, his wife told me that I would never understand America if I traveled across the country by plane. She made me promise to travel by road if it was in any way possible.

Perhaps this is a good time to explain who the Plymouth Brethren are. This sect, if I may call them such though they resent this appellation, was started in the late 19th century in Ireland by a dissident clergyman of the Church of Ireland (which is the Irish equivalent of the Protestant Church of England) J.N. Darby. He was an erudite scholar who translated the Bible from those original sources to which he had access. He added annotations and cross references in the margins. Perhaps influenced by the letters to the churches as written in the first two chapters of Revelations, he believed that the church as organized had departed from its original teachings. It should revert to the original way the Christians were set up by the Apostles. His idea was of a system of small groups (50 to 100) based on the groups that were fed by Christ at the feeding of the five thousand. It should be without "clergy" or paid ministers. Groups would sit down together on Sunday mornings to celebrate the Lord's Supper. There was no set organization of the service but prayers and scripture readings were given spontaneously by any of the brothers who felt that they were moved by the Spirit. A loaf of bread was broken and passed around followed by wine. Hymns could be sung but without instrumental accompaniment. There were various other services such as a Bible reading and study and a Gospel preaching on Sunday evening. It is very important to understand the emphasis that they put on the teaching that Christians, though in this world, should not be 'of this world'. Worldly pleasures are a distraction and must be avoided. This applied to all public entertainment such as the theater, cinema, dances and similar activities. After this sect had been in existence for a few years, it developed several differences of opinion as to how these strict requirements should be interpreted. As a result, this sect split into several groups. The two sects I was aware of, where called the Open and the Exclusive. My parents belonged to the latter though they were somewhat more liberal and much less judgmental in their outlook than many others in the group. Only fully fledged members could participate in the services and partake of the bread and wine at the morning service which was called the 'breaking of bread'. In order to become a member of the brethren it was necessary to apply. Then the applicant was interviewed by several of the brothers to determine his sincerity and depth of commitment. Before I left school I had become a member. When a member traveled from one area to another, a letter of introduction to the 'meeting' in that area was given. This was how we got to know the people in New York and in Boston. While in Boston, though I had started to attend the Meeting on Sundays, I became increasingly dissatisfied with their exclusivity. It seemed that they felt that they were the only true Christians. Not only did this seem to me to be wrong, it seemed to represent one of the deadly sins, that of pride. I came to realize that I could not continue with a group with whom I had developed some fundamental differences of opinion. Yet I admired many of the Brethren who I met both in England and in the States. I had great respect for their sincerity and the way they lived up to their convictions. It took time, a great deal of heart searching and some mental anguish before I eventually decided that I could not continue where I was not truly committed. It was after I had left America that I formally resigned from the Brethren.

During the latter part of that year, though most of the work consisted of lectures and lab work, we were given some exposure to patients and taught the elements of physical examination, which we performed on each other. However our exposure to clinical work necessitated visiting hospitals. Harvard used several different hospitals and this meant that the students had to travel to the various sites to which they had been allocated. We had been split up into groups so that there were not too many students in any one group. This traveling presented some problems as the hospitals; mainly the Mass General and the Boston City Hospital were some distance from Vanderbilt Hall where many of us lived. Several students had cars so finding a lift with one of them was a premium occupation. Otherwise it was necessary to take a streetcar. Fortunately several of the students who had cars were very willing to help those without, some even lending their cars.

During that year we had a course called dog surgery. We were divided into groups of four and provided with a dog that we had to operate on. We were expected to perform four operations on each dog and our duties rotated. One was the surgeon, one the assistant, one the scrub nurse handing the instruments and sutures and one was the anesthetist. These dogs were kept in the animal lab and we were expected to look after them. They seemed very friendly and were always delighted to see us when we visited them to assess their progress. In retrospect this seems a very cruel activity but I learned a great deal from the experience. I felt much more competent when I had to operate on humans. We had an excellent surgeon running the course, Dr. Champ Lyons, who subsequently became a Professor of Surgery at another University. The first thing we were taught was how to scrub correctly, i.e. to sterilize our skins by washing. This was done by making us dip our arms up to the elbows in a mixture of lamp black in oil. Then we had to scrub all the black off. I discovered that there was an area at the back of my forearm that I had probably never washed before. I was quite sure I was clean until someone pointed out that there was a black streak up the back of my arm. Dr. Lyons was insistent that we did not put our noses into the wounds that we were making. Anyone getting his head too close to the wound was threatened with his hook technique. This consisted of a tape attached to the forehead which ran over the back of the head, down the back and between the legs to be attached to the scrotum with a sharp hook. Ducking the head led to dire consequences. During this course I learned to tie surgical knots rapidly with one hand, a skill which has stood me in good stead ever since. I do not think that this course has been continued and I know of no other school that has a similar one. I am sure it would be outlawed now on the basis of being unjustifiably cruel to animals.

Though the work load was considerable and there were many ongoing tests besides the examinations at the end of each course, there seemed to be time to fit in a few extracurricular activities. These divided themselves into two main categories, the intellectual and the strictly social though they sometimes overlapped. It was possible to sign up for Symphony concerts at a reduced rate as a Harvard student. The theaters were excellent and not too expensive. The Museum of Fine Arts was within easy walking distance and was worth many visits.

Female companionship was available from at least three sources, Wellesley College, Radcliffe and Pine Manor Junior College. The medical school itself was not coeducational at that time but there were the nurses with whom one had some contact. I pursued one young lady from Radcliffe quite ardently during that first year. She was from England and turned out to be very interested in going on the stage. Though she had some auditions in New York, she found that her visa did not allow her to take a job. We had many interesting discussions about art and literature. My ardor was somewhat cooled when I noted on one occasion that though her shoulder was warm, that was as far as it went.

During the fall a notice was posted offering a job as a medical counselor for an organization taking a group of children skiing for a few days in New Hampshire. This was to be right after Christmas. I applied for the post and was lucky enough to be accepted. This necessitated acquiring some skis. These I bought for what seems now to be a very reasonable price, boots $10.90, skis $15.95 and harnesses $4.50. In November it got quite cold but we did not get any snow until December. Then I got my first chance to try out the skis. Alex and I went out to ski in Fenway Park which was very close by. It took me some time even to start to navigate at all, but fairly soon I learned the most basic elements. While the weather was so cold the tennis court in the center of Vanderbilt Hall was flooded and provided an excellent skating rink. My skating experiences at Cambridge enabled me to enjoy this.

Because of the war the authorities decided that the four-year course at medical school would be compressed into three years. This could be done without curtailing any of the teaching, if the long vacations were eliminated. The largest cut was to the summer vacation which was reduced to five weeks. The Christmas vacation was preserved and Alex invited me to spend it with his family in Philadelphia before going to the ski camp immediately afterwards. Alex and I got a train from Boston to New York with my friend from Radcliffe as she was also going to New York. It was a very crowded train and seating was at a premium so the young lady had to sit on my knee for quite a bit of the journey. The train was held up on the way because the train ahead of us had run into a furniture van and we had to wait while the debris was removed. We got into New York later than we had planned. Alex wanted to take me to his old college, Princeton, on the way to Philadelphia. We were just in time to catch the last train to Princeton Junction where we arrived about midnight. There we found an eating place where I was introduced to Philadelphia Scrapple, a mixture of cornmeal, ground pork and spices. We were both hungry and Scrapple with eggs tasted very good. I have liked it ever since. Alex's brother was still an undergraduate at Princeton. He was on his Christmas vacation and we had arranged to borrow his rooms for the night. The next day Alex showed me around Princeton which I found a most impressive and very beautiful place. That afternoon we took the little train to Trenton where we joined the New York train to Philadelphia and from there by a local to Chestnut Hill where Alex's family lived. His family welcomed me warmly and I found them to be charming people. His father was the Professor of Urology at the University of Pennsylvania and his mother, a Needham, came from one of the oldest Philadelphia families. There I spent a restful couple of days with the family, going with them to the midnight service on Christmas Eve. On Christmas Day I found they had arranged a stocking for me filled with thoughtful gifts. After a sumptuous dinner I had to depart as I was due to go on the skiing trip from Boston the next day. I took the train to New York, being invited by a rather inebriated gentleman to join him in the Pullman car. The overnight train to Boston was very crowded and spending the night crunched up on my suitcase was not the most comfortable way to travel. I just had time to collect a few things, including my skis, before reporting to the skiing party back at the station by noon.

The skiing party consisted of about 40 young boys and girls. We stayed in an inn near the ski slopes. My duties consisted of running a clinic for those with minor ailments and chaperoning where and when necessary, including dormitory duty. I had plenty of time to try to ski. After a very shaky start I improved slowly during the week but was rather slowed down because I wrenched my hip on the second day. It was interesting to meet a group of American teenagers and to learn of their interests. They seemed very keen on playing card games in the evening rather than dancing or other more organized activities. The week went very quickly but by the time we had to return to Boston I felt that it had been a very worthwhile experience.

The rest of that academic year was spent completing the preclinical studies. The Professor of Pharmacology was a German, Otto Krayer. I heard later that he had come from Berlin. When my Cambridge teacher, Feldberg, had been forced to leave Germany where he was a professor of Physiology, because the Nazis did not tolerate Jews, Krayer was offered his post. Though Krayer was a German of Prussian ancestry and ideologically acceptable, he refused to take the appointment under the circumstances and left his country. Few people are prepared to put their principles on such a high level. Pitting his conscience against his national loyalty must have been agonizing. The Germans lost another very good man. He was a superb teacher, an excellent lecturer and ran a strict but inspiring department

During the third year the clinical teaching started in earnest. The class was divided into groups as we were assigned to study different subjects in separate hospitals. The basic lectures continued to be given in the mornings in the main buildings but then it was necessary to go to the hospital for the clinical work. During this period of clinical teaching we were assigned to obstetrics. As students we were responsible for delivering babies in the homes of indigent mothers. This required traveling to some rather seedy parts of Boston at short notice. There was a senior resident who was available as a backup if we, or the patient, seemed to be in trouble. A nurse went with us. She was invaluable as she knew far more than we neophytes. One of our colleagues was unfortunate enough to have the baby slip out of his hands as he delivered it. At that moment the burly husband barged into the room. He was incensed at seeing his baby on the floor. Fortunately it was not damaged. With great aplomb our colleague said; "Oh, we sometimes have to do that three or four times to start the little devils breathing!"

There was an alternative to this situation. Two or three students at a time were allowed to go to the Providence Lying in Hospital in Providence, Rhode Island, instead. It was a two week assignment. Alex and I applied to do this and were allowed to go. There we acted as junior residents, living in the hospital and taking part in all the medical activities. We delivered babies and took care of them and their mothers. It was our first chance to really feel that we were doctors. Most of the patients who were assigned to us were Portuguese women and were multips, i.e. they had had previous babies. Besides being responsible for the actual deliveries, we had to do some of the usual lab work and sometimes were called upon to give the anesthetics. We assisted the senior obstetricians with their cases, including the Cesarean sections when these were necessary. When the vaginal opening seemed to be too narrow for delivery of the baby without tearing, it was necessary to perform an episiotomy. This consists of making a slit sideways to enlarge the opening and thus prevent a random tear which, if it goes straight back, can damage the rectal sphincters. After the baby is delivered the slit has to be sewn up. It is customary to give an anesthetic for this whole procedure. While Alex was delivering one lady, the nurse who was responsible for giving the anesthetic, asked him if he needed to do an episiotomy. Alex replied rather casually "Good God, no. One could drive a truck up here". Regrettably, he did not realize that the nurse had not given any anesthetic so the patient was awake enough to hear his comment. These patients were a wonderful group of people and we appreciated our experience there. There was one very sad episode where a young woman was having bleeding and a miscarriage late in her pregnancy. The placenta was misplaced in the uterus and when the fetus was delivered and the placenta came out it was not possible to stop the bleeding. The patient died on the table. Neither of us was involved with the care of this case though we were present as observers. It was the first time I had watched a young and otherwise healthy person die and it was a very harrowing experience.

During that April I tried to make plans for the abbreviated summer vacation. I was anxious to drive across the country to the West Coast. This would fulfill my promise to the lady in New York and allow me to gain a better insight into America. There were advertisements in the papers from automobile dealers looking for drivers to take cars west. Owing to the fact that very few passenger cars were being made because all the factories were turning out military vehicles, there was a sellers' market for good second hand cars. It seemed that there were more available in the east and better prices could be obtained in California. I contacted another Rockefeller Student, Rex Whitworth, who had been sent to Iowa Medical School. He was an old friend from King's College, Cambridge. I suggested that if I could get a car to drive to California I could pick him up in Iowa City on the way. He was enthusiastic. I was not anxious to drive from New York to Iowa by myself and hoped that Alex would come with me. He had other commitments so I advertised in the Harvard press. In this way I found an Egyptian, Kahlil by name, who was studying at Harvard College. We met and agreed to team up. By answering an advertisement I obtained a car from New York to drive to Los Angeles. Kahlil and I met in New York to pick up the car. It took quite a bit of the morning to make all the necessary arrangements and do the paper-work. As a result we did not get started until almost noon. We were told we had to check in to the company's branch office in Chicago in order to get coupons for the necessary gas to go the rest of the way. During the war gas was rationed with a system of coupons. Every car owner got a basic allowance of coupons and extra coupons were given for special needs.

Having got the car we studied the map and decided we would drive to Cleveland the first day, spend the night and then drive on to Chicago. There were no fancy Interstate highways built at that time and we had no real concept of the distances and the time it would take us. As we were driving along a fairly deserted road with Kahlil at the wheel, there was a loud bang and the car was difficult to control. Kahlil stopped the car and we got out to inspect. It was obvious that at least one of the back tires was a 'retread' and its outer casing had come off. This also accounted for the curious noise that we had heard for a few miles before the loud bang. Fortunately the car had a spare tire and we were able to put it on. Evening was drawing on by the time we got to the Delaware Gap. We ate there before deciding to drive on. We were alternating the driving chores. Once it got dark, I realized that Kahlil was used to driving across the Egyptian deserts but not American roads. His night driving was too nerve-racking for me so I decided to drive the rest of the way to Cleveland. By midnight I was getting rather tired and sleepy. We came upon a curve in the road as I dropped off to sleep. I woke up just before the car went off the road. I did manage to get round the bend, though on two wheels. The fright woke me up so thoroughly that we progressed safely to Cleveland. There we arrived at about 3 am. On making inquiries we were told of a hotel downtown where we could stay. We found it in a rather seedy part of town. We took a look at the recommended hotel, assessed the people going in an out and decided that it was not for us. I remembered that another Rockefeller Student had been sent to the Medical school at the Cleveland Clinic. Perhaps we could talk our way into getting them to let us sleep in their Emergency Room. We found our way to the

Clinic and went to the Emergency room. When I explained who I was and why I was there they welcomed us with open arms. We had comfortable beds, met Peter, the other Rockefeller student, and were given a great breakfast before being allowed to leave for Chicago. There we arrived in the evening and spent the night at a hotel. The next morning we drove north towards Milwaukee to look at some of the millionaires' estates in Lake Forest, before checking in to the firm for which we were driving the car. When we got there we were in for a rude shock. We found that there were four or five other people waiting for cars to drive west but there was no way of obtaining the necessary gas. I made a great deal of fuss about the way we were being treated and the fact that we had contracted with them to drive to Los Angeles. They eventually agreed to pay for our hotel and that we should see them again the next day. That evening we decided to look around where we were in Chicago. It turned out to be Cicero, which is scarcely the most delectable part of the city. It was full of night-clubs and some rather seedy joints. Kahlil and I decided to inspect a few. We would go in, stating that we were looking for some friends. Once we had seen what was going on we left each one stating that we could not find our friends. (Rather crude strip-tease was not my cup of tea). This was a cheap education for an innocent like me and solidified my taste for what I considered better things.

The next day we returned to the car company only to be told that there was no gas available and that we were stuck. There was only one thing to do. That was to see if any other companies would help us. Several inquiries led to the information that company X would be getting cars through if anyone was. I went round to that company and was met by a very good-looking, business-like lady. She agreed that they had cars that they wanted to get driven to California and that the difficulty was getting gas. She suggested that I might try to get the necessary coupons myself. She offered to help me to fill in the requisition form. We decided that the purpose of my going west was to go to Berkeley Medical School and that I was driving the car for its owner who lived in Los Angeles. This was true because the owner of the firm did live in LA. The lady then told me which was the most lenient rationing office in Chicago and how to get there. Off I went, wearing a Cambridge blazer, and presented my application to the girl at the desk. She said; "You're English aren't you?" I admitted as much. She then told me that the supervisor was English and that she was sure she would like to talk with me. I was introduced to this lady who had been born in Liverpool. After the usual small talk, she asked what I needed. I told her as much of the truth as seemed expedient and explained that I had been told I would need 200 gallons to get to California. She asked how soon I needed it. I told her I was expected to pick up another friend in Iowa City that night. She said that it was too far and that I would never get there but agreed that I needed the gas right away. Then she said that she did not think that 200 gallons would be enough. She immediately gave me 240 gallons worth of coupons and wished me luck. After expressing my most sincere gratitude, I returned to the X Company. The lady there looked a little surprised but showed us the car that she would like us to drive for her company. It was an almost new white Pontiac convertible. We climbed in happily and set off for Iowa City at once.

We did get there that night but it was almost midnight. We found Rex Whitworth still celebrating the end of his school year. We joined the party and met his friends, including Bill who was to join us on our trip west. Bill was a classmate of Rex and he had never been out of Iowa. He was enthusiastic about coming with us and was looking forward to seeing the sea for the first time. It was revealing to realize how far the Midwest was from the oceans and to consider how this distance could alter an appreciation of the world in general. The isolationism that was so prevalent before World War II was much easier to understand.

We started our trip in a white Pontiac Convertible

We spent the rest of the night in beds in the dormitory before packing up to move on. Bill had arranged for us to have a meal with his family who lived nearby by Midwest distances. They gave us a wonderful meal before we left in the afternoon to drive to Sioux City. There we had a meal before driving on all night with only a 2 hour stop, sleeping in the car. While in Sioux City a friendly character showed us how to disconnect the speedometer. This was a very simple process that could be done by loosening one nut under the dashboard, which could be tightened to return it to normal function. This was most helpful because the car was not expected to have too many miles on the odometer when it was turned in to the Los Angeles garage. The only disadvantage was that it was impossible to know for sure how fast we were driving when we were going through areas with speed limits.

That day had been very hot, terminating in a real Midwest electrical storm with thunder, lightning and torrential rain. It was my first experience with any weather as awesome as this and gave an insight of the conditions that the pioneers must have endured as they trekked west.

The next day we were in South Dakota. After breakfast in Draper we drove on through the Bad Lands, stopping to wander a little through these. It was scary to realize how easy it would be to get lost among the hills and valleys of the bare sand without apparent evidence of any vegetation. We went on through Dinosaur Park to the Black Hills. The weather had improved and these hills seemed incredibly beautiful. The Rushmore Memorial with its monumental mountain carving of four Presidents was interesting and unique. The weather changed to rain again before we got to Hot Springs but the country had been exciting with its constant changes and varying beauty. At Hot Springs we had a meal and found a tourist camp. It was not easy to get to this because the rain had made the roads slippery. There were cabins which could be rented for four dollars a day and bathing facilities were available. We took advantage of this and had a very good night's rest. Early the next morning we started off on the wrong road. It was still raining and the road of mud and gravel made driving difficult, but we got back onto the right road and set out to go over the Teton Pass.

Before leaving Boston my roommate, Alex, told me he knew a lady from Philadelphia who had married a cowboy and was living in Cora, Wyoming. He suggested that we should stop there and visit with them. He wrote to them warning them that we might be coming. It sounded like a wonderful opportunity to see a real working ranch in the Wild West. We had to get over the mountains to get there. None of us had much idea what we were letting ourselves in for. When we got to the base of the pass we found that it was officially closed. Not deterred we continued a short distance, before finding a ranch where we asked about the situation. A young lady explained that the pass was closed because of snow and not even the mailman could get through. This was at the end of May. This lady told us that the only way to get over the mountains was to take the South Pass. On the map the roads did not look very inspiring. We had discovered that most of the minor roads were dirt surfaced. When dry they were quite good but when wet they were very treacherous. Fortunately they were dry as we wound up over the snow line and down the other side. The scenery was magnificent but we did not get into Pinedale, Wyoming, until after dark, about 10.30 PM. We were looking for somewhere to eat and sleep as it was too late to drive on to Cora which looked, on the map, very close by. At Pinedale we found a very small town with little more than a couple of buildings at a cross roads. There was only one building with lights on and we looked through the window hopefully. It was a bar and around the table sat some cowboys' playing cards. They had piles of silver dollars in front of them and they had taken their guns off and laid them on the table. This did not look very encouraging. We decided that discretion was the better part of valor and that we would go to bed hungry. There was a sort of motel made of log cabins on the opposite corner and we managed to get beds there.

The next morning we got breakfast and very good it seemed. When the people there found that three of us were medical students they asked us to examine a cowboy who had fallen off his horse the night before. They did not realize how green we really were. We did our best, could detect no serious injuries and decided his chief problem was a severe hang over. We got directions for the road to Cora which turned out to be a single store without any other habitation in sight. From this store we got directions to the O Bar Y Ranch, which was our destination, from an outspokenly Anglophobe character. We were told we could not miss it. We drove along a dirt road happily though cautiously, until we came to a fork. This was a disconcerting surprise as we had not been warned that there was a divide in the road. After tossing up, we took the right fork. Some little way along we came to a ranch building where we met a very pleasant old man. He was most talkative. He seemed to live alone on his spread. After a lot of conversation, he explained that we should have taken the left fork. We backtracked to take the other fork and, after a few miles, arrived at O Bar Y Ranch. Alex's friend Cita and her husband

Dick Dew gave us a wonderful welcome. We asked about their neighbor who had set us on the right road. He had seemed such an interesting loner. It turned out he was a retired cattle rustler.

We were the first people the Dews had seen since they had been snowed in the previous fall. They were a most attractive couple. Cita's life must have been quite a contrast from her upbringing as a Philadelphian debutante. Their isolation was inconceivable to us. Cita had delivered her baby at home with the only possible outside care being provided by the local doctor who would have had to fly in. Being so isolated tests a relationship in a way that few experience, perhaps fortunately. An inner fortitude and self-reliance is necessary to survive but there are those who thrive in such settings. This couple seemed to be examples. They had the cattle to care for but the winters were long, cruel and must have seemed interminable. Dick spent some of his time making beautiful silver inlays on the leather harnesses that he had to use. The only other person we met while we were there was a cowboy who helped Dick care for the cattle.

In the course of conversion they found out that I had done a lot of riding but never in a western saddle. I confessed that I would love to ride with Dick while he was rounding up and checking on some of the cattle. The cowboy generously offered to lend me his horse and saddle. Since he was shorter than I am and the stirrup leathers on the saddle were not adjustable, I found myself riding with short stirrups on a western saddle. This may not seem much of a problem to those who are not horse riders, but the technique for riding using the different saddles requires considerable adjustment. This is most marked when trotting as one does not post in a western saddle but sits down, seeming to bump along. Actually it is very comfortable and much more restful over a long period of time. The other difference is noticeable when cantering or galloping. Owing to the presence of the pommel or horn on the front of the saddle, which is used for roping, rising on the stirrups and leaning forward can be exceedingly painful and even mutilating. Riding the cowboy's horse was an amazing experience. The horse was very well-trained, and nimble, being able to negotiate some rough ground with ease. When one of the cattle broke away from the herd I swung around to see where it was going. As I swung my head, the horse turned instantly and took off after the stray. It took me so much by surprise that I nearly fell off.

When we returned to the stables, the others joined us. They had been walking with Cita and climbed the nearby hill to admire the view. It is wonderful country. What appear to be hills are really the top of mountains. It is hard to realize how high above sea level it all is. We were warned that, because of the altitude the atmosphere is somewhat rarefied and it is easy to find oneself out of breath. Also a little alcohol goes a long way. Even Rex, who had been President of Athletics at Cambridge and an international hurdler, got short of breath walking up the climbs.

Back at the stables Dick tried to teach us how to use a rope, spin a loop and to use it as a lasso. We were not very apt pupils. Even when we made the loop we could seldom get it to drop over the post that we were using as a target.

Though the weather had not been too good, we found this short stay with such hospitable people a great relief from the driving. Rex even tried a swim in one of the mountain streams. The sound of his gasps and the sight of him shivering discouraged the rest of us. The melting snow feeding the stream was not appealing. It was still raining the next day so we spent the morning cleaning ourselves and our clothes before setting off after an excellent midday meal. When we tried to settle up for our stay, we were made to feel that we were insulting them. Such is the true western hospitality. They had given us a wonderful time and a truly memorable experience.

Setting off that day in the drizzle made driving on the wet dirt road a nightmare. Rex, who was driving the car, skidded off the road at one point but no damage was done. We got back onto the road without too much difficulty. We stopped at the store at Cora where we again found the character that had made it abundantly clear that he despised all Englishmen. This was quite a change from our reception at the ranch. As we went on through Pinedale towards Jackson's Hole the weather cleared allowing us to appreciate the beauty of the scenery. We had the Teton Mountains on one side, snow covered and rising above the clouds, yet reflected majestically on Lake Jenny. We spent the night at Jackson Hole before setting out in filthy weather to go over the Teton Pass. It was disappointing to miss what we realized must be some magnificent views. Once over the mountains we decided to drive south to Salt Lake City. There we found a hotel and looked up a Harvard colleague and his family. We had an opportunity to see the Mormon Tabernacle from the outside but not much else as it was raining. There was one inch of rain that day, the greatest rain fall that Salt Lake City had had in 65 years.

The next day we backtracked north as we were making for Portland, Oregon. Our plan was to drive down the coast from there to Los Angeles. At lunch time we stopped to get gas and something to eat while the car was having an oil change and grease job. It was a very successful stop as the food was good and cheap. Furthermore they forgot to ask for the coupons for the gas and I am ashamed to say we did not remind them. We had been driving the car hard and, at times, fast so we felt that it deserved some TLC. After entering Boise in another rain storm we set out for Weiser. Soon after we left Boise we found ourselves running beside the railway with a passenger train going our way. I was driving and decided to race the train. Some of the passengers in the train were waving encouragement and we were driving somewhat over the speed limit. At that time there was a national speed limit set with the idea of saving gas. As we got into Weiser we thought that we should get off the main road lest someone might report the way we had been driving. On the map we noted a small town called Cambridge just to the north. Since both Rex and I were Cambridge men we decided that it would be fun to see the town. We noticed that the map showed a road running west from Cambridge to a ferry across the Snake River. This would bring us near Hells' Canyon which sounded as if it would be worth a visit.

We got to Cambridge, which was somewhat of a disappointment, and set off towards the ferry. By this time it was almost 8.30 in the evening but it did not look far to the river. In June the days were long. After a short distance the road deteriorated so much that we wondered if we were on the right route. We found a house and, to our inquiry, were assured that we were. The road was dirt and wound round the side of a small mountain. There was a sharp drop-off on the left side with no obvious edge to the road and rocks narrowing the road on the right. At one point we had to have one of us in front watching that the left front wheel did not drop over the edge while another, at the rear, watched to see that we did not scrape the right back fender on the boulder. After that little excitement we progressed safely though somewhat slowly to the river where we arrived about 10:30 PM. By the ferry crossing there was one building. We inquired about getting across the river but were told firmly that the ferry did not run at night. We debated among ourselves as to what to do. Going back on that road at night did not appeal. Since the people at the ferry station had not offered any hospitality we decided that further intrusion would be unwise. The only alternative was to sleep in the car until morning. It was cold and we had not had anything to eat since lunch, but we did have a couple of chocolate bars. We built a fire, sat around it, told stories and ate the chocolate until after midnight. Then we climbed into the car to try to sleep until dawn. Our sleep was somewhat disturbed by the calling of the coyotes who sounded very close by.

Crossing the Snake River on the Ferry

When the sun got up we understood why the ferry did not run at night. The ferry consisted of two narrow boats fastened together with planks. To get on or off this ferry planks were put between the sloping bank and the ferry so that they were under the wheels of the vehicle. You had to drive up these planks. Once aboard the crossing was accomplished by using the current of the river. A rope attached to the front of the ferry was shortened while the rope attached to the other end was loosened. Thus the ferry became diagonal and the current swept it across to the other side. All went well until we got to the other side. Here the ramp, up which we had to go, was at a sharp angle. The planks were placed and we started off. It was necessary to turn the front of the car sharply as it hit the bank. I was trying to drive slowly and carefully but the engine was cold and kept stalling out. The car stalled again just as I got the front wheels onto the ramp. I got it started again but had to gun the engine to get up the hill. This got the back wheels in rapid motion. The result was that the planks shot out from under the car and the rear end dropped into the water. Fortunately it was not too deep, the wheels gripped and up the ramp we went. We climbed into the car and started off only to notice that the car was not driving very well. Inspection revealed that one of the back tires had a big gash in it. No problem as I knew that we had a brand new tire as a spare. We got out the tire but our discomfort was complete when we found there was no jack or lug nut wrench. There was no alternative except to walk until we could find some habitation where we might borrow the necessary equipment. We were hungry, a little tired and I was more than a little unpopular with my traveling mates. Within a few miles we found what we were looking for, borrowed the equipment, changed the tire and got started off again.

We never did get to Hells' Canyon as we were told that it was a 20 mile drive down the river and then a 10 mile hike or horse-back ride to the canyon itself. It did not seem to be a practical proposition for us. We went the other way seeking a town where we could get something to eat. The first place we came to was Richland and there we stopped for breakfast. We were famished but Rex and I were on a tight budget and Bill was not exactly rich so we looked to see what was the most we could get for the least money. It turned out to be pancakes and syrup with eggs on top. It was a mixture that I had never had before but was one of the best breakfasts I have ever eaten. It is wonderful how circumstances can influence your opinions.

From there we set out for Portland via Pendleton. While buying food in Pendleton the local Sheriff became curious and asked what we were doing with a fancy convertible carrying Illinois license plate in Oregon. Obviously we were four bums in a stolen car. By dint of telling the truth and explaining that we were medical students driving a car west for someone else, he seemed satisfied. Fortunately we had enough papers to prove this, so he allowed us to proceed. However this experience alerted us to the fact that we might be stopped and questioned again now that we were in more populous country. To our surprise Rex told us that he did not have an American driver's license. He had been taking his turn at the wheel as we were spelling each other regularly. The car had a bench type front seat and the gear shift was on the steering column. We usually drove with three in the front and only one in the back. On the way between Pendleton and Portland we noted that there was a police car behind us. Rex was driving and I was sitting next to him. We did a flying change. This consisted of Rex pulling forward and my sliding under him into the driver's seat to take over without slowing the car. It is not a maneuver that is recommended by safety experts but it works. Obviously the police did not notice as we were not stopped.

The drive along the Columbia River to Portland was very beautiful. The weather had improved and we were able to enjoy the scenery. On the way we saw an army sergeant hitchhiking. We stopped to pick him up. He was trying to get to his home in Portland. We dropped him off there and decided to go on north as we were anxious to see Mt Rainier before turning south. It was dark by this time. After we left Portland we came to a T junction and had to decide whether to turn left or right. There was no signpost but it was a beautiful starlit night. I knew that we had to go north. In spite of my most rudimentary knowledge of the stars I could recognize the Big Dipper and the North Star. It was to the right and we went that way. In the early hours of the morning we found a small town with a hotel where we could get accommodation. Wearily but happily we turned in for the night, sleeping until 10 the next morning.

We drove to Mt Rainier admiring the countryside. There we fed the deer in the park and tried a climb in Paradise Valley. Rex made it to the top but we others tried a short cut that led to nowhere. We finished up sliding down a very steep incline on the seat of our pants. The beauty of the whole place made our detour well worthwhile. We would have liked to spend longer there but we had to get on south to deliver the car. We returned to Portland for the night.

After we had eaten there, we looked for somewhere to stay. We could find no place with empty accommodation. Portland, at this time, was bustling with activity as it was one of the main shipbuilding ports in the West. There, Kaiser was mass producing ships at an unprecedented rate. In desperation we decided to sleep in the car. We found a side road, parked the car and settled down. Bill was in the driver seat with Rex beside him and Khalil took the back seat. Being the smallest I lay crosswise on the floor in the back. We were all very tired and slept soundly in spite of being somewhat cramped. In the middle of the night there was an imperious tap on the window beside Bill's head. He woke to find two police men one on each side of the car. He wound down the window and they opened the door. I was still asleep. As they opened the door they saw my head and demanded to know what Bill was doing with a body in the car. At that moment the body woke up. The police wanted to know what we were doing with the car in Portland. I explained that we were driving it from Chicago to Los Angeles. "By way of Portland", they demanded incredulously. I tried to explain that because I was an Englishman they had given me extra gas. They shook their heads but accepted the truth. We had a pleasant conversation with them. I told them that I was sorry that we had not seen them before as we could have committed a minor offense so that we would be locked up for the night. There we would have had a bed. After cautioning us about the danger to which we were subjecting ourselves by sleeping in the car, they drove off.

The next morning it was imperative that we find some toilet facilities. Inspiration struck and we found the Bus Depot. There we managed to wash and shave before driving to the house of the family of our hitch-hiker. He had been most pressing that we call on them. He told us that some of his family worked in the ship yards and would take us to see the ships being built. When we got to their house, they enabled us to change our clothes before they took us round the Yards. This was a special treat for Bill who had never seen the sea or any big ships. After this expedition they wanted to set us on our way south. As it was a Sunday and they did not have to work, we found that they had decided to drive with us a little way so that we could all have a picnic together. We had wanted to buy them lunch but we found that they already had the picnic lunch prepared.

They knew the countryside and we stopped in a pleasant park to eat. It was a magnificent repast that they had prepared. It was about 5 PM before we left them to drive on. Much to our embarrassment they insisted on stuffing the car with more food so that we would have an evening meal as well. Little did any of us think that we would be so richly rewarded for giving a lift to a hitch hiker? Their generosity and that of the family on the ranch at Cora revealed to me an aspect of the American character that has left a permanent impression.

After we left this hospitable family we set off for San Francisco. We picked up an army hitch-hiker for a little distance and then a young sailor who said he was serving in a submarine. He confessed that his ship had been in Tokyo harbor. This was somewhat of a surprise to us but we did not express our skepticism. We spent that night at an auto park which we found very comfortable. The next morning we got going early as we wished to see the Redwoods and to take the coast road. The redwoods lived up to all that we had heard about them. It was quite an experience to drive through the middle of a tree. We wandered a little off the road to examine the flora under these enormous and ancient trees. It was all most interesting. The coast road gave some magnificent views of the cliffs and the Pacific Ocean. The road was tortuous in parts and there were some fog patches so going was slow. It was almost midnight when we got to the Golden Gate Bridge which we went over to get to Berkeley. There we found a cheap and nasty hotel for the night. We had stopped for gas just before getting to San Francisco and there had another example of the local generosity as they gave us about four pounds of delicious cherries.

Having had a quick look around Berkeley we went into the Chinese area of San Francisco for breakfast. We had been told to be sure to visit Gump's, a famous shop specializing in Chinese art, especially Jade, if we got to S.F. We dutifully went there. While we were looking around, a gentleman came up to ask if there was anything he could do for us. This surprised us as we thought we were a rather scruffy looking bunch after all our traveling. After we explained who we were and that we were not in a position, financially, to buy anything, he asked if we would like to see some of the better pieces of Jade that they had. We jumped at the offer, so he unlocked an inner room and took us inside. It is unlikely that there was a finer collection of jade anywhere in the world outside of China itself. We were spellbound by the beauty and the workmanship exhibited by the various pieces, and by the extent of the collection. It seems that it had taken many years of oriental trading to assemble so many rare objects of art.

We left in the early afternoon determined to get to Los Angeles before we stopped again. It was only 400 miles and we did not think that it would be too difficult. As we left, there was a real San Francisco fog. When we stopped for gas we could only just see enough to drive. The garage man who was filling the car realized that I was English and asked how I could manage to live in a country so notorious for its fogs. Rudely, I lied to him, telling him that I had no idea what a fog was really like until I encountered the one that I was in at that moment. The coast road was winding and we kept running into more patches of fog, or should I call it 'thick sea mist'. We were not allowed to use the headlights because of wartime restrictions so driving was much slower than we had planned. We did not get into L.A. until early the next morning. There we went straight to the YMCA to check in and get a cleanup.

At the YMCA we found that we could stay there so we booked for four nights at 75 cents a night. We were also told that there was a standing invitation from Jeanette MacDonald, the Hollywood singing star, for all overseas guests to be sent to see her at her house. Much to our disappointment she was out of town and we missed this privilege. At that time I was a great admirer of hers. Having driven the car to Los Angeles safely or at least without any serious mishaps, all we had left to do was delivering it and then get back East. We spent one day driving around viewing the sights and the film stars' houses before getting the car washed and turned in to the garage which owned it. They seemed very happy to have the car and even returned us $5 from our original deposit. They did not charge us for the tire we had ruined getting off the ferry. As a result the cost of our transportation across the States was about $25 each.

Each of us had to make our own plans for the return journey. I tried to hitch a ride on a plane using my RAF connections through my father. I drew a complete blank there. I found that the cheapest form of public transportation was the bus. If I could get to Philadelphia I knew I could stay with Alex's family as I had already been invited there. Four and a half days continuous travel by bus did not sound very attractive but it was cheap, $50. After a couple more days looking around LA, I caught the Greyhound bus at 7:15 in the evening for the first stage to Albuquerque. There we arrived after midnight the next day. The bus was very full but I had managed to get a seat and slept fitfully. The next day we drove through Arizona and the Painted Desert. The weather was good and the scenery interesting. After a delay in Albuquerque, the next bus took us to Las Vegas. We progressed across the country with various stops for food and other necessary relief but the whole journey is a vague jumble in my mind. I have a hazy memory of a stop in the early hours of one morning in St Louis where I drank as much as I could with hope to numb the weariness. I had started on a Saturday evening and found myself in Pittsburgh at 8 am on Thursday. I just managed to catch the bus to Philadelphia and had a seat until lunch time. The bus kept collecting more people until there was barely enough room to stand. I gave up my seat and stood or sat on the floor the rest of the way. We got into Philadelphia late that night. I managed to catch the local train to Chestnut Hill where the Randall's welcomed me with a bed and some rest.

There were still almost three weeks of vacation left before courses started again in Boston. I decided to spend 10 days with the Randall's and then the rest in New York where another of the Rockefeller students would put me up in the intern's quarters at the Presbyterian Hospital. Philadelphia that summer was a very interesting experience for me. Alex's sister, Virginia, was Coming Out, i.e. being officially introduced to Philadelphia society. As her brother he was invited to a number of parties and I was allowed to tag along. Because of the war, there was a shortage of eligible males and so the various hostesses were pleased to have an extra one. In this way I received an introduction to Philadelphia Society. I met the 'right people', learned that you should go to Saunderstown for the summer and that God lives in Rittenhouse Square. I was asked by one young lady whether I did not find the class distinctions in England intolerable. Since I was attending a most exclusive dance at the time and had been carefully vetted by the hostess before I was allowed in, I was rather surprised at the question. I replied that I had not fully appreciated how exclusive Society could be until I came to Philadelphia. Perhaps I had been moving in the wrong circles in England. It was revealing to try to understand the different customs. At one dance I had met a very attractive young lady. I found out that she lived not far from the Randall's so I arranged to call on her one evening. When I got there I met her parents. After chatting with them for a short while the young lady and I were left alone. Sitting on the porch together I noticed that she was wearing a ring on the fourth finger of her left hand. Presuming that it was an engagement ring, I asked her about her fiancée. She whipped off the ring and informed me that she did not have one. We spent a very pleasant evening together and I found out that she was only 17 and that she liked Englishmen. When I talked to Alex about the ring, he told me that the girls only wore them to scare off all but the more determined suitors.

Alex and I did not spend all our time at these social events. We visited the hospitals with Dr. Randall, made rounds with him and watched some operations. It was a rather strenuous routine as it was difficult to get up in the morning if one had been partying half the night before.

One episode revealed to me that human nature is much the same everywhere in the world. If you are a caring altruistic person there are those who will take advantage of you. It happened to Dr. Randall. In his usual generous manner, he had operated on a man as a charity case. Making rounds Dr. Randall decided that the patient was ready to go home. At once the patient called the nurse over and told her to call his chauffeur to bring his car.

There is a most unusual story with regard to the actions of a grateful patient. At the time when there was prohibition, the actions of the gangs who supplied liquor were notorious. One gang was centered in Trenton, just across the river from Philadelphia. The leader of this gang developed severe abdominal pain and had to be hospitalized. He chose a hospital in Philadelphia where he rented a whole floor and posted his own security guards. With more than a little trepidation the surgeon operated on him. The operation was a success and the patient's account was settled. This was not the end of the matter as about once a month a case of liquor was left at the door of the doctor's house. Finally a man called at the door asking for the doctor. He said to the doctor that his employer, the gangster patient, wanted to know if there was anyone that he, the doctor, particularly disliked. If so he only had to say who it was and he would see him no more.

After ten hectic days overlapping hospital visits with the doctor and social engagements associated with 'coming out' parties, I took the train to New York. The Randall's had been most generous and had made me so welcome that I felt totally at home. A fellow Rockefeller student, Robert, who had been assigned to Columbia Medical School, agreed to put me up on the day bed in his room at Presbyterian Hospital. I had an ulterior motive for my stay in New York. I wanted to see more of the young lady, Anne Colcord, from Wellesley to whom I was very much enamored. She was at home with her parents who lived in Scarsdale. I managed to spend one day with her, visiting the Metropolitan Museum and the Frick art collection. Then we went to the Lewisham Stadium to listen to Paul Robeson before taking her to Grand Central Station so that she could catch the last train home. The next day Robert and I went to see The Skin of Our Teeth. We found this a rather confusing experience. The play itself was not too comprehensible at first, but our confusion was exacerbated by the fact that we went outside at the intermission. When we returned everything seemed even more bizarre. It took us a few minutes to realize that we had returned to the wrong theater. On that street in New York there seemed to be a string of theaters and they all looked similar from the outside. When we confessed what had happened to some friends later, we were informed that we were not the only people who had made this mistake.

I spent one more day with Anne. I took the train out to her house where I met her parents. Then we cycled about 10 miles to a beach and spent the day there before returning to her parents' house for supper. We spent the evening talking. Besides being a beautiful young lady, she was clever and very well read. We had many intellectual interests in common and I thought that if she would marry me we could have a good life together. However I came to realize that a successful marriage depends on mutual love. This 'love' is a thing which is very difficult to define except that it has to be 'two way' to be really meaningful. Without reciprocal devotion, a relationship cannot last as it is built on a false foundation. Unrequited love has been the subject of great literature and the basis for many tragedies, literary and otherwise. It is better to be a realist than the subject of another tragic story. I think that it was at this time that I realized that, though Anne liked me, she could never love me. From then on we were just good friends.

Two days later I returned to Boston for my final year at Harvard Medical School.

Chapter 4

THE LAST YEAR AT HARVARD MEDICAL SCHOOL

My final year at medical school started quite routinely and without any premonition that it would be, in many ways, the most significant year of my life. Having started with the thought that I would like to be a physician because I did not like the idea of surgery, I finished up with the determination to try to be a pediatric surgeon. I had spent the first year in Boston chasing a number of young ladies and finished my last year with a fiancée to whom I became happily married after I returned to England. The fourth year started at the beginning of July but it was not until the spring of the next year (1944) that these changes began.

When I got back to Boston, Alex and I found ourselves busy with lectures and visits to the hospitals for clinical teaching. I started with a rotation in General Medicine. There was a considerable amount of hands-on examination of patients. We were given new patients to 'work up'. This entailed taking a very detailed history, examining the patient and then writing up all that we had discovered. At the Brigham Hospital, where I was assigned, the study of one patient took most of a day and part of the night. The next morning the 'attending' (the physician in charge of the patient) made rounds. The student had to present his case and was criticized on the history and the physical examination. Thereafter the attending would quiz the student about the patient's condition and what the diagnosis might be. He was expected to have read up about it the night before and even to have looked up some of the current medical literature. There was one attending who quoted the current literature extensively, giving chapter and verse for his quotes. This was a little too much so, on one occasion, we took down his quotes and their references to check them. When we did this, we found that they were more than somewhat inaccurate as to details. I found this all rather tedious though in retrospect, I realize that I learned a lot as he was a stimulating teacher.

Besides this clinical exposure which extended to various outpatient clinics, we had a series of lectures on a wide range of subjects. Some of these were given by very eminent doctors who were the recognized leaders in their fields. Unfortunately erudition in a field does not necessarily endow one with the ability to lecture well. Some lectures were very dull and uninformative but this was the exception rather than the rule. Later when I went through the notes that I had taken I was amazed to discover how much I had been told. When I got back to England and went over these notes during my residency there, I found them very valuable. It was not until I was confronted with practical problems that I appreciated how very thorough was the teaching to which I had been subjected.

Because I was to return to England when I graduated from Harvard I was anxious to see as much as I could about American medical practice. I discovered that it had been permissible to transfer from one medical school to another and get credit for a course taken there. It was not a very common practice and was not done during the war. I decided to ask if I could avail myself of this privilege. I should explain that the final year was divided into periods when specific subjects were studied. Since I was not particularly interested in surgery, I thought this would be a good time to see if I could get permission to transfer. I decided that Johns Hopkins, because of its reputation, would be most interesting. I negotiated with the Dean at Harvard and the Rockefeller Foundation and found that Hopkins would accept me. After getting this permission, I also got permission to spend two weeks studying anesthesiology at a hospital near Philadelphia where Dr. Randall, my roommate's father, worked. I arranged to do this in the spring.

There were two other memorable events in the first part of that last year. When I first got back, Ed Lerner and I realized that the lack of a car was cramping our style. We set about trying to find one which we could afford. At this time cars were difficult to come by as no new ones were being sold to the public because of the war. There were some old ones available though mostly in rather poor condition. We turned down a Ford which was offered for $50. There was a Chrysler Airflow for $175. Someone told us that the passenger seat could be folded down to make a bed. On the basis of this information one of our colleagues offered to contribute if he could borrow it on occasion. When he discovered that we had been misinformed about the front seat, he cried off and we could not raise the money. Ed and I eventually settled for an old Nash for $50. It was not the most reliable car and often had to be pushed to get it started. However it usually got us to the hospitals and to Wellesley College for our social encounters. On one occasion a couple of RAF pilots who were training in Canada came down to visit. I took them in our car which we had named Beelzebub, out to Wellesley College to meet some of the young ladies there. On the way, there was a loud explosion. My passengers looked for their parachutes to bail out, but finding none, sat tight and prayed. We had blown a tire and were stuck since we did not have a spare. Getting a replacement was no easy task during the war but we did manage it. We got my passengers safely to the college where they seemed to have a good time. The campus is very beautiful with a lake where one can canoe and admire both the scenery and the company.

The other important event was my introduction to a lady who became the next best thing to a foster mother to Alex and me. Mrs. Lefferts was the wife of the headmaster of a prestigious private school. Her husband was serving as an intelligence officer in England and she was living in an apartment overlooking the Charles River. Aunt Betsy, as we came to know her, offered us a home from home where we could visit when we needed a change from life at the medical school dormitory. She was a very generous, wise and exceedingly well-informed lady. Alex had been introduced to her through his Philadelphia connections. Through her we met many of her relatives both of her generation and that of her nieces. They proved to be a remarkable group of people, well-to-do, very bright and rather nonconformist. Aunt Betsy herself was someone to whom I found I could open up easily. She was a good listener, nonjudgmental and full of sound advice. It was she who said to me one day, when you are married there will come a time when someone, other than your wife, will seem far more attractive. Before you do anything stupid, consider what it will be like with that other person in a few years time." Is this thought a corollary to Kipling's quote: "The more you have known of the other, the less you will settle for one" But perhaps the truth of that remark has become abundantly manifest in the 1980s and 90s. With the sexual promiscuity that has become, if not acceptable, at least widely condoned, lasting marriages are increasingly rare.

We spent many pleasant evenings at her apartment being very well entertained, and we went to quite a few concerts and shows with her. We also visited her brothers in Connecticut. One was called Uncle Swill. He produced a bottle of Rye whiskey which had been matured by being taken round Cape Horn in a barrel before being bottled. Very smooth it was and we drank more of it than was wise.

The other was Uncle Dan Barney. He was an alcoholic, diabetic, poet and photographer with private means. One time his family packed him off to a sanitarium to be dried out. When he got there, he was offered a drink which he refused. When they inquired as to why he did not wish to have a drink, he replied that it was because there were so many interesting people there to whom he enjoyed talking that he was not bored and did not need a drink. When he returned home he reverted to his habit of starting the day with a couple of ounces of neat whiskey. On one occasion I went down to New York with him and shared his hotel room. In the middle of the night I was awakened by his stentorian breathing. I could not rouse him and was in a quandary. I did not know whether he was merely sleeping it off or whether he was slipping into a diabetic coma. Fortunately it turned out to be the former.

One evening during the fall while I was playing squash before going to bed, I pulled off a magnificent shot from the back left-hand corner while turning the other way. Unfortunately it was not the only thing I pulled. I gave my back a severe wrench. Since the pain the next day was crippling I went to see the local physician who sent me to Dr. Green. He was an outstanding orthopedic surgeon and a great favorite of our class. After assuring me that I had not ruptured a disc and that I should not let anyone operate on my back, he recommended rest. He put me in hospital at the Brigham for a few days. This was not too much of a hardship as I was given a private room and was visited almost continuously by many friends, both male and female. They were not averse to bringing in a few things to cheer me, and them up. The hospital was probably glad to get rid of me as my visitors were not always quiet and I played classical music audibly on the radio. Perhaps the night nurse missed me most as she used to come to sit and chat whenever she had a spare moment. They fitted me with a back brace and let me get back to work and limited physical activities. By Christmas time, I was feeling sufficiently recovered to accept an invitation to go to Canada.

Through RAF friends of my father who were stationed in Montreal I had been introduced to a very generous lady, a Mrs. Duckett. She invited me to spend Christmas that year in Montreal as her guest. There it was the coldest I had experienced, being well below zero at night. Mrs. D took me and her niece to various shows and an ice hockey game. She also took us to a very memorable restaurant called "Au Lutin Qui Boeff" (I am told that this can be translated the little Gnome who teases). As one entered the restaurant the cuts of meat were laid out in a case to one side, on the other there was a tank of fish. One was expected to choose one's menu which was then cooked to order. While this was being done, there was a little piglet that ran around the floor. It could be picked up and it thoroughly enjoyed being nursed with a baby's bottle of milk. I remembered this restaurant so well that many years later, when I was visiting Montreal for an International Pediatric meeting, I decided to take a couple of my pediatric surgical colleagues, one from Australia and one from England, to eat there. No one at the meeting seemed to know about the place or where it was. One of the hostesses at the convention was the French Canadian wife of a local doctor. She knew of the place but explained that it was in one of the suburbs. She told us how to get there and that we would need to take a taxi. Neither the food nor the piglet was a disappointment. I still have the picture of Nicky, my English colleague, with the piglet on his lap while he fed it from a bottle. Nicky Nixon became the leading Pediatric Surgeon in England. When he came to Washington as a visiting consultant, I had the picture made into a slide and had it shown at the start of one of his lectures.

After Christmas Mrs. Duckett, bless her, took me with her niece to a ski resort up in the mountains for a week. The weather was excellent with sunny, clear days. I was surprised to find how cold it was at night but how warm in the sun during the day. I found myself skiing in shirt sleeves and getting a little sunburn. Though I twisted my ankle the first day, it did not seem to be very serious. With some expert lessons, I learned to ski sufficiently well to enjoy some of the more difficult runs.

After this pleasant break I returned to get back to work, little realizing all that the rest of the year would have in store for me. At first it was very much as it had been before the break. A lot of work studying and as many social activities as could be squeezed in. Alex and I listened to a great deal of music, read outside of medical subjects when we could, and had the usual learned discussions that young men often think are so important. These latter were aided and abetted by Aunt Betsy who always seemed to be available to hear us out. The major change came in the early spring when it was time for me to take the courses that I had arranged, anesthesia in Philadelphia and surgery at Johns Hopkins in Baltimore.

I went to stay with the Randall's for two weeks, going to Abingdon Hospital just outside Philadelphia where Dr. Randall had some of his patients. He introduced me to the anesthesiologists' who took me under their wing. As the only student there, I had a wonderful time and much individual attention. It was a real learning experience with much practical teaching. At the end of those two weeks I went on to Johns Hopkins in Baltimore. There, there was another Rockefeller Student and he had arranged for a place for me to stay.

Alan Parks was a very bright and charming person who had been at Oxford before winning his studentship. After his return to England he had a very successful career, becoming President of the Royal College of Surgeons and acquiring a Knighthood. I found that he was living in the Pithotomy Club. This was an informal club in a house right opposite the front entrance to the hospital. I am not sure who owned the building, but Alan had become the manager which allowed him to live there free. The other medical students who lived there paid for the privilege. It was staffed with a cook and a house cleaner. The club was used by other students who came regularly to take a break from their studies. There was a permanent poker game which went on almost continuously with players cutting in and out. Not being much of a gambler, I did not get involved in the poker though I did play a few games of cribbage. The Pithotomy club was so named from a Greek derivation: pithos, (a keg) and otomy, (meaning to open). It was not a dry establishment. It also had a tradition of putting on a show once a year. This show pilloried the teachers in a very cruel and totally uninhibited way. The teachers were always invited and most took the ribbing in good spirit.

Harvard Medical School had a similar tradition and some memorable skits were produced. The Ballad of Chamber Street was still quoted when I was there, though it must have been at least twenty years old. Mayor Curley, who had been reelected mayor of Boston while still in jail, did not escape unscathed. Professor Irving who was head of the Lying in Hospital was a real autocrat. He was known as God but he did not escape attention from the irreverent students. There is a wonderful story that is almost certainly true. The wife of a very prominent Proper Bostonian was pregnant and about to be delivered by Dr. Irving. As her husband was taking her to the hospital she went into labor and proceeded to deliver the baby on the entrance lawn. She was admitted and all went well for both mother and child. When the husband got the bill from the hospital he found that there was a charge for 'delivery room'. He felt that this was not right. He went to Dr. Irving and explained that, as most of Boston knew, his wife never got to the delivery room. Dr. Irving agreed that there was a mistake and took the bill back. He wrote on it and handed it back. The total remained the same. 'Delivery room charge' had been crossed out and 'Greens Fee' inserted instead. The husband was delighted, paid the bill and then had it framed.

When I arrived at Hopkins Alan Parks had arranged for me to live in the Pithotomy Club It was in the middle of the year and I felt rather lost. The system seemed different and I did not know anyone, nor did I know my way around. Because of the war there was a shortage of interns and I found that they were looking for fourth year students who would act as substitutes. Nothing loath, I volunteered and was accepted as what was known as a 'strike surgical intern'. It meant that I lived in the hospital and was fed for nothing. I even got my laundry free. I was assigned as the intern to the Private and Semi-private surgical service. These services were staffed by a senior resident, a junior resident and an intern. As the 'intern' I had to work up all the new admissions and do the essential laboratory studies before surgery, i.e. the blood counts and the urine exams. I had to shave the patients where necessary and was somewhat surprised to find that this included perineal shaves on the female patients. I am not sure which of us was more embarrassed but I did get very expert with a razor. Besides these routine duties I had to start the intravenous infusions on all the surgical patients who needed them. We were not allowed to run more than one infusion (i.e. one liter of fluid) through any needle, so this entailed setting up an intravenous on some of the patients twice a day. I got pretty good at finding veins with so much practice. Since I was expected to be in the operating room, scrubbed and gowned, before 8 am, ready to assist or second assist the attending surgeon, life became rather hectic. Almost as soon as I started work the junior resident got mumps and disappeared. This left only the senior resident and me. While it increased my work, it greatly increased my responsibilities. It was utterly exhausting but, at the same time, tremendously exciting. I found myself assisting some of the great names of Hopkins surgery; among them, Blalock who developed the 'blue baby' operation and was one of the pioneers of cardiac surgery, though he did not confine himself to this field. Firor was always a perfect gentlemen and a superb, thoughtful surgeon. Reinhoff, nicknamed 'Wild Bill' was fearless but an excellent technician. All this activity was in sharp contrast to the leisurely discussions and seeming inactivity of the medical service to which I had been exposed in Boston. The results of surgery were swift and, whether successful or not, determinate. They depended on technical skill as well as thoughtful planning. The whole atmosphere was intoxicating for a budding physician. It was here that I changed my mind and decided that I wished to become a surgeon. I still liked children and saw the possibilities of combining both my interests by being a pediatric surgeon.

At that time blood transfusions were far less common than they are today. Patients who required these transfusions were expected to pay for them, particularly if they were private patients. It was a source of income for medical students who were often hard up. I got the opportunity to give one while at Hopkins. I was paid $50 and had it in my pocket when I went to change for the operating room the next day. When we had finished and I went to change again the $50 was gone. I was very upset as it meant a lot to me. Somehow one of Blalock's wealthy patients heard about my loss and wished to reimburse me. It was strictly forbidden for any of the resident staff to accept monetary remuneration or gifts from patients. Blalock stepped in and accepted the gift from the patient and then gave it to me. In retrospect working in the operating room with Blalock was a great privilege. His cases were often unusual and he had to devise new, innovate treatments.

I was exhausted most of the time. Nurses would ring me up in the middle of the night to ask for a medication order on a patient. I would give it over the phone and would have to sign the order the next day. I must have given some in my sleep because there were occasions the next day I had no recollection of the incident. Fortunately the nurses were very competent, knowledgeable and caring. In those days they did not spend most of their time filling out forms! The orders that I approved for them proved to be beneficial and no harm was done. On one occasion I was sitting in a patient's room taking a history from her so as to write up her record. I asked her a question and then was surprised to hear her laughing. When I asked what was so funny, she said I had been sound asleep for the last hour but she had not wished to awaken me because I looked so tired. I had no idea that I had dozed off. Once in the operating room assisting Blalock I realized that I was getting very light-headed and was afraid that I would fall into the wound. I asked to sit down but the nurse in the room pulled down my mask and shoved a lump of sugar soaked in Spirits of Camphor into my mouth. It made my hair stand on end but was a real wake-up call and I was fine for the rest of the case.

The food that was supplied for the resident staff was good but I had little time for breakfast. Working for the private and semiprivate service had another advantage. There was a special kitchen for these patients. Some of patients were unable to eat, but their food was available. By making friends with the staff in this kitchen it was possible to persuade them to cook a sumptuous meal for a poor intern at midnight. When you are tired and hungry this is a godsend.

One day a private duty nurse came to me to say that the patient that she was taking care of was a young lady who was anxious to talk to me. I assumed that this patient was anxious to talk because I had found that a number of Americans were fascinated by my English accent. Rather reluctantly I went to see the patient. (Later I found out that the patient had never asked to talk to me. It had all been a scheme of the nurse to try to cheer up the young lady for whom she had developed affection.). I found a very beautiful young lady lying completely encased in Plaster of Paris from the neck to the feet. Besides being very beautiful she had an enchanting smile and was obviously very friendly. I enjoyed that first visit and returned whenever I had the chance. I discovered that she had osteomyelitis as a girl and it had settled in her hip. As a result the whole top of her femur had sloughed leaving her with a totally unstable hip. A local orthopedic surgeon had attempted to reconstruct the hip in Washington. This was unsuccessful and so she had been taken to Hopkins. She begged the surgeon there to try again. Somewhat against his better judgment he consented but this also failed. At the time I met her she was having the joint fused so that it would be stable and enable her to walk with a cane. It was not until later that I learned the full extent of her misfortunes. At the age of eight she had a septic sore on her foot. There were no antibiotics in those days and she developed septicemia. The bugs settled in her bones, those of one foot, her hip and her jaw. She was desperately sick for four years and confined to bed. Much of the time she could not or would not eat. The only treatment available was blood transfusions. The residents from a local hospital in Washington where her surgeon (not the orthopedic surgeon) worked would come out to her parent's house to give these transfusions. It was a popular thing to do because not only were they paid, but her father replaced the blood they had given with Bourbon whiskey. She maintained that she knew clearly when the donors had recently eaten a meal well laced with garlic! When the first of the antibiotics became available she was one of the very early patients treated with Sulfonamide. Her parents were utterly devoted and spent much time and effort taking care of her. Her father was fairly well off and had a number of influential friends in Washington. Also they had a surgeon for her who was not only a very competent physician but one of the finest characters I have been privileged to meet. His sympathetic approach and devotion helped her and her parents through many crises. After the four years of acute sickness she had been able to return to school and then to be admitted to Vassar College. Because of difficulty in getting about her father had persuaded the authorities at the college to let her have a three-wheel motor cycle there. When I met her I found her utterly enchanting. She was very bright, loved good music and we found that we had many interests in common. Her misfortunes had not embittered her in any way. It was not long before I realized that I was hopelessly in love with her. Because of her father's influential friends in Washington she was enabled to have a phone in her private room at Hopkins. This was a great advantage because I found myself visiting her more and more and I could sign out to her phone number. This worked well until she was called at 3 am one night by someone looking for me. She had a phonograph in her room so we could play a lot of the classical music that we both enjoyed. Every evening I had to write up the charts of the new admissions for which I was responsible. This was a considerable chore but it was far more pleasant to do it in her room. Soon we worked out a system whereby I dictated the patient's history to her while I was writing up the physical exam. Though probably not totally ethical, it worked very well and no one complained. If the records are still available you will find that many of the patients on the private service at Johns Hopkins in the spring of 1944 have records that are written in two different handwritings. Before I had to leave to return to Boston I had been delighted to find that she reciprocated my affection and wished to continue our relationship. She persuaded her parents to invite me to spend a weekend with them in Washington. I tried to make a good impression on them but I am not sure that I did. I did meet her sister with whom I went to a party where I met some of her friends. Her parents were living in an apartment, having rented their house farther out of town because of the gas shortage. Actually their house was still in the District of Columbia. It has now been torn down and has been rebuilt to become an ambassador's residence.

Rather sorrowfully I returned to Boston to resume my studies there. My exposure to the thrill and satisfaction of surgery at Hopkins convinced me that I really wished to be a surgeon. I do not recall too much of the work of the rest of that year. I was concerned about how Agnes, the young lady in Hopkins, and I were going to work out our future. It was obvious that there were many obstacles not the least of which was our families. In the meantime Don, my Peruvian classmate, had decided to follow me and second himself to Hopkins for his surgery course. Needless to say, I had not been reluctant to tell my friends about the wonderful young lady I had fallen in love with. When Don got to Hopkins he went to see Agnes and was equally smitten. He offered her an enormous diamond engagement ring, (he came from a very wealthy family), but I was delighted to learn that she turned him down. One of my other classmates came from Washington and knew the family. He gave a very glowing opinion of the young lady's character.

After Agnes got out of Hopkins she returned to her family in Washington before returning to Vassar to continue her studies. She was majoring in the History of Art. She was still having to use crutches to walk but could use her motor tricycle. Before she returned to college I went down to Washington to visit her and her parents. While there I asked her parents for permission to marry their daughter. They were shaken by this request and more than somewhat reluctant to give their permission. They were not happy at the prospect of their invalid daughter marrying an unknown young man who was proposing to take her to live in England. They had no idea of my background or of my prospects. They set about trying to find out something about my family. I had told them that my father was an official in the Air Ministry. Through contacts that they had with the British military delegation in Washington they found out that he was well known and very highly regarded. This helped a little but my prospective father-in-law decided to write to my father. They were both equally surprised and horrified at the plans that we were trying to make. They were convinced that we had not known each other long enough and had not realized all the implications of what we were proposing. We were both equally sure that we were in love and wished to spend the rest of our lives together. The upshot of many discussions across the Atlantic was that we could be engaged. I would return to England after I graduated from Harvard, as required by the conditions of my Rockefeller Studentship, and there get my medical degree from Cambridge. When the war was over, if we both felt the same way, Agnes would come to England to visit for six months. After that period, if we were both determined that we wished to marry each other, they would give their blessing.

While this was going on Agnes returned to Vassar where she shared rooms with five other girls. They were very curious to learn about the Englishman who had captured her fancy. When one of them asked, among other things, how tall he was, she innocently replied that she did not know because she had only seen him in bed. She still had a year before she could graduate and this would occupy her while I was returning to England to graduate from Cambridge.

Having returned to Boston to complete my last year, I found it was rather an anticlimax. Needless to say I discussed the new twist that my life had taken, not only with Alex and my other medical school friends, but with Aunt Betsy. She was sympathetic, wise and understanding. She arranged for Agnes and me to visit her brother, Uncle Dan, in Connecticut. He also became very fond of Agnes after a short time, insisting on photographing her and giving her one of his books of poetry. I had to study for the final exams. These I passed, though not with flying colors but in the top third of the class. By the conditions of my studentship, I was not allowed to receive my MD degree until after I graduated from Cambridge. As I had no intention of practicing in America I did not bother to take the National Board exam which would have entitled me to apply for a license to practice in almost any State in the country. This subsequently proved to be a nuisance because I had trouble getting a license to practice when I did decide to return to the States.

Aunt Betsy decided to give a party as a graduation present for Alex and me. She was lent a house on the coast near Gloster by a friend of hers. She decided to take some of our friends up there for a long weekend and invited Agnes as well. It was a big house with a wonderful view over the water from the cliff. Though empty it was furnished so we had to open it up. While looking for such supplies as sheets etc. we found a cupboard with a shelf full of bottles of Haig and Haig 5 star Scotch. I am ashamed to say we were not reluctant to help ourselves to some, with Aunt Betsy's permission. This was a wonderful time for me as I was able to enjoy Agnes's company.

After this weekend I had to make arrangements to return across the Atlantic. There were no passenger ships because the war was still in full swing. It was necessary to get a passage on a freighter taking supplies to England and traveling in convoy. The battle of the Atlantic was continuing unabated. The Rockefeller Institute made the arrangements for me to sail from New York. I had two or three days to kill before the boat sailed, so I arranged to meet Agnes in New York. She stayed in a hotel there and I found a room at the YMCA. I figured that I had just about enough money for the couple of days if we were careful. Those days went very quickly and we had a fond farewell as she dropped me at the dock.

When I got to the dock to which I had been told to report, I found no evidence of the ship. On making inquires no one seemed to know anything about it. There I was on the dock, with my baggage and no money as I had spent it all. The only thing to do was to contact the Rockefeller Institute and ask what was going on. When I got through to them, I found that they had been trying to contact me but did not know where I was. The ship I was supposed to sail on had been canceled and they had arranged for me to sail a week later. I explained that I was stuck in New York with no money. They agreed that if I came round they would give me some more to tide me over. I rushed round and collected the money. It was not difficult to decide what to do at that point. I rang up Agnes at Vassar where she had just returned. I explained the situation and told her that I was catching the next train up to Poughkeepsie where her college was. Could she find me a cheap B & B nearby? She said she could and I met her again that evening. It was a very convenient and pleasant B & B within easy walking distance of the college.

    I spent a very interesting week attending lectures and generally enjoying my time at a girl's college. The faculty did not seem to mind my presence and even involved me in some of the discussions. Perhaps I was the first male student at Vassar, though it has now become coeducational. Agnes's popularity with both the faculty and the other students had a lot to do with my being accepted. I had the opportunity to meet Agnes's roommates. They were a most interesting group with very varied backgrounds and habits. One of them was an ardent horsewoman who had her own horse there. She arranged for me to go riding with her a couple of times. This was no great hardship as she was an exceedingly beautiful young lady. I traveled around college with Agnes on her motor tricycle much to the amusement of the other students. She still had to use crutches as her new hip was not totally stable. Need I say how much I enjoyed being able to be with her for that week. Unfortunately the week went all too quickly and I had to say goodbye.

    I returned to New York to my ship. This time there was no mistake. It was another freighter not unlike the one I had come over on. To start with the weather was quite calm as we joined a convoy and started zigzagging across. After a couple of days we ran into the tail end of a hurricane with waves well over the height of the mast. By this time I had gotten my sea legs and did not mind the motion during the day though the nights were rather trying as I slid up and down the bunk until my skin was sore. It was not the cleanest ship. We had to knock the cockroaches off the table at mealtimes. Otherwise the food was quite good. I found a fellow traveler who was congenial and an ardent chess player. I knew a little about playing chess but was no expert. Since we were at a loss for something to do we played chess every day even taking the board onto the top deck when the weather improved. There was one very exciting experience. At the end of the storm we were running with a heavy swell following us and the ship pitching. One swell caught the rudder and swung it at right angles to the hull. There it jammed causing the ship to turn sharply and wallow in the troughs between the waves. The crew could not correct this at once. Because we were sailing in convoy every ship had to keep its exact position relative to all the others in the convoy. With a jammed rudder we were out of control and swung across the bow of another ship. By great good fortune we got across it without being rammed though we seemed to be within a hair-breadth. This occurred during the day which may have helped minimize the potential of disaster but allowed the passengers to appreciate what nearly sank us.

After this the rest of the journey was uneventful and we arrived safely in Plymouth. There I was met by my parents and returned to our house just south of London. We had a lot of catching up to do, filling in the gaps which my letters to them had left. Needless to say they wanted to hear more about Agnes, especially because they feared that she would always be an invalid and a burden to me. They were not overly enthusiastic about my decision but were prepared to meet the young lady before making any final judgment.

Then I had to get busy organizing my return to finish my medical studies at St. Thomas's hospital in London prior to taking my final exams at Cambridge.

Chapter 5

GETTING MY ENGLISH MEDICAL DEGREE

As soon as I got back to England I had to set about getting my medical degree from Cambridge. To do this I had to attend courses at an English hospital. Because I had tentatively enrolled at St. Thomas's Hospital in London and been awarded a scholarship there before I accepted the Rockefeller Studentship to Harvard, they allowed me to join their courses. I was able to live at home in Cheam, Surrey, with my parents and commute to the hospital every day. There was a good train service or I could hitch a ride with my father when he was being driven up to his office in town. Fortunately his route took him right by the hospital.

The teaching and the courses at St Thomas's Hospital were startlingly different from those at Harvard. Instead of having patients assigned to the students, there were ward rounds with one of the attending physicians or surgeons. The attending doctors were Consultants appointed by the Board which governed the hospital. These Consultants were not paid. Their recompense was the kudos attached to being a Consultant at a teaching hospital. Their income came from their private practice, the extent of which depended on the reputation they acquired in their charitable work at the teaching hospital. This was before the National Health Service came into force. Each attending or Consultant was responsible for all the patients in one ward, or if the ward was large, one half of a ward. Though the patients in that ward were the responsibility of that attending, their day to day care was performed by the senior registrars, (American senior residents). The students saw the patients at set times during the day when the 'Sister' in charge of the ward allowed them in. Two or three times a week the Attending would make rounds. These were very formal. Sister would have the whole ward cleaned up with all the beds beautifully made and the patients lying demurely, neatly tucked in. Following the Attending would be the senior registrar and the rest of the house staff, Sister and her nurses and finally the students. After the senior Registrar had briefed the Attending about the current state of the patient, with help if necessary from Sister, the Attending took over. If the case was interesting he often turned to one of the students, asking them questions before finally dictating the further management of the case. On one occasion the Attending turned to a rather lackadaisical student and asked him to put a hand on the patient's abdomen and tell him what he found. The student said that he felt a mass. "Good," said the Attending, "What do you think it is?" The student said; "An aneurysm of the left renal artery". The Attending laughed and shook his head at the presumption of this extraordinary diagnosis so glibly offered. The next day the patient was taken to the operating room and low and behold the patient was found to have an aneurysm of the left renal artery. At the next rounds the Attending admitted that he had never seen one before and wanted to know how the student had made the correct diagnosis. The young man replied; "It came to me in a dream, Sir."

Sister was in charge of a ward which had about 30 beds in it. She was responsible for everything in her ward 24 hours a day, seven days a week. She had a deputy who held the fort when she was not there. No one was allowed into the ward without her permission. This included not only the students, but the junior house staff as well. She had a little sitting room at the entrance of the ward and served coffee to those who were fortunate enough to be in her good books. In my experience the care that the patients received under her management was superb, understanding, sympathetic and very professional. Some of the Sisters were real tartars and could give the nurses under them a hard time. The nurses were known as Nightingales as the school had been founded by Florence Nightingale. The doctors, and students, were not allowed to talk to the nurses except on the ward and about the patient's needs. They were not allowed to socialize even in the corridors. Since a number of the nurses were both attractive and well educated, keeping this rule strictly adhered to was like keeping the two poles of a magnet apart. It presented a real challenge which neither the nurses nor the students found totally insuperable.

The nursing side the service was under the control of the Matron. She was a most formidable person. The nurses were terrified of her and even some of the sisters. The title of Sister had nothing to do with any religious affiliation but was given to the nurse who was responsible for a ward or department. There is a story about a somewhat irreverent senior surgical registrar who was operating one day. During the case a junior nurse contaminated the operating field. After things were straightened out and the operation proceeded the young lady did it again. The surgeon, who was not known for his forbearance, said; "Go to the devil you silly bitch". Sister, who was assisting the operation, was furious that anyone would speak to one of her nurses like that. She laid down the instruments that she was handling and walked out. The surgeon had to get one of the house officers to take her place. At the end of the case, while the surgeon was changing, a porter knocked on the door and announced that Matron wished to see Mr. Mitchner who was the surgeon involved in the case. (Surgeons in England are always called Mr.). After he changed he went to see Matron. She said, "I hear that you told one of my nurses to go to the devil!" To which he replied; "and I see that she has". This surgeon went on to have a very distinguished and always colorful career. He had a reputation for sticking up for the little guy and deflating the arrogant or snobbish. When one of his surgical colleagues was given a Knighthood in recognition of his distinguished reputation Mr. Mitchner was reputed to have said, when meeting him shortly thereafter in the hall of the hospital; "Congratulations, Sir. Perhaps some may have merited the Honor more, but I am sure that no one could enjoy it more." During World War II he became the senior surgical consultant for the Army. This required his visiting various stations around the country. One day he found himself staying with one of the Guards Regiments. He was always reluctant to wear anything but battle dress. Before dinner the Colonel of the Regiment who was entertaining the surgeon who had the honorary title of General, explained that it was customary for officers to change for dinner. It was obvious that the visiting General was expected to do the same, even during the war. Nothing daunted, Mr. Mitchner disappeared, only to return in his underwear, announcing; "you told me we were expected to change and this is all I had to change into."

Not only did the students have ward rounds but they attended outpatient clinics. These were held in small rooms designed as amphitheaters where the students sat in the seats while the Consultant sat in front. Each patient was brought in to be seen, diagnosed and treated as necessary. The students were asked questions and taught about the cases. At my first attendance a man was brought in with a lump on his neck. I was asked what the matter with him was. True to my Harvard training, I asked if I could take a history from him and examine him. The reply was curt and to the point. "Didn't they teach you anything at Harvard? Can you not recognize Tuberculous Glands of the neck from across the room?" It was a rude awakening to the fact that medicine here was practiced in a different way and that I had better learn it as quickly as possible. These outpatient sessions were most instructive and I came to enjoy them greatly. I learned to examine the patient concentrating on what was their complaint and to draw the obvious conclusion before looking for other possible problems.

Final examinations at Cambridge could be taken in two parts. Some of the subjects could be taken at one time and the others at another. The exams were held twice a year; before Christmas and in the summer. I decided that I would take some of the subjects that Christmas and the rest the next summer. If I passed the first lot, so much the better, but if I failed, at least I would have a more informed knowledge of what was expected. All the questions required answers of the essay type. That I managed to pass the first lot was a relief and gave me more confidence for the next lot. My Harvard teaching had been very thorough and the notes I had taken gave me a far more detailed and scientific background than my English colleagues.

At St. Thomas's I found my old Cambridge roommate, Hugh. We resumed our friendship which enabled me to work in with the other students and not to feel like a total stranger. Life was very much more leisurely than it had been at Harvard. There was no apparent requirement for attending any of the rounds or clinics. Learning was left up to the students and 'beating the books' was usually left up to the last minute before the final exams.

In London there were several 'teaching' hospitals. Each of these had teams which played each other at various sports. Rugby and cricket were the major ones but I managed to join the field hockey team. Not only did we play the other hospital teams but we also played some of the city clubs who were made up of young businessmen, often from one of the city banks. My father's youngest brother, who was twenty years his junior, was a rugby enthusiast. He played for a team called the London Irish, one of the typical London sports clubs. He was invited to play in the final trial for the Irish international team. Unfortunately he was kicked on the head and concussed. This not only eliminated him from being chosen for the final International Irish team but also prevented him from returning to the bank the next working day. It did not improve his standing at that Bank. He decided to go abroad where he worked for the Imperial Bank of Persia, which became the Imperial Bank of Iran and then the Imperial Bank of the Middle East. After all these changes of name, he decided that it was time for him to retire and he returned to England.

Not only did I renew my friendship with Hugh, but also with a young man who I had known from my school days, Arthur Peters. He was a member of the Plymouth Brethren and we had been introduced by a mutual friend. We had found that we had many interests in common. His home was in the Isle of Wight where his father had a house with a small holding attached, i.e. a very small farm. Actually it consisted of a couple of meadows where they kept a cow or two. I stayed with them several times and remember the wonderful butter, cream and milk. Their pastures were full of buttercups so the cows gave rich creamy yellow milk. Their butter was so yellow that their cowman was accused, much to his indignation, of adding color. During the war Arthur could not go along with those of the Brethren who were conscientious objectors so he joined the RAF. He underwent training as a navigator, some of which was in Canada. While there, he managed to visit me in Boston. He became one of the Pathfinder navigators who were in the lead planes on the night raids over Germany, marking the targets for the following planes. Fortunately he was one of the lucky ones who returned safely. These nights raids were very hard on the crews. There was the anxiety on the way over avoiding the flak and the occasional intercepting enemy planes. Then the target had to be identified and a bombing run made through the flak. Few planes returned without at least some flak damage. The relief set in on the return journey. The planes were equipped with George, the name they gave the automatic pilot, which took over at that point. Because of the earlier tension and the relief of still being alive, everyone on board became very sleepy. Tragically they did not always wake up in time to answer the calls for identification as they returned over England. At least one was shot down and others either crashed or narrowly avoided disaster. While I was at Cambridge they were experimenting with drugs to give to some of the crews to keep them awake. I was a guinea pig for a new drug called Dexedrine. The ideal dose was still experimental. I was given a dose right after I had taken one of my final exams. Then I had to drive a marker on a rotating drum between two lines. Every time I touched one of the lines it was recorded. I was so hyped up that I hit the lines frequently as I overcompensated for every curve. I was quite unable to sleep that evening. At 4 am I was still going strong and talking a blue streak to anyone I could find who would listen. Then I collapsed and it took me another full day to recover. Obviously the doctors found that the dose they gave me was larger than necessary but the drug, in a more appropriate dose, would work.

Arthur had an older brother who was a vet on the Isle of Wight. I became very friendly with him and when I could get time visited with him and helped him with his practice. On one occasion he had to operate on a dog and asked me if I could give the anesthetic. He was shorthanded and did not have an assistant. I assured him that I had anesthetized dogs during my course of dog surgery at Harvard and I would be happy to do so. At Harvard I had been taught to use open ether and not the intravenous drugs which are used now. The technique is to make a cone stuffed with cotton and pour ether into it holding it over the animal's nose and mouth. It is rather wasteful of ether and one gets a pretty good dose oneself. About half way through the operation which was progressing nicely I asked for another can of ether. Arthur's brother, Gerald said he did not have one! I had to fly up to the nearby pharmacy to get another, leaving my patient, hoping it would not wake up before I got back. It didn't and we finished the operation successfully.

It is impossible to predict when some piece of seemingly irrelevant information will be useful. One day Gerald was called to see a cow which was 'down' in the pasture. We went over; Gerald took one look and said that it had milk fever. This comes about when cows which are very good milkers, have calved and are supplying excessive amounts of milk. This exhausts their calcium and they develop tetany. The treatment is to stop the milk production and give some calcium intravenously. To my amazement Gerald got out a bicycle pump with a blunt needle on the end. He inserted it into each of the teats on the udder of the cow and blew it up. This stopped the gland making milk and gave the cow time to recover. Later on, when I was working as a resident in Norwich, England, we got a call from the emergency room. The doctor there had a young lady who was having severe fits. I went down with some colleagues and, after taking one look, said that I thought she had Tetany. Her fingers were curled up and in spasm and she was rigid. The question was why she would have developed tetany which is caused by a deficiency of calcium in the circulating blood. I looked around. Her husband had brought her in and he had a two year old with him. I asked what they were feeding the youngster. He said that he was still breast fed!

He was a fine well-grown two-year old and his mother was a little bit of a girl who did not look as if she weighed 80 lb. I told my colleagues that she had Milk Fever just the same as some cows develop. Her child had depleted her calcium and she would be all right if we gave her some intravenous calcium. Within half an hour of starting the infusion her spasms all disappeared and she was fine. After explaining what had happened and forbidding her to breast feed any more, we were able to discharge her. My veterinary experience with Gerald had really paid off and benefited that young lady. It is an example of the difference between modern medicine as we see it practiced here and the much more clinical medicine that was practiced before we had laboratories working 24 hours a day using machines which can perform multiple tests in a few minutes. Nowadays we would have run a battery of tests to prove the diagnosis before instituting the treatment. It would take longer and be vastly more expensive. Now, in one of the emergency rooms of a Washington hospital where I have worked, there is a notice which reads; "When all else fails, examine the patient".

After Christmas I resumed my studies at St. Thomas's Hospital until June when I sat and passed the rest of my final exams. This gave me the degree of MB.BChir but it was necessary to serve as a house officer at a hospital for one year before going out into practice. The house jobs varied from hospital to hospital. At St. Thomas's the first year was divided into two six-month periods. During the first six months three months were spent as a Casualty Officer at the main hospital in London and the second at the country branch at Hydestyle, south of London, taking care of 'in-patients'. It was necessary to apply for these jobs and there were not enough vacancies at the teaching hospital for all the graduates. I applied for the job at St. Thomas's and was appointed. The job did not start until the fall so I had a little time to relax.

Hugh, who had also graduated, and I decided that we would spend a couple of weeks sailing in the Falmouth Inlet on the south coast. His parents came there and stayed in a hotel but I found a nice cheap lodging house. We rented a local sail boat which was quite heavy and very sound. It was not the most exciting sailing but we found some female companionship and had a lot of fun. One day we decided to go out of the inlet to go round to the next one west. When we got out we found that the sea was much rougher than we expected and there was a heavy swell coming in with a strong south wind. We thought that discretion was the better part of valor and decided to return. The problem was that we were heading into the wind and had to put about. The boom and the sail were quite heavy and reversing course meant jibbing. With the amount of wind blowing, it seemed that the boom would snap around violently and we were doubtful if we could control it. Neither of us was a very experienced sailor. We decided to tack into the wind with the sail on the side where we wanted it when we started to run before the wind. If we then continued to let the boat fall off the wind we would turn until the wind was behind us and the boom would be on the correct side. We managed to accomplish this and ran back into Falmouth at great speed and with much relief.

During my last months at St. Thomas's we enjoyed a baptism of fire with first the V 1s, and then the V 2s. The V1 was an unmanned plane with a limited amount of fuel and an explosive on it. When the fuel ran out the machine crashed and exploded. The V2 was a rocket with an explosive head. With the V1s when the noise of the engine quit you knew it was about to come down. The only thing to do was to lie flat and pray. However if one heard the explosion without the preliminary engine noise it had to be a V2. Because you heard the explosion and you were still alive you knew it had missed you. The one gave you some warning, the other dealt death and destruction without any prior alert. Though this led to an atmosphere of subconscious tension it was astonishing how everyone adapted to the uncertainty. They went about their business with seeming nonchalance. Fortunately there were not too many V 2s because the Allied bombers had delayed their production and damaged their launching sites.

Then the end of the war came in Europe. The celebration in London was memorable. Piccadilly Circus seemed to be the center of activities. There were plenty of St. Thomas's students there and even a friend who played the Bagpipes. Though it had been obvious for some time that we were winning the war, the final declaration that it was done, after five years of hardship and the shedding of so much blood, so many of our friends never to return, it is hard to remember all the mixed up emotions that flooded over us all..

All during this time I had been writing to Agnes almost every day and she wrote letters back. Neither of us had changed our minds. Her parents kept their promise and arranged for her to come over on one of the first boats sailing to Europe to pick up American soldiers and repatriate them. She was to stay in London and if we were still of the same mind in six months, they would come over for our wedding. My father and I went down to Plymouth to meet her ship and to drive her back to our house. It was a joyous reunion for us. She was just as beautiful and lovable as ever. My mother, who had told me before I left for America, to be sure not to return with an American bride, was sweetly and warmly welcoming. It took her very little time to become very fond of my choice. After a stay with my parents, her parents had arranged for her to stay at a wonderfully stuffy hotel in London, less than a block from the south entrance of Kensington Gardens. By this time I had started work at St Thomas' hospital as a house officer and could visit her most days. This was my first year as a doctor, 1945-6.

Chapter 6

POST GRADUATE TRAINING

The job at St. Thomas's, during the first three months, had two aspects. As the house surgeon, there were duties taking care of the patients on the ward to which one had been assigned, but there was also a rotation in the Emergency Room. I was assigned to Nuffield ward which was run by a sister known as Nora Nuffield. This was not her real name and it was only later that I discovered that she was Miss Sheldon. She was a very small person but a real dynamo. The nurses who served under her were all scared of her as she was very demanding but they respected her because everything that she did and expected to have done was directed at trying to achieve the maximum of comfort and well being of her patients. I found that whenever I went to the ward to attend to the patients I had to report to her first. She would come with me to see each patient. After I had gotten to know her better I asked her why she always came with me. She told me it because she was afraid of what I might, as a neophyte, say to HER patients. She taught me more about the niceties of patient care than could ever have been learned at medical school

St. Thomas's Hospital is situated on the bank of the Thames exactly opposite the houses of Parliament. At that time, right after World War II, it was still showing the signs of the damage that had occurred during the Blitz. The east end of the hospital complex abuts the south entrance of Westminster Bridge. At that end the Private Wing had been demolished by the bombs which had missed the bridge. There were a series of blocks of wards separated from each other by quite wide spaces. They ran at right angles to the river. Some had been slightly damaged but all except the top floors were usable. The 'pavilion' plan had been designed to try to minimize cross infection at a time when this was a major problem in hospitals and wounds were expected to heal with 'laudable pus'. The hospital complex stretched for one mile along the south bank of the river. The east half mile of the area was the hospital itself and the west half mile, the medical school. There were two long wide passages, one above the other, at the side opposite the river. The upper one was only half a mile long but the underground one stretched the full mile. This passage was a truly spooky place at night as it was dimly lit and haunted by the ghost of the Grey Lady. She was supposed to be a lady who had committed suicide by jumping out of a ward window. The morgue was over the west end of the underground passage. One night a young hospital porter had to take the body of a still born baby from the hospital to the morgue. He was carrying the baby along this dark passage but when he got under the morgue he heard footsteps coming from the morgue above him. In terror he dropped his bundle and fled back from whence he had come. It turned out that a Jew had died the day before and his body was in the morgue. According to orthodox Jewish custom the body must not be left unattended so a rabbi was in the morgue and had been walking up and down. This accounted for the footsteps. A posse went down to rescue the body of the baby but had a hard time finding it because it had dropped behind a board.

The other aspect of my job was duty in the Emergency room. This was once every third night. My first night on duty taught me how little I knew about the practice of medicine. I made three terrible mistakes. The first occurred when a man came in with acute urinary retention. He was in severe discomfort and I decided that I had better catheterize him at once. I could not pass the soft rubber catheter so I tried a stiffer one made of gum elastic. I failed again. Nothing daunted and still determined, I looked around and found a sterile metal curved instrument that looked like a catheter. With consummate skill I passed this into his bladder and gave him immediate relief. He left the hospital a very happy man, only to return early the next morning in retention again. He was admitted and taken care of properly. Later that night a young lady was brought in who had fallen backwards off a truck onto her head. She had a cut on her scalp which had stopped bleeding when I saw her. I sent her down to the X-ray department to have her head X-rayed. While this was going on another patient arrived who had attempted suicide by cutting his throat. There were gashes on his neck but they were not actively bleeding so I put a bandage on them and left him for the senior registrar to see in the morning. That next morning when the senior registrar came down, (they lived in the hospital), the enormity of my crimes was explained to me in no uncertain terms. Patients in acute retention are admitted, patients with lacerations of the scalp are sewn up first as they may start to bleed again at any time and patients who have cut their throats are seen by the senior registrar at once as the potential of deeper damage could be fatal if it is not thoroughly assessed immediately. The only mitigating factor in this humiliating experience was the fact that the registrar expressed surprise, tinged with admiration, that I had managed to pass the metal catheter without causing any bleeding or doing any other damage.

The Emergency room at that hospital was a very interesting place to work. St. Thomas's hospital took care of the Metropolitan Police force and therefore had a special relationship with their members. In order to avoid arresting drunk and disorderly persons who were suffering from more serious illnesses rather than the effects of alcohol, the police would deliver them to the emergency room. After they had been examined and found only to be drunk, the hospital porters would throw them out onto the street. There the police would be waiting to pick them up again. In this way they were arrested outside the hospital and when prosecuted, the hospital staff would not be involved in the court case and the police would not be responsible for the arrest of someone who should have been in the hospital.

The porters were a very important part of the hospital and most helpful to the young doctors manning the emergency room. They were a very stable force and had been around for a long time. They not only knew the routines but they knew the chronic old lags that came wanting a bed for the night. These old lags knew the hospital routine and knew when the new house staff came on duty. They would come in at the time of the change over hoping that the new staff would be more gullible, but they had to come by the porters. The porters cooperated with the staff. One evening an old lag returned at the time of the change of medical staff. The porter came to the new doctor and told him that this patient was well known to him and that he was looking for a bed for the night. He advised the young doctor to give him an ounce of H.S.Co and send him out. (H.S.Co was the hospital formulary for a 'never fail' laxative). The patient did not realize that the doctor had been tipped off by the porter. Knowing that the new doctors rotated and that there would be a different doctor the next night he returned that next night. Unfortunately for him that doctor was taking the duty again, standing in for a friend. The poor man got two ounces of H.S.Co and was sent out. Not deterred he returned for a third try. Unbelievably the same doctor was taking duty again for another friend. This time he got three ounces of H.S.Co and was never seen at St. Thomas's again.

On the side of the hospital opposite the river was a road. It was an interesting road because it was occupied by brothels, a pub (often frequented by medical students and the resident staff) and the Bishop of London's palace. Detectives who had been detailed to observe the activities of the brothels used to come into the hospital Emergency Room from whence they could observe the activities across the street. They were always welcomed and could expect a cup of tea from the nursing staff. They usually had many intriguing stories to relate. A very close relationship had developed between the police and members of the hospital which was most beneficial to both. The police were treated as VIPs at the hospital and members of the staff were treated with leniency when they committed minor infractions of the law.

All this was before the National Health Service was introduced. These hospitals were run as charitable institutions. They were financed by their endowments, some of which went back many years, and by contributions from the public often raised by 'Flag Days'. They ran 'in the red' as this was an incentive to ask for more contributions. Their services were not free to all comers. The patients were expected to pay but only according to their ability. This was assessed by a team called 'Lady Almoners'. These would go into the financial circumstances of each patient, taking into consideration all aspects of their income and obligations. They would then decide what each patient would be required to pay. It was felt that everyone would be expected to pay something though sometimes it only amounted to sixpence a day. In this way no one was allowed to feel that they were charity patients. They regarded the hospital as their doctor and were both proud and loyal. There was a feeling that some of the more chronic indigent patients belonged to the hospital and the hospital took care of them in ways beyond their medical care. At Christmas time the wards were always full as the Sister in charge made sure that her chronic patients were admitted so that they could be given a good meal and some Christmas cheer. There was a turkey carved on each ward. It was a great honor if Sister invited you, as a resident, to carve the turkey on her ward. There was always some small gift for every patient, if necessary, bought by Sister with her own money.

The senior visiting staff gave their time and were not paid either for their services to the patients or for their teaching assignments. Their income was derived from their private patients who were referred to them by the general or family practitioners. They were called Consultants and were specialists known generically as either Physicians or Surgeons. The former were entitled Doctors and the latter Misters. The volume of their private practice from which they derived their income depended on referrals from General Practitioners. This, in large part, was influenced by the reputation that they built up caring for their charity patients. This had the effect of keeping the standard of charity care at a high level. Though the Consultants did not do all the work themselves and delegated much of it to the resident staff, they were responsible. As in every other walk of life, they varied in their conscientiousness where these obligations were concerned. The resident staff was very poorly paid. Their reward was in the teaching and experience that they got from the job. The senior resident staff, the senior registrars, had several years of postgraduate work and had advanced degrees in their specialties. They were waiting for a vacancy to occur at a hospital where they could have an appointment to have their own charity patients and build up their own private practice. As a house surgeon/casualty officer I was paid about 100 pounds (at the rate of exchange then, $400) a year.

The pub opposite the hospital was much frequented by the resident staff. It was unofficially known as The Annex and the residents would tell the porters that they would be in the annex if they were needed. It was also frequented by the morgue attendant Mr. Stet, commonly known as Death. He was responsible for overseeing the autopsies. His occupation was well known to frequenters of the pub. On occasion he would drop something into his beer and announce that a little bit of meat improved the flavor, implying that it had come from one of his 'patients', i.e. a corpse. Actually it was a rabbit kidney but it served to turn the stomachs of the uninitiated.

After the first three months at the main hospital in London I was sent down to the country branch at Hydestyle about 20 miles south and in the beautiful Surrey country. Here I was made the house surgeon for the male and the female surgical wards. My duties included taking care of the patients postoperatively and assisting in the operating room. The surgery was done either by the residents or one of the consultants who came down from London. One day I was assisting the senior registrar and picking up the stitches that he was putting in. I immediately tied the knots using a one handed technique which I had learned during my dog surgery course at Harvard. He was astonished and said "My God, a house surgeon who can tie knots. Where did you learn that?" He was very happy to have me help him in future and even let me do a case which he thought would be simple. I found that it was not as simple as I thought and I had to ask his help.

This was a time at the end of the war and so many doctors were still in the military service that those who would otherwise have retired were still working. We had one elderly anesthetist named Zeb who had been a general practitioner. In England anesthetics were always administered by doctors as opposed to the American custom at that time when most were given by nurses. Zeb was a delightful character though somewhat primitive in his methods. We asked him how he had become an anesthetist. In his youth, when he was a general practitioner it was customary for the surgeons to asked the general practitioner who had referred the patient to give the anesthetic. Zeb told us that when he was giving an anesthetic to a Duke he had killed him. He said that the notoriety was such that his practice never looked back and he became in constant demand.

One day, while sitting around in the doctor's quarters, I listened to the medical registrars discussing a patient with diabetes. They were having a problem controlling the patient's blood sugar levels and her reactions. I got out the notes I had taken while at Harvard where there was a very advanced diabetic service. To my surprise the problems that this patient was exhibiting were described and the recommended management outlined. I mentioned this to the registrars who were looking after the patient. They were interested and decided to try the recommendations. They worked. I realized how much the teachers at Harvard had tried to teach me, and though I had taken notes, how little had sunk in.

During this time Agnes continued to live in Kensington and had obtained a job. While at Vassar she had majored in the History of Art. She had become very friendly with the Professors there. When they found out that she was going to London, they recommended her to their friends who were working at the Warburg Institute cataloguing European art treasures which might be lost or destroyed during the war. These experts were very happy to have her help them. She thoroughly enjoyed working with them and it kept her from being bored while I was working. They even paid her a small sum which she discovered was less than their telephonist earned. These experts increased her knowledge of various art treasures and where they could be found. On one occasion we were visiting the National Gallery in London where there was, on exhibition, a famous painting by Vermeer. Agnes was not always very sympathetic with the ignorance about art of her fiancé. I decided to provoke her to see what would happen. I said that I could not see what was so great about that painting. The result was astonishing. She gave me a lengthy lecture on all the aspects which made that work so outstanding. It took quite a long time and while she was doing it she was quite oblivious to her surroundings. When she finished we realized that there was a large group of other visitors around us who were as fascinated as I was. Standing in the door of the exhibition room was the director of the gallery with a big smile on his face. Agnes was very embarrassed. She never seemed to realize what a gift she had for communicating her knowledge and enthusiasm. She never would accept work as a docent at an art museum though she had a real talent. Her enthusiasm was infectious and this is the mark of an outstanding teacher. Though I benefited and my appreciation of paintings increased it seemed a shame that her ability to spread her knowledge was wasted.

At the end of my six months at St. Thomas's I had to apply for another six months as a House surgeon before I could do my National Service. I was anxious to get started in the field of my special interest, Pediatric Surgery. My father knew Sir Stanford Cade who was the senior Surgical Consultant to the RAF. He offered to introduce me to the staff of Great Ormond Street Hospital for Sick Children, the premier hospital for children in England. Though I was offered another six months at St. Thomas's I applied at Gt. Ormond Street and was awarded a House Surgeon appointment to work with Denis Browne.

Sir Stanford Cade was a Polish immigrant who was born Stanislaus Kandinsky but changed his name. He became Vice President of the Royal College of Surgeons and a very influential advocate for the RAF. During the Battle of Britain he was most concerned for the pilots who were shot down over England. Many of them sustained severe burns and were taken to the nearest hospital. These local hospitals were not equipped to treat major burns. Sir Stanford organized a special burn service at an RAF Hospital. He then told the Government to announce immediately on the radio that all burned RAF pilots were to be transferred at once to this special hospital. If they did not make this announcement that night, he threatened to hire, with his own money, Sandwich Men with placards stating that the Government was neglecting the best care for the RAF heroes. He would have these men march up and down outside Parliament carrying their message. As a result the announcement was made that night. On another occasion he was being driven on an inspection tour through Flanders in Northern France after it was 'liberated'. As they were going through a town, he told the driver to turn off towards a damaged house. He disappeared into the house and came out with a painting. The driver remonstrated and pointed out that looting was illegal. Sir Stanford said that it had been his house and he thought that the painting which was of his father was rightfully his. When visiting

America with his wife many years later they stopped at a small town in the Middle West. When they signed in at the local hotel, they signed in as Sir Stanford and Lady Cade. The clerk at the Registry desk remonstrated because he said that they were not that kind of hotel. If he would sign as Mr. and Mrs. Stanford he would overlook it. A very tragic thing happened to them when they were to visit South Africa after the war. The plane made a stop in West Africa and while they were there Lady Cade was bitten by a malaria carrying mosquito. She developed Black Water Fever and died in 48 hours. Sir Stanford never really recovered from this loss.

By the time I got the appointment at Gt. Ormond Street the six months waiting period that Agnes's parents had demanded was up. She said that she still wanted to marry me. Her parents agreed that it was impractical for us to return to the States to get married so they said that they would come over for the wedding. House surgeons at Gt. Ormond Street were not allowed to be married in those days and I was not when I applied for the job. After I got there I knew that I was going to get married while I was still there so I took the bull by the horns and invited my bosses to the wedding. To my delight they both accepted the invitation and raised no objections.

Agnes had moved from the hotel in Kensington to a small flat on the top floor of a house near Baker Street. We thought that we could both live there after we were married. When her parents arrived they were horrified to find her living on the top floor where she had to walk up and there was no fire escape. They set about trying to find more suitable accommodation. I found that her father had friends in London through the Mergenthaler Linotype Company of which he was a director. We met a number of these friends including a family who owned a Reversionary Auctioneering business. The family became good friends and was always very kind to us. They were very fond of Agnes and gave us much helpful advice. They found a mews which was for sale and we were very keen to acquire it. Her father who was a mortgage banker in Washington thought that it was overpriced. Agnes had a small trust fund and her father was the trustee so he had the last word. We finished up finding a very pleasant flat in Chelsea which satisfied everyone. We discovered afterwards that the mews had been resold after we turned it down for very much more than we would have had to pay for it. Her parents stayed at the Connaught Hotel where they had stayed on previous visits to England. It was a treat to visit them there and to enjoy the luxury. They were also introduced to a little restaurant in Leicester Square, Mr. Bellometti's Perroquet. Churchill often went there during the war. The food was superb and the service outstanding. Mr. Bellometti took a shine to Agnes and when we went there subsequently we always got special treatment. Right after the war restaurants were not allowed to charge more then 10/6, or half a pound (about $2 at the then prevalent rate of exchange) for a meal. They could charge what they liked for drinks. If one did not drink a lot, this meant that poor house surgeons could go out for dinner occasionally. When we did, we went to Mr. Bellometti's. We even took a party of our medical friends on one occasion. Not only did my parents become very fond of Agnes but all my friends welcomed her most warmly. She got called the Duchess because she walked with a cane and looked very proper. They were delighted to find that she had a great sense of humor, was by no means a prude and entered into all our parties with enthusiasm.

Shortly after I started work at Gt. Ormond Street came my wedding day. Agnes and I had been going to a rather evangelical Church, St. Paul's, in Portman Square where we had gotten to know the minister. We decided that we would like him to marry us and made the necessary arrangements, including having the Banns read for three successive Sundays. Her parents were agreeable and arranged for a reception afterwards. Since I was working as a house surgeon, I was not entitled to any time off. These jobs were officially 24 hours a day, seven days a week, though one could get a colleague to stand in if there was no special emergency. The authorities, i.e. my surgical chiefs, were most sympathetic and allowed me a long weekend. We were able to be married on Friday and I did not have to be back until Tuesday. Both my parents and hers attended the wedding and a friend of Agnes who happened to be visiting England from Washington was her bridesmaid. My best man drove me to the wedding in his ancient Bulldozed

Morris. This was a soft top car of the twenties vintage. On one occasion we were driving through Hyde Park where there was a twenty five mile an hour speed limit which we were exceeding. We were stopped by a police man who said "I do not know whether to congratulate you or give you a ticket". He was nice enough to let us off with a caution.

After the wedding we borrowed my parent's car and drove to a wonderful old pub at a village called Pishill on the old coaching road from London to Oxford. The village was probably named because the coach horses were allowed to stop there to relieve themselves. We were married on April 5th. My new mother-in-law had always been interested in horse racing. The next day April 6th was the Saturday of the running of the Grand National so they went to see it. None of us had the intuitive foresight to bet on an outsider called April the Fifth. This horse won at odds of about 100 to one. Such is our usual luck. The pub at Pishill was all that could be desired. We had a marvelous old room with a four poster bed and a private bath. We were the only resident guests in this small pub and were royally treated. The honeymoon was all too short and I reluctantly returned to work on the Tuesday. I still had three more months at Great Ormond Street before I would have to go to do my two years military service.

Great Ormond Street is a remarkable hospital. It was the first hospital in England to care for children exclusively. It had been founded in 1852 largely due to the efforts of Dr. Charles West. Its foundation coincided with the awakening of the Victorian conscience to the neglect and abuse of children. This was exaggerated by industrialization and urbanization. In London in the mid nineteenth century the death rate is recorded as about 50,000 a year, 40% who were children under the age of ten. The hospital was founded with 20 beds for inpatients to supplement an outpatient clinic. It grew steadily over the next century due to wide spread support both by dedicated physicians and enlightened lay individuals. By the mid twentieth century it had become known throughout the British Empire as the primary children's teaching hospital. Until the National Health Service took over in 1948 it was supported by charity. It was extremely well endowed. One of the major donations was given by Sir James Barrie, the author of the Peter Pan stories. He donated the copyright of Peter Pan. Since this donation covered stage, television, play and book rights its value was incalculable. One of the members of the Board of Directors of the hospital was Lord Southwood who was a newspaper magnate. Through his office the hospital got continuous, almost daily, publicity and this greatly increased its ability to raise money. Just before World War II it had completed a new building which housed the in patients and operating rooms. There were plans for new outpatient facilities but they had not been built. At the time the hospital was founded it did not accept accident victims because these could be looked after in adult hospitals. This tradition persisted and the hospital concentrated on the treatment and study of diseases both congenital and acquired. It became a referral center for almost the whole of southern England.

When I first went there in 1946 as a House Surgeon/Intern the resident surgical staff consisted of a senior surgical registrar, a senior ENT registrar who had to help out the senior surgical registrar and two house surgeons. Though there were several Attending Surgeons only two had confined their practice to children, T. Twistington Higgins and Denis Browne. I was assigned to Denis Browne. He was a most remarkable man. He had started life in Australia and had been a doctor with the Australian troops at Gallipoli in World War I. He was fortunate to be evacuated from there to England. There he decided to devote his career to the surgery of Children. He started at Gt. Ormond Street Hospital and remained there the rest of his active life. When he arrived there relatively little work had been concentrated on the surgical diseases of children and the repair of congenital deformities. Denis Browne (D.B. as he was always known) decided to concentrate on these problems. He developed the idea that many of the orthopedic deformities were caused by the position of the fetus in utero. Compression forces therein could prevent the normal movement of the fetus and thus cause deformities. If this was so, treatment should be aimed at devising methods to actively reverse the stresses that had caused the malformation. At the same time it was necessary to develop muscles that would reinforce and continue the correction. For this he devised various splints which would cause the infant to manipulate itself towards the corrected position every time it kicked or moved. He was a most original thinker who took nothing for granted. Everything he did had to be thought out de novo. This attitude was most stimulating to a young resident. It was impossible to do anything without being asked why you were doing it. Even the simplest procedures had to be logically defended. He accepted nothing because it was customary unless he could justify it on the basis of sound scientific evidence. This attitude had a profound influence on my thinking for the rest of my career. Because he was virtually alone in his concentration on the surgical problems of children, and because there were at that time so few sub-specialists who worked primarily with children, his field of activities was very widespread. He devised operations for harelips and cleft palates. He took care of club feet and congenitally dislocated hips. He devised a simple method for taking care of tuberculous glands of the neck which were still all too common He devised a simple, fool proof, operation for hypospadias, a condition where the end of the male urethra terminates at the base of the penis and not at the end. I was lucky enough to be working with him when he was devising this operation. It was fascinating to observe his efforts and his reasoning. He taught me to consider the differing reactions of different tissues to healing. Some heal with scarring and some show little evidence of scarring. Tissues grow and heal at different rates. His operation for hypospadias was devised as a result of taking all these factors into consideration. It was educational to watch other surgeons try to modify his operation without understanding the basis upon which it was founded. As a result the operation did not work well in their hands and they condemned it. A Swedish surgeon came to observe D.B.'s results. He was allowed to examine our results and was so impressed that he went home to apply D.B.'s principles to adult patients with comparable problems. There he had great success.

It was a time when surgical practice was undergoing remarkable changes. Not the least of these was a greater understanding of the physical changes induced by anesthesia and the delicate physiological balance of babies. When I was at St. Thomas's there was a baby with pyloric stenosis, a condition where there is an obstruction at the outlet from the stomach. This causes the baby to vomit everything that it is given by mouth, a situation which drives a mother to distraction and if untreated causes death from inanition. Sometimes this can be cured with medicine which causes the spastic muscle responsible for causing the obstruction to relax. This does not always work and unless the muscle is severed surgically the baby will die. The pediatrician at St. Thomas's was convinced that surgery would kill the baby. He persisted with the medical treatment until the baby was moribund before allowing surgery to be attempted. He was right as the baby did die. When I got to Great Ormond Street I found that there were quite a few babies admitted with this problem. After a short trial of medical treatment they were turned over to the surgeons. D.B. realized that giving a general anesthetic to a severely ill baby was dangerous. Working together with the pediatricians and anesthetists he decided that it would be much safer to perform the operation under local anesthesia. He devised a method for doing this which became the standard at that hospital I do not think we lost a single baby. (Many years later, in America, I successfully performed D.B.'s operation under local anesthesia as an outpatient in order to save the impecunious parents the cost of hospitalization.)

Gt. Ormond Street was a very friendly hospital and a wonderful place to work. The nursing care was superb. The children were on wards with glass enclosed cubicles for the babies and small rooms with six beds for the older children. Each ward was run by a sister. One example will show the devotion of these ladies. D.B. was doing his rounds one morning. When we went into Sister's office for a cup of coffee it was obvious that this lady, who was responsible for the ward, was not her usual self. She looked exhausted and on the verge of tears. When asked what the matter was, she confessed that she had not left the ward for the last 48 hours because we had a sick baby and she would not trust the care to anyone else.

In spite of the hard work and the responsibility inherent in taking care of these children, it was a very happy place to work. Everyone helped everyone else whenever they could. When we were not working social life was informal and at times quite riotous. The only adults around at night were the staff and a few nursing mothers so the social life tended to be rather uninhibited. The hospital was designed with a balcony which stretched around the wards so that the children could be pushed out when the weather was suitable. As residents we were assigned rooms in the center of the block with access to the balcony. On warm nights we would push our beds out and sleep under the stars. We were taken care of by a couple of wonderful 'maids' who were responsible for feeding us and keeping our rooms cleaned. If they knew we were going to have a party, one of them would inquire as to whether we wanted to have breakfast in bed the next morning. If the answer was yes, we were asked if we wanted breakfast for two.

The nurse's home was in a separate building behind the main hospital The main hospital had been hit by a couple of bombs which had destroyed part of the top floor but the rest was still working. The top two floors did not have patients because of the potential danger of further bombing. They were occupied by the operating rooms and as quarters for the residents. Besides the surgical residents there were medical (pediatric) residents and an anesthetist resident. The parties that we had were often held in the nurse's home. There was one very rowdy party there. Matron came down the corridor in her dressing gown to reprimand the carousers. Attending the party was a surgeon of remarkable talents. For some reason he had never been able to pass the exam to become a fellow of the Royal College of Surgeons but he had invented a special knife with a guard on it which facilitated taking a very thin layer of skin to use as a graft. This was before we had mechanical devices which now are used to do the job. Mr. H was somewhat unconventional but held in high regard by his colleagues. When Matron appeared to protest the party, he picked up a poker which was handy and was seen chasing Matron down the hall screaming "Go away, you un-enjoyed old bitch". She did. Because he was an attending surgeon this episode was never officially recorded.

At the end of my six months there, I had to do my National Service for two years. Since I was determined to become a surgeon it was necessary to become a Fellow of the Royal College of Surgeons. This required the passing of the exams which the College ran. These exams were divided into two parts. The first part consisted of exams, written and oral on the subjects of Anatomy, Physiology and Pathology. The second part was on the clinical aspects of surgery. I was anxious to pass the first part before I went into the RAF to do my service. The next exam was a month after my job at Gt. Ormond Street finished. I got permission to postpone my call up for that month. I met an Australian, Ray Last, who was also trying to get his F.R.C.S. We decided to study together. We spent every evening, usually at my flat, with a box of bones and the text books. I had a very thorough grounding in Anatomy at Cambridge so did not have too much trouble revising the subject and polishing my knowledge of the details. Ray had a much more difficult time and had to understand why everything was where it was. Once he grasped that he had no trouble learning and remembering.

Ray had a very interesting and somewhat traumatic background. He had been a surgeon in Australia before World War II. In 1938 he decided to come to England to become a Fellow of the Royal College of Surgeons. Before sitting the exams, he and his wife took a year off to relax and enjoy themselves. War broke out before he got around to taking the exams and he decided to join the Army. He was told that he could not join in England and that he would have to return to Australia and join there. He bought a lot of clothes and surgical instruments in England and boarded a ship to return home. Their ship got as far as the coast of Iceland when it was torpedoed. He and his wife managed to get into a lifeboat where they drifted for a few days. Ray thought that they would die of exposure and dehydration. He struggled to find a knife with which to put his wife out of her misery and to commit suicide. Before he found the knife their lifeboat was bumped in the dark by a steamer. The steamer was on its way to England and stopped to pick them up. Ray and his wife and a cabin boy were the only survivors. Ray decided that he was damned if he was going to try to get back to Australia again. At this time the British had thrown the Italians out of Abyssinia and were trying to reinstall the Emperor, Haile Selassie. Ray met the Ethiopians in London and the Emperor asked him if he and his wife, who was a nurse, would take over and run the hospital in Addis Ababa. This they did for the next couple of years before returning to England at the end of the war. Their experiences there, both medical and social, were incredible. They kept my wife and I enthralled on many occasions. They told us that one time the chief orderly who helped Ray run the hospital did not turn up for work. Ray found out that he was in jail because he had murdered his wife. On making further inquiries Ray discovered that he could get the man out of jail if he paid the blood money to the relatives of the man's late wife. Apparently it was perfectly all right to murder someone if one paid the blood-money to the relatives. Because the man was a good worker Ray paid the necessary money. Ray asked him how he, Ray, could be sure that he would not murder the Memsahib, i.e. Ray's wife. His simple honest reply was that he could not afford to do that because the blood-money would be more than he could ever afford to pay. Ray tried to ensure that he never had sufficient money. It seems that the amount of blood-money depended on social status. On another occasion they were invited out to the country estate of one of the local magnates. They were to have dinner and spend the night. After dinner, when they were getting ready to retire, Ray realized that they did not know where the facilities were for his wife to relieve herself. Ray inquired of his host who informed him that this had been prepared for and that there was a privy at the end of the walk outside. Margaret was somewhat apprehensive about going outside in the dark in the wilds of Abyssinia. When she got outside and saw that the walkway was lined with soldiers, who came smartly to attention to guard her both coming and going, her fears turned to embarrassment.

My having to work with Ray helped me to concentrate and master many details that I might have overlooked myself. We learned a few genomics which were useful in remembering the order in which anatomical parts related to each other. One came in very handy during the oral phase of my anatomy exam. I was being examined by a surgeon and his fellow examiner, an anatomist. The surgeon asked me about the ligaments of the knee that attached to the top of the tibia. I remembered my gnomic, "Treves is an excellent surgeon especially in highly pregnant women". The initial letters of these words gave me the names of all the ligaments and their branches in the correct order. The result was a detailed answer which floored the surgeon. He turned to the anatomist and asked if I was correct. The anatomist said that I most certainly was though he seemed surprised. I was then shown a partially dissected body with a band of muscle running, in segments, from the chin, down the neck over the chest and abdomen to the pubic bone. I had never seen this continuation of muscle over the chest. I said that I did not know what it was called but that it occurred in some primates and had been rarely found in man. The anatomist was delighted and asked me where I had learned that. When I said "in your book, Sir" his expression assured me that I had passed that part of the exam. Both Ray and I passed this exam and so I set off for the RAF with that hurdle behind me.

Ray, who was an experienced surgeon went on the pass the Final and clinical part of the exam at the next opportunity thus becoming a Fellow. For some reason he decided neither to return to Australia nor to continue surgery. He was offered a job teaching anatomy at the Royal College of Surgeons where he became famous as a superb teacher. He was sought out by many overseas candidates. He wrote a book which was considered the bible for those trying to learn detailed anatomy because it was so clear. It was easily memorable because it gave the reason why everything was where it was. He became the Professor of Anatomy at the College and the Warden. When he retired he was invited to lecture and give courses as a visiting professor. He was invited to give a course at a Southern California Medical school. At the end of the course the students gave him a standing ovation. I am told that this had never been done before. I was indeed fortunate to have studied with him while he himself was learning. My next move was into the RAF.

Chapter 7

MILITARY SERVICE

Going into the RAF was a real change of pace. After working at the Hospital for Sick Children, (Great Ormond Street), for six months and then studying hard for the Primary FRCS exam, putting on a uniform and being subject to military discipline took a little getting used to. At first several other young doctors and I were sent to a country estate that had formally belonged to the Rothschild's but had been taken over by the RAF. There, for two weeks, we were put through our paces and taught the rudiments of military life, before being assigned to various stations. It was a congenial group, each of us being determined to make the best of the disruption to our careers. One of the fellow inductees had been a chorister from St. Paul's Cathedral and was an excellent pianist. He entertained us with some most enjoyable classical piano music.

At the end of this training I was assigned to an RAF station with a small hospital which was under the command of a Wing Commander. This gentleman, who shall remain nameless, was a most unusual character. My father had known him in Baghdad in the early 20s. Even then his eccentricities were noted. Some of the prescriptions that he wrote were so bizarre that an edict was passed preventing any of his prescriptions being filled unless countersigned by another doctor. He had risen to be a Wing Commander by the beginning of World War II. He finished the war without being given a promotion, the only man known to have achieved this distinction. My duties were not particularly onerous as they consisted of running a clinic and doing some ward rounds on the few inpatients that were there. The Wing Commander thought that it would be good for morale if he entertained his officers in the evenings. He would have a very mediocre type of buffet and then make us play parlor games. Such a reversion to our childhood activities did not sit too well with most of us.

Fortunately I was rescued from this assignment quite quickly. When I was taking the Primary FRCS exam I had met an RAF Group Captain Dixon and become friendly with him. He found out who my father was and knew of him. He was one of the permanent senior surgeons in the RAF. Through someone's influence I was transferred to a job as a surgeon at Ely Hospital. This was one of the two main RAF hospitals. It was a general hospital and had been one of the main burn units set up to treat burned pilots, many of them casualties from the Battle of Britain. Though the treatments were relatively primitive by our modern standards they were, at that time, the state of the art. Some of the best English plastic surgeons worked there. Since the war was over by this time, we had relatively few burn patients and our accident victims were due to motorcycle crashes rather those of aircraft. We spent most of our time taking care of general surgical problems such as one would expect in any civilian hospital. My boss was the Group Captain who I had met before while taking the Primary Fellowship exam. He acted as a visiting surgeon and I as his resident. We became very good friends, so it was a pleasure to work with him. He sometimes brought with him, when visiting, the senior consultant surgeon of the RAF who was Vice President of the Royal College of Surgeons and chief at the Westminster Hospital in London. Between the two I was lucky enough to be able to continue my surgical education.

After I had to go into the RAF, Agnes and I gave up the flat in Chelsea. She went to stay with my parents until we found out where I would be assigned. This allowed my parents to get to know her much better. My father had been appreciative of the pretty girl I had chosen from the first time he had met her. My mother, because of her generous nature, had been most welcoming but had held back her final judgment. She had not wanted me to marry an American and was worried because she was a cripple. After Agnes lived with them for a few weeks, mother came to realize that my new wife was a very determined character who would not allow her disability to stand in her way. She was always helping my mother with the chores and they quickly became life-long friends. My mother was a very special person. She was kind hearted and utterly honest.

She epitomized the person who hated the sin but loved the sinner. My American in-laws became very fond of her and were delighted to entertain her when, in the future, she visited America. My father, though very successful in his career, was somewhat of a pessimist. He was always sure that we were going to the poor house. He kept very careful accounts of his personal finances and expected my mother to do the same. She had to keep track of the household expenses and balance her books. When father was going over her accounts one month he was pleased to see that they balanced accurately. However there was one item that perplexed him. "What is this item, SPG?" He asked. "Oh!" she replied, "that stands for Something Probably Grub". Father was defeated, took the teasing with good grace and they had a good laugh. Because of his cautious approach to financial matters he left my mother reasonably well off when he died. Both my parents spoiled me and were always there to help when I got into trouble.

After I was assigned to work at Ely Hospital in the RAF, Agnes and I had to find somewhere we could live which would be near the hospital. Ely is 17 miles north of Cambridge. We decided that it would not be too far for me to commute from Cambridge if I had a car. Also we would be able to enjoy the University life in our spare time. I still had a few friends there. We found a small rooming house in the town and rented a couple of rooms with a kitchen. I found an old car which I could afford. It was a little sports car called a Wolseley Hornet Special. It was a very open car since it was a convertible which had lost its roof. Instead it had a piece of old barrage balloon which served as a cover. The only trouble was that this could not be used when the car was moving as it blew off. We discovered that when it rained we were all right as long as we kept moving as the rain was diverted over us by the wind-screen. It did necessitate some careful clothing. I had a leather flying suit which could be put on over my uniform and I wrapped Agnes up in a blanket, lined leather boots and a fur hat. The car turned out to have one major disadvantage. The cylinder block and the cylinder head did not fit perfectly so occasionally the cylinder head gasket leaked. This did not immobilize the car but did not help its performance. Actually it ran quite well and had a good turn of speed. Although petrol (gas) was still rationed at that time, I was able to get enough coupons to be able to drive to the hospital and have a little left over.

The rooming house proved to be unsatisfactory. Our rooms were over the landlady's living area and she complained that Agnes's stumping around with her cane disturbed her. In fact she had a number of complaints. Through an advertisement we heard of a little cottage for rent in a nearby village. When we went to see it, we were both intrigued. It sat at the end of a village called Great Wilbraham and was next to a farm. This village was about 5 miles outside Cambridge and just off the road to Ely. It consisted of a kitchen and living room with an attached addition. From this latter there was a staircase, little more than a ladder, which led to the bedrooms. There were two bedrooms but one had to go through the first and duck under the main cross beam to get to the second. It had one of the few baths in the village, though this was in the kitchen. It was supplied with hot water from a gas heater. There was no toilet but the outside privy was close to the back door. The living room had a fire-place which was the only source of heat in the house. The cottage was owned by a lady who was suffering from severe migraine and had decided to live with her sister. When we inquired as to the rent, she told us that she wanted two pounds a week (approx $8) and this would include a man to bury the dead, i.e. empty the privy once a week. The cottage was ancient, made with wattle and daub walls and had a heavy thatched roof. The cross beam between the bedrooms was curved and must have come from a ship wrecked on the coast. This meant that the floor upstairs was also curved which made for an interesting tilt to our bed. We were enchanted and decided that the charm and situation, to say nothing of the price, were well worth the lack of modern conveniences. It did not take us long to decide and move in. It turned out to be a wonderful honeymoon cottage which we enjoyed for almost two years.

My duties at the hospital required me to stay at the hospital some nights and some weekends. I did not like to leave Agnes at the cottage alone as it was somewhat isolated and she did not drive. Anyway she did not have the car. We found a very pleasant rooming house in Ely well within walking distance of the Cathedral. Since she had majored in the history of art at Vassar she was delighted to have the opportunity to explore the cathedral thoroughly. She met the Verger who was happy to find someone who was really interested and knowledgeable. They became good friends and he showed her many things that the normal visitor would never have noticed. At the crossing of the nave and the side aisles is a famous octagonal tower built by Walsingham in the 14th century. It is a remarkable structure as it sits on eight half arches so it appears to have no substantial support as the arches do not meet. The tower is built of wood and consists of timbers 40 ft long and 4x4 ft at their bases. These pillars rest on the apparently unsupported tips of the half arches. Walsingham must have been a mathematical genius to have figured out the engineering design which allowed his plan to work. Time has proved how right he was. Builders still marvel about it. After the verger got to know Agnes, he asked if she would like to go up and inspect the bases of the tower pillars. It necessitated climbing up the spiral staircase in the West end and then going along a catwalk over the Choir to the base of the wooden tower at the crossing. Then one could walk on to one of the half arches to the base of the pillars. At this point one seemed to standing on nothing with the floor of the Cathedral seemingly miles below. Agnes achieved this feat in spite of walking with a cane. Afterwards she admitted to me that she had been scared to death but having once started, her innate determination would not allow her to give up.

Both Agnes and I became very friendly with my chief, Group Captain Peter Dixon. When we invited him to come to have dinner with us at our cottage, he would spend the night so as not to have to drive back to London. Because meat was rationed and in short supply, we would try to harvest some game from the country-side. There were plenty of rabbits and hares but it was not easy to get within range to shoot them. Peter, as I came to know the Group Captain when we were not on duty, and I solved the problem. The solution was not exactly legal but it was effective. We would get into my car at night and drive down the main road which ran through the country between Royston and Six Mile Bottom. Because of the petrol rationing there was very little traffic on that road at night but there were plenty of rabbits. It was possible to put the windscreen flat on my car. This we did so that we could shoot over the top of the bonnet when the rabbits were caught in our headlights. In this way we could enhance our meat supply. When carefully cooked in a casserole, rabbit is delicious. We sometimes topped off the meal with apple pie and brandy butter sauce. It is even better than pie with either custard or ice cream.

Beside the rabbits there were hares though we rarely managed to shoot any. However there was a field beside the cottage which belonged to the neighboring farm. One day in March Agnes and I were walking along the edge of this field when the meaning of the March Hare became apparent. The field was alive with hares dancing around and paying no attention to us or anyone else. Periodically they would sit up on their hindquarters with their long ears straight up and their forepaws hanging in front as if begging. This was in broad daylight. It was obvious to us that in the mating season hares do really go mad. They seem to lose all sense of self preservation.

The soil around that part of East Anglia consists of rich loam. This is because the area was largely marsh before it was drained many years ago. With the advice of Dutch engineers a complicated system of drainage channels was constructed which left the salvaged land deep in soil which is incredibly fertile. We found that it was very easy to grow flowers and vegetables. When we planted a row of peas, the disadvantage of living beside a farm became apparent. The chickens which ran free in the farm-yard came and enjoyed our seeds. Someone at the hospital told me that, if one soaked them thoroughly, dried peas became pleasantly edible. I bought a pound of dried peas and soaked them but was disappointed with the result. I left some in a saucer and forgot about them. In a few days I noticed that many of them had started to sprout. Since I had the best part of a pound of the peas left, I decided to plant them to see what would happen. There were more than the chickens could demolish and to our amazement the next spring we had a great row of pea plants which bore masses of pea pods. We enjoyed all the fresh peas that we wanted. We had also planted a row of spring onions. I think every one of these seeds germinated and we had to thin them. The little shoots that we were thinning looked so good that we ate most of them. This was a mistake as a large number of baby onions can cause considerable indigestion.

Not only the garden which we were trying to grow flourished but so did the grass. It grew so tall that it was not easy to cut. We did not have the fancy mowing machines that are now available, so I decided to cut it with a scythe. I knew the correct technique for swinging the scythe and how to keep it sharp. What I had not realized was that the movement required to swing the scythe was one that was alien to me. Though I got the grass cut, I also got an acute tendonitis in my right wrist which was very uncomfortable.

While living there we acquired a couple of stray animals. The first was a kitten. We had to leave it in the cottage when we both went to Ely overnight. When we returned there was never any mess in the house. This was how the kitten acquired the name of B.C. which stood for bladder control. One day on the way out of the hospital, as I was passing the guard house at the entrance, I noticed that they had a very small puppy. I stopped and found out that it was a stray which they had picked up and fed. It had obviously been very hungry and had eaten so much that its stomach was dragging on the ground. The men did not know what they were going to do with the little creature, so I offered to take it home with me. Agnes, who was a great dog lover, was delighted with our new addition. She called it Barnaby after one of her favorite cartoon characters. We came to love it and took it with us where ever we went. Soon after acquiring it, we went down to my parent's house. We were driving in our very open car with Agnes all wrapped up in coats and a blanket. Barnaby traveled on Agnes's lap as he was still very young and small. As we were going along Agnes said that he seemed to be getting very restless. We thought that he might have a full bladder. It was at night. I stopped the car, picked up Barnaby and set him down in front of the car in the headlights so that I could keep an eye on him. The moment his feet hit the ground he let forth such a flood that I thought the car would float away. Thereafter we had an uneventful trip to my parents' house where he immediately made friends with the dog that they had. Unfortunately Barnaby developed Distemper and died in spite of our best efforts.

One day we noticed clouds of smoke billowing up from a little distance down the path that ran beside the field between us and the farm. There was a railway line that ran across the end of the path. I went down to see what was happening. I was joined by half the villagers who had rushed out thinking that our cottage was on fire. We had never met any of these villagers before but they were rushing to help what they thought was a neighbor in distress. We went down the path together and were soon fighting some very acrid smoke. It was coming from a railroad wagon parked on a siding. The burning posed no danger as there was nothing else around to catch on fire but the smoke started to irritate us and burn. We fled away quickly. It turned out that it was some kind of chemical like a mustard gas that had been left there after the war prior to organizing its proper disposal. I had been wearing my RAF battle dress which was a thick woolly overall. That gas got into the cloth so that, even after professional cleaning, it continued to be rather irritating to wear.

While working at Ely hospital I decided that it would be a good opportunity to study for my final FRCS exam. Many evenings I would sit in our living room in the cottage with a surgical textbook. This was not very exciting for my wife. Eventually she announced that she was fed up with being married to the back of a book. My studies gave me a good theoretical knowledge but I was woefully lacking in practical experience. I decided to have an attempt at the exam. I got leave to go to London to take the exam. I stayed at my parents' house from whence I could get to the Royal College of Surgeons easily. After the last day which consisted of the orals, I went to stand at the bottom of the stairs at the College hoping that my number would be called and that I would be able to go upstairs to sign the book. I was not called and I realized that I had failed. Though I should not have been surprised, I was disappointed. I went back to my parent's house before returning to the hospital at Ely the next day. When I got there the next afternoon, I was sent for by the Group Captain who was in command of the hospital. He gave me a thorough dressing down because I was late returning. I felt that this was somewhat unfair and did not improve my mood after my disappointment at the exam. I related all this to my surgical boss, Group Captain Dixon, who was very sympathetic. He went to the hospital commander who had no control over a consultant of equal rank. There he told this gentleman what he thought of him and I had no further trouble.

While at Ely I was allowed a vacation. Some of my father's friends had a small cottage just south of Chichester on an inlet of Southampton Water. They kindly let us use the cottage and lent us a small sailing boat. We had a very pleasant time there for a few days until Agnes, who was in the early stages of pregnancy, started to bleed. I rushed her to the hospital in Chichester where she aborted. This was the most devastating experience of our married life. For me, besides the disappointment, it was very educational. It gave me an insight into how differently similar events affect people both physically and mentally. Though I was unhappy and disappointed, I did not realize how it would affect Agnes. As we sat together afterwards, she suddenly burst into tears. I had never seen her cry before. Then she said, between her tears; "I can't even have a baby". The realization of how much she had suffered and overcome because of her osteomyelitis and the subsequent disability became so much clearer to me. I developed an even greater admiration and love for her. I think it made me a better husband and probably, if not a better doctor, at least a more sympathetic one.

After my two years in the RAF I was demobilized. Besides giving me a set of civilian clothes they gave me a month's leave with pay. I decided that I had to pass the exam to become a Fellow of the Royal College. There was also the opportunity to become what was known as a Supernumerary surgical registrar at a teaching Hospital. I chose to return to St. Thomas's hospital. They ran a course to prepare candidates for the final Fellowship exam. It had the reputation as the best course in London. The exam at that time had a 20% pass rate, but candidates who had taken the St. Thomas's course had a 70% pass rate. The next course started about a month after I got out of the Air Force so I postponed accepting the Supernumerary surgical registrar job until that time. Not knowing when I would ever get another opportunity to take a similar vacation with pay, I decided that we would visit my in-laws in Washington. I sent Agnes by boat ahead of me so that she could have a longer time with her parents. I planned to fly over as soon as I was finally demobilized.

Chapter 8

VACATION WITH MY IN-LAWS IN THE US

Having put Agnes safely on the ship to sail to the U S, I set about arranging for my own travel. I had decided to fly over on a BOAC plane (the predecessor of British Airways). It was the summer of 1949. Having said good bye to my parents at Heathrow Airport I found that the plane could not fly from that airport because of the fog. With my fellow passengers, we were put on a bus and driven south to Gatwick, which was not much of an airport at that time. There we boarded the transatlantic plane, a four-engine monster much like a modified wartime heavy bomber. Before midnight we took off. The noise of the four powerful piston engines was very tiring and not conducive to peaceful sleep or any other relaxation. After a few hours the pilot informed us over the speaker system that we were encountering head winds. We were supposed to land either at Goose or Gander in Canada to refuel. These were two refueling stations used during the war for fueling planes being ferried to Gt. Britain from the USA. We were told that there was some uncertainty as to the weather at these places and we did not have enough fuel to go anywhere else if they were closed. We would have to stop in Iceland to top up our tanks. This we did. I did not see much of Iceland, only the airport where we were allowed to disembark to stretch our legs. Then we were off again to Gander. As it turned out we arrived there early on a beautifully clear cold morning. As we came in to land the scenery was dramatic and beautifully wild. After the stop over there we flew on to New York where we arrived almost 24 hours late. Or perhaps I should say 24 hours after our expected time of arrival in New York. I had to change planes there to get a flight to Washington DC. I had managed to communicate with Agnes's family as to my delayed time of arrival. They were there to meet me. That plane went on to Texas.

I was shattered to see that my wife had altered her appearance. Instead of the wonderful head of long hair that I loved so much, she had much of it cut off. As a girl she had long hair that came down to her waist but when I married her it was only shoulder length. This was even shorter and it took me some time to get used to. We had to collect my luggage and were most unhappy to discover that my main suitcase had not been unloaded. It was still on the plane going to Texas. My father-in-law took over at that point and negotiated with the airline. They assured him that my suitcase would be returned on the next flight and delivered to his house the next day. Sure enough it was. It was indeed fortunate as my in-laws had arranged a big party for the next day to introduce me to their friends. It was a black tie cocktail party and my dinner jacket was in the missing suitcase.

When I had first visited my prospective in-laws in Washington, they had been living in an apartment in town and had rented their own house on the edge of town. My Father-in-law had built this house on 12 acres fronting onto a dirt road. His father told him it was crazy to build so far out in the country. Agnes had grown up in that house and told me that when they looked west from the back of the house all they could see was the light of a farm house in the distance. For those who know Washington, it may be surprising to realize that it was on Nebraska Avenue just north of Ward Circle and is now the site of the Japanese ambassador's residence. During the war, because of gas rationing, my father-in-law had decided that it was too far out and had moved into an in-town apartment. At the end of the war they had moved back into their own house. I was delighted to get there and be able to get a real night's sleep. Their collie recognized Agnes when she returned and had taken up her old sleeping quarters, on the other half of Agnes's bed. Tammy, the dog, resented my taking her place.

The next day we had the party. It was a very hot day at the end of July. My father-in-law served his mint cocktail. This is a wicked concoction which consists of bourbon, crushed ice, sugar and mint. This is shaken in a cocktail shaker and served in wine glasses. On a hot day it is insidious and extremely intoxicating. I am sure that I had too much of it but I understand that I did not totally disgrace myself. I was introduced to a large number of people but could not remember who any of them were afterwards. Fortunately, when I met them again, they introduced themselves by name. I discovered that this is an American custom which is, regrettably, very un-English.

In August the family took me and my mother, who came over to visit, with them up to a Lodge in North Wisconsin. They would drive the car there. It was a long trip and took three days. There was none of the fancy turnpikes and through-ways in those days. We had various overnight stops on the way. There is quite a history to the lodge. It belonged to my mother-in-law's family. She had come from Milwaukee where her father had been a judge. In the mid 1870s he had joined with some other fishermen to fish a small stream called the Brule which ran north from near the source of the St. Croix River into Lake Superior. The stream had in interesting history as it served the Indians and later the French Canadian explorers and trappers as the main route between Lake Superior and the Mississippi. From the headwaters of the Brule there is a portage of about one mile to the headwaters of the St. Croix which flows south into the Mississippi. The fishermen found that this stream or river was loaded with trout and there was wonderful fishing to be had. It was relatively unknown and not easy to get to. There was a railroad that ran from Chicago to the town of Superior at the head of the lake. This railroad crossed the Brule River on a trestle bridge. Passengers could get the train to stop there. The fishermen could then canoe up river to camp and fish. After a few years a fishing club was built there and the fishermen started to bring their families. Three of the families joined together to buy about 20 acres on either side of the river and make for themselves more permanent camps. These acres were bought for the astonishing price of one trout to be caught and delivered by one to the ladies of the group. My wife's grandmother, the judge's wife, was one of those who built a camp on this ground. The other two families built their own camps. I gather that my wife's grandmother was an extremely strong-willed and determined lady. She chose a spit of land where the river took a sharp bend and the land was elevated twenty or so feet above the river. There she would take her family of one son and four daughters for the summer. They would get off the train and be taken up stream in canoes by the local half-caste guides. Their food and heavier equipment was transported by oxcart. They had their own canoes which were locally built of cedar by a man called Joe Lucius. These canoes were 17 to 21 feet long, moderately broad with no real keel. They were designed to be sturdy and accommodate an armchair seat in the front for the fisherman. As the river had several rapids, they had to be strong enough to withstand the occasional bump on rocks. There are still a few of these canoes on the river. Since they are over 100 years old, it is irrefutable evidence of the skill of Joe Lucius. The standard technique in using these canoes was to pole them upstream and paddle them down. In the 1920s the camp that Grandma had built caught fire and burned down. She set about rebuilding. She had two assets. The first was the determination to build something that was attractive and big enough for her expanding family. The other was a son-in-law who was making a fortune and could afford to subsidize her plans. The result was, not a camp, but a lodge. It consisted of a living room two and a half stories high with an enormous fireplace. Around this was a screen porch on three sides about 12 feet wide. Over the porch were six double bedrooms with three bathrooms. These were entered from a balcony which jutted out into the living room. At the back was the dining room, kitchen, butler's pantry, icehouse and a separate dining room for the children. Over this area were four more bedrooms. Over the dining room was another bedroom with its own fireplace. This was Grandma's room. A boat house and dock was also built and a guide house where the help could live. This whole place was built entirely with timbers shipped in from Oregon and hand-trimmed. There does not seem to be a single nail in the whole structure either inside or out. This was where my wife had spent most of her summers when she was growing up. It was to this place that my in-laws took me. When I saw the place I was spellbound. It was something that I had never imagined; the smell of the pines, the 40 to 50 ft tall Norway pines standing beside the building and the building itself. Then there was the river which was so clear that one could see every detail of the bottom and so clean that one could, and did, drink it. Admittedly we often added a little bourbon, of course, merely for safety's sake.

There I had to learn to trout fish with a fly and to navigate a canoe. I rather disappointed the family because they put me in a canoe and gave me a pole and waited for me to fall out. They did not realize that I had spent some time on the Cam poling punts and sometimes canoes which were much less stable than the Lucius canoes. I had much less trouble with the canoes than learning to cast a fly effectively. The river varied in width and in places opened out into lakes of varying sizes. Between these lakes there were rapids. Some were longish stretches running over rocks and a few were quite steep and short. My family and their friends were quite expert at poling up these rapids and at avoiding the rocks coming down. I found that these skills took a good deal of mastering and I never became as proficient as my brother-in-law. When he found that I was interested in learning to fish with a fly, we became good friends. We would go up river in a canoe with one guiding, i.e. sitting in the back poling or paddling, while the other sat in the front and fished. As the guide I had to learn to put the canoe in such a position that he could cast his fly exactly where he wanted it to land. This was not too difficult in the calm stretches or the lakes but often the best fishing seemed to be in the faster water. This necessitated holding the canoe in the fast water. This was done with two short poles called snubbing poles, one on either side of the canoe and tucked under the armpits. Since my brother-in-law weighed considerably more than I did the bow tended to be down in the water and the stern, where I was, up almost in the air. It made holding the canoe much more difficult. In many of the areas where we wanted to fish, the river is quite narrow and the trees lining the bank designed to catch the fly on the back cast. Jim, my brother-law, informed me that the fish were not up in the trees but he was most tolerant of my many hang-ups and helped me rescue quite a few flies. One of the most exciting things to which he introduced me was night fishing.

The Family Lodge on the Brule River, Wisconsin

By the time I first went to the Brule the abundant supply of trout had diminished considerably. Unless you knew the best places and the best technique it was difficult to catch many. The river had native brook trout and brown trout and was being stocked with rainbow trout. The brook trout could be fished by tempting them out from under the fallen logs at the edge of the river but the browns tended to feed at night. The technique was to drift down the river at night and cast a large fly or bug near the bank, letting the current swing it out in front of the canoe towards the middle of the river. The darker the night the better for fishing but the more difficult it was to judge where the bank was. It was very exciting as one could not see the lure. The first sign of any fish activity was a loud splash as the trout came after the fly or mouse. Then one attempted to set the hook. If successful, which was not always the case, the rod bent and the line ran out. Then there was the fight to play the fish into the net and thence to the live box in the canoe. These canoes were built with holes in the bottom in the center which were covered with a box which prevented the water from flooding the canoe. Fish which we caught could be put in the live box and taken back to camp. There they could be put in a live box, a wire screen enclosure, built under the boat house. If no one wanted to eat them they could be released.

The reason that the river is so clean and clear is that there is neither industry nor agriculture contaminating it. From the town of Brule upstream, i.e. south, there is a series of privately owned camps or lodges which occupy the banks up to a big lake. One of these is our lodge, the Noyes Camp. Beyond big lake there is a big estate called Cedar Lodge where President Coolidge used to go for summer vacations. It consists of about 40,000 acres of woods on either side of the river. It has its own fish hatchery and harvests its timber in a most selective manner. Some of the owners of the lodges on the river had made picnic sites up the river where one could go for lunch or evening suppers. These consisted of a roofed picnic table and a fireplace for cooking. Because my in-laws had been going to the river for so many years they knew most of the owners of the other lodges, including Cedar Lodge. We had access to any of the picnic grounds though we usually used our own. Some of the evening parties included friends from other lodges. These parties became quite hilarious at times as a good deal of alcohol was used to ensure the safety of the drinking water!

When I got to the Brule for the first time, there were five branches of the family entitled to use our lodge. These were Grandma's children. Grandma had died before I visited for the first time. I am sorry that I never met her as she has always sounded like a very interesting person. As a matter of fact many of the family and the caretaker are convinced that she still haunts the place. Certainly her spirit remains dominant. Each branch was entitled to one month in the summer. The lodge was not winterized and had to be closed after the hunters left in early October and be reopened in time for the spring fishing. Agnes's family shared August with her mother's favorite sister. This lady, Aunt Katherine, was the widow of the gentleman, Donald McLennon, who had provided most of the money to build the present building. She had been left very well off and lived both in Lake Forest near Chicago and in Palm Beach, Florida. She was quite autocratic and the rest of the family seemed rather in awe of her. Fortunately she was fond of Agnes and I found that she was very friendly and had a great sense of humor. We got along very well. She and my mother-in-law ran the lodge from the catering point of view with the help of some local ladies who cooked and cleaned. My father-in-law seemed to look after the upkeep of the buildings and the pump which provided water to the house from the river.

I had a marvelous time that August and when the time came to leave I found that we were invited to break the journey back to Washington at Aunt Katherine's house in Lake Forest. It was a wonderfully luxurious place. Among other servants there was a butler who insisted on taking my clothes at night to press them. Aunt Katherine had several cars. One she kept for visitors to use. Since I was going to go back to Washington for another month before returning to England she insisted that we borrow this Cadillac so that we could use it until I left the country. When I asked about how we would get the car back to her she said that we should not worry as she would get her chauffeur to pick it up in Washington and drive it down to her in Palm Beach. Agnes and I drove the car back to Washington making a detour through parts of Tennessee on the way.

My mother made a great hit with all the members of the family because she was so even tempered and was always ready to fit in with any plans that were made. She had to return to England before Agnes and I had to. She was to sail on a Holland American Ship from Hoboken, so we drove up to New York the day before. We stayed at a hotel near Central Park and had the car checked into their garage. I was driving Aunt Katherine's car with Illinois registration plates. The next morning we ordered the car to be able to drive across the river to where the ship was docked. We waited and waited but no car was delivered from the hotel. Eventually, two hours later, the car came. This meant that we had less time than we had planned to get mother to her ship. We started off to take a ferry across only to find that the ferry that we planned to take had been discontinued. We had to go further south on Manhattan to take the only ferry that was running. There we found a very long line of cars and trucks waiting to get on the ferry. In desperation I drove to the front of the line where there was a policeman. I explained our predicament because by that time the ship was due to sail. The policeman approached the truck in the front of the line and asked the driver to let us go in front of him. I heard him say; "I have seen everything. Here is an Englishman driving an Illinois car in a hurry in New York". We got on the ferry and as it was crossing the river we heard the ship tooting to signal its departure. We roared off the ferry to the dock and arrived just as they were removing the last gangplank. This they held for us to rush mother aboard. As we heaved a sigh of relief we met one of my father's friends. He was enormously relieved to see us. Unbeknownst to us my father had arranged for a fur coat to be delivered as a present to my mother. It was to be delivered to her on the ship. This friend had it delivered to the ship and did not know what would happen if my mother was not on board. My mother got home safely with the coat. We returned to the hotel emotionally exhausted.

When I got back to Washington I still had a few more weeks before I was due to sail back to England. I had been introduced to Dr. Lyons, the doctor who had taken care of Agnes when she was sick as a child. He invited me to visit the Emergency Hospital where he was the surgical chief. It did not take me long to discover that he was one of the finest characters I had ever met. Everyone at the hospital loved and respected him. He had the gift of knowing and remembering everyone. He would, for instance, ask about the elevator operator's family and he treated everyone with equal respect. I started to attend the surgical rounds that he ran. He introduced me to the leading urologist in Washington. This man had been trained at Johns Hopkins. Besides an extensive private practice he was a professor at Georgetown University Medical School. My exposure to urological surgery had been meager in England so I asked him if I could tag along with him. When he found I had a very nice car, and since he hated to drive, he asked if I would drive him around. This I did and had the opportunity to watch him operate and to attend his teaching sessions.

On one occasion he was asked to consult on a problem presented by General Marshall and I tagged along to meet the great man. I learned a lot and it stood me in good stead in the future.

Agnes was pregnant again. I was to sail back to England and she was going to stay a little longer with her parents. Just before I was due to sail Agnes started to bleed. We were scared that she was going to miscarry again. We put in an emergency call to her parent's gynecologist who came in a hurry. He gave her an injection and put her to bed. I was not willing to leave her until I knew what was happening. I called up the Holland America line and they agreed to allow me to transfer to one of their ships sailing a week later. During that time Agnes seemed to have settled down and I accepted the later sailing. This was on one of their older ships, the Veendam, which stopped at Bermuda on the way.

When I got on board I found that the cabin class was full and they had to put me in a first class cabin. Because the ship was old and did not have all the facilities of their more modern ships they made up for it by providing the very best food available. The ship was slow and made the detour to Bermuda. Unfortunately it only anchored offshore to unload passengers so I did not get to see around the island. It was a rather boring trip but I found a very congenial gentleman with whom I became friendly. He had been in the RAF and so we had plenty to talk about. As we were approaching Southampton he asked if there was anything he could do to help me while we were disembarking. I asked him what he meant. He confessed that he was an official of the line. Ralph Mace proved to be an invaluable contact whenever we crossed the Atlantic. When he knew that Agnes was coming over shortly on one of their ships which would call at Southampton before going on to Rotterdam, he told me that it would not dock at Southampton but anchor off-shore to unload the passengers destined there, by tender. He offered to take me down with him on the tender to pick up Agnes. I took him up on this offer. It was a most interesting trip. On the trip down Southampton Water we had the customs and immigration officials with us. The custom officials told us many intriguing stories. When ships dock, they station an officer in uniform at the bottom of each ramp. The average passenger does not notice them. Those that are trying to smuggle something tend to eye these officers. When they do that, the examining officers are alerted and subject these passengers to a very thorough search. One examiner found a passenger trying to bring in a very large bottle of perfume. When he was told how much the duty would be, he was incensed. In his fury he took the bottle and broke it over the officer's head. The man was not hurt but his wife would not let him back in their house for quite a while. Some perfumes are powerful and lingering. They also told us that they station an officer at the exit to the customs shed. On one occasion a lady dressed as a Nun cleared customs but just as she was leaving she started to 'ring' loudly and clearly. She was brought back and stripped by one of the female examiners. Under her habit were found pinned a number of alarm clocks. She had foolishly forgotten that they were still wound up. Drug smuggling was much less of a problem in those days and they had not started to use dogs to sniff for contraband.

When we got to the ship I was taken aboard and introduced to the Purser. He was supplying his official guests with Holland's Gin. This was the real stuff and was served neat in small glasses. When they found that I had never had any before they insisted on serving me some. I found that I disliked it because it had a rather oily taste. I was careful not to say so at the time, though I did refuse seconds. I met Agnes on the ship and we came back to land together on the tender. Agnes had brought back with her a good deal of furnishings for our flat. These had been packed in crates in Washington by a professional moving company. We had their inventory and the crates were bound with metal strips. When we got to customs we were subjected to a very thorough search. We had offered to pay any duty that they thought necessary on any of our possessions. The officers demanded that the crates be opened and informed us that they would not do them up again after they had inspected the contents. They would not accept the bill of lading from the packing company. They started to rip the metal straps off and undo one of the crates. At this point Agnes burst into tears. This disconcerted the officer and after undoing only one crate and not riffling through it, he did have it done up again. We had to pay some duty even though they were all our own possessions. We got everything shipped home eventually. I do not know what the officers were looking for, but they must have been tipped off that there was some illegal shipping on that boat. We were not the only ones that day to be subjected to intensive examination. Thank goodness few men are not softened by a pretty girl walking with a cane bursting into tears, seemingly due to your having harassed them.

Chapter 9

GENERAL SURGICAL TRAINING

After I returned from my vacation in the States, I got down to serious work to try to obtain my Fellowship in the Royal College of Surgeons. Under the National Health Service there was a carefully devised system of training for those who wished to become specialists. After the first appointment as a House Officer for a year and military service, it was necessary to obtain jobs as Registrars. The Registrars were divided into three groups, Junior for one year, Middle Grade for two years and then Senior for four years or until one could become a Consultant, a lifetime appointment. Because of the pyramidal nature of the system it is obvious that there are fewer and fewer vacancies at each level. Consequently the competition is keener on each move up. Just because one got onto the bottom rung of the ladder there was no assurance that one would be able to progress. If one did not, one had to give up and go into General Practice. The jobs were awarded by the individual hospitals and each candidate was interviewed locally and appointed by the staff already working at that hospital. If you had service in the military and had obtained a postgraduate degree it was possible to skip the

Junior Registrar grade. If I wanted to become a surgeon it was essential that I obtain my Fellowship.

Perhaps this is a good time to explain some of the background of the machinations that occurred when the National Health Service was instituted. At the end of the war the national election returned a Labour Government. This government was elected with the idea of a national health service as one of its foremost platforms. Nye Bevin had been appointed Minister of Health and became responsible for devising the plan. The medical profession in general was opposed to the whole concept. The General Medical Council which predominantly represented the general practitioners refused to negotiate with the minister. The presidents of the two major specialist organizations, the Royal College of Physicians and the Royal College of Surgeons appreciated the fact that the Health Service was the new law. They decided to cooperate and try to make it as good as they possibly could, particularly for the specialists who they represented. They did a very good job because Bevin, who had no experience with the practice of medicine, was delighted to find two such prominent people prepared to help him. As a result the specialists found that they could recommend a scheme which would be satisfactory for them. The Consultants had lifetime appointments to hospitals where they could work for a number of sessions. Each session was a half day and the week was divided into eleven sessions. If the specialist worked the maximum of eleven half days, he was regarded as full-time and was not allowed to undertake private practice. If, on the other hand, he accepted no more than nine sessions he could have private patients as well, provided this did not encroach on the time committed to the National Health patients. The specialist was paid according to the number of sessions that he worked. If he worked nine sessions he would be paid nine elevenths of a full-time salary. He was allowed four to six weeks vacation on full pay and could apply for study leave beyond this to attend meetings. The general practitioners who were represented by the General Medical Council, which had refused to cooperate, got a very much less satisfactory deal. They were to be paid on a per capita basis according to the number of patients who signed up with them. There was no provision for them to have any vacation. If they took time off they had to provide a locum to cover their practice at their expense. There is a lesson to be learned from this. It is that it is wise to cooperate with the inevitable, or to put it crudely, if you are going to be raped you might as well lie back and enjoy it.

I had organized to attend St. Thomas's Hospital as a supernumerary registrar, an appointment provided for ex-service men to get extra training. St. Thomas's Hospital ran an excellent course for surgeons. It was organized by a young surgeon, Mr. Charles Robb, one of the youngest men to obtain a Fellowship himself. He was very dogmatic, demanding, and a good organizer. He devoted a lot of time to the people he was coaching. He subsequently became chief surgeon at another hospital before emigrating to become Professor of Surgery at an American Medical school. The course that he ran consisted of sessions where we had to write answers to questions which he would set. We were given one hour to write the answers. After we handed them in, he would go over them with us, giving us not only factual corrections, but also criticism as to the construction of our answers. In fact he taught us how to organize what we knew and set it out in a logical way. He also organized clinical sessions with others of the surgical staff and relevant specialties. In these we sat around and had questions fired at us which we had to answer as if we were in an oral exam. Since some of these teachers were examiners for the exam itself, both the questions and the atmosphere were very helpful. The exam itself consisted of one day of written questions and one day of orals. The written exam consisted of four questions, two for two hours in the morning and two for two hours in the afternoon. There was no choice of questions.

On another day there were a series of orals. Each oral was before two examiners, one of whom was supposed to ask the questions and the other mark the candidate. The subjects of each oral were different, surgical pathology, the recognition of surgical specimens and the description of how the candidate would perform a specific operation. This latter is much more difficult than actually performing the operation itself. The candidate was allowed to ask the person ushering him in for the oral to which of the examiners he had been assigned. The course at St. Thomas's was particularly helpful here as we were told of the pet hobbies of some of the examiners that we might face. Some were reputed to have very set ideas which were not always generally accepted. If one was forewarned one could avoid getting into a discussion which might irritate the examiner. The importance of knowing who the examiner was is well illustrated by one candidate's misfortune. He made two mistakes. He did not know who his examiner was and he added more to his answer than was needed. He was asked if he knew the underlying cause of a specific condition. He gave the usually accepted theory, but when the examiner asked if he knew of any other theories, he said that there was another one. He outlined it but added that it was considered ridiculous and totally discredited. When asked if he knew who had proposed this theory, he hesitated for a moment and then said that he thought he could remember because the doctor had a very curious double-barreled name. Then he remembered the name but added that this doctor was long dead. Since the discredited and long dead doctor happened to be his examiner, his answer did not sit very well. There was one curious rule at the College. Once one was a Fellow one was allowed to attend any of the orals as an onlooker. I did this once and it was a most enlightening experience. I watched a candidate who looked as if he was very knowledgeable. He was asked a relatively simple question, but he appeared to assume that there was a catch, so he stumbled with his answer. The examiner asked an even simpler question which convinced the poor man that it was a trick question. The whole exam continued this way. At the end the two examiners discussed the problem, realized the situation, but agreed that there was no way they could pass him as he not given a single correct answer. It was sad to see a promising candidate fail himself.

When I took the exam myself I found that I was well prepared to write answers to three of the questions but the fourth was set to test the candidate's ability to think for oneself. It was; 'Discuss the influence of antibiotics on the practice of surgery'. Antibiotics had only recently become available and so there was no precedent for answering this question. It was necessary to think this out de novo. Some of the overseas candidates felt that this was an unfair question as there was nothing in the books which they had studied to help them. I am sure the answers revealed a great deal about the candidates ability to deal with an unexpected situation.

When I had the orals one of my examiners was an Attending surgeon at Great Ormond Street and he knew I had been a house surgeon there. The first question he asked me was about rectal bleeding in children. This was very easy for me and got me relaxed so that I could cope with the rest of the questions more easily. The exam was terrifying as a single examiner could give a failing mark and this was the end. One had to come back another time.

A young aspiring surgeon that I met was extremely knowledgeable. He had been attending rounds at Great

Ormond Street as a visitor when we were discussing a case that was baffling everybody. He spoke up and said that it was a case of X which was written up in a specific book on page so and so. He was right. His book knowledge was phenomenal but he had no common sense. This was known to the examiners at the College when he went for his Fellowship exam. During the oral on operative surgery he was asked what he would do if a specific problem arose while he was operating. His answer would have caused a major disaster and so he was failed. This was what those who knew him hoped would happen. He would have made an excellent consultant but would have been a menace as a surgeon.

At the end of my day of orals I went to the Royal College itself, taking Agnes with me. There we stood with the other candidates who had taken their orals that day. We stood in the hallway at the bottom of the stairs. One of the college servants stood on the staircase and started to read out numbers. Each of us was known by number and the numbers ran consecutively. If your number was called, you went up-stairs to sign the book of Fellows amid the cheers of those still below. As the numbers came nearer to yours the tension was devastating. So much work had gone into preparing for the exam and the day of orals had been exhausting. My number was called and I tried to go up the stairs in a dignified manner as I was now a Fellow. There I signed my name in a book and shook hands with the President of the College. Returning downstairs to my wife was an exhilarating experience. One I will never forget. She had suffered at least as much as I had. She had put up with my studying because we both realized that our future depended on the result. We went out to celebrate. There was a Marx brother's movie showing nearby and there we went to laugh uproariously at the most mundane jokes. Others in the audience must have thought that we were crazy and in a way we were.

When I first came back from my vacation I had moved in with my parents and commuted to St. Thomas's hospital. When Agnes returned we acquired a small flat in London. While still in the RAF, I had sold the little open sports car and bought a second hand AC convertible coupe. After I had the engine partially rebuilt, it proved a very satisfactory car. It meant that we were mobile and could visit my parents, which we frequently did. The alarm we had over the threatened miscarriage seemed to have settled down. I put her in the hands of one of the Obstetricians at St. Thomas's. She mentioned that her hands were swelling and that she had trouble with her rings. She went down to one of the fancy jewelers on Bond Street to get a larger wedding ring. She did not realize until she got there that it might seem unusual to buy a wedding ring when you were obviously pregnant. She became very embarrassed. In those days in England there was a stigma attached to unwed mothers. Because of the unusual swelling in her hands, she saw the obstetrician again. I was too dumb and inexperienced as a doctor to jump to the obvious diagnosis.

As soon as Mr. Bowes, the obstetrician, saw her he realized that she was getting eclampsia. Both she and the baby were in trouble. There was only one thing to do. Though she was only seven to eight months pregnant and the baby would be premature, her own life was in danger. He put her in Lambeth Hospital and performed a Cesarean Section to deliver the baby. During the operation the Matron of the hospital chatted with me. She asked if I hoped it would be a boy or a girl. She was startled by my reply. I said that I did not care which it was as long as it was one or the other. I then had to explain that while working at Great Ormond Street we had to deal with several inter-sex babies. These presented serious problems. Mr. Denis Browne had to decide which sex to try to make them. At that time we did not have the chromosome testing available to determine the true sex. The only thing we had to go was the external appearance of the genitalia. My boss, Mr. Denis Browne, decided to make them all boys. This led to at least one mistake which became apparent subsequently when we had to do a bilateral mastectomy on a boy scout.

Our baby girl weighed 3 1/2 pounds but seemed otherwise healthy and determined to survive. This all happened very suddenly while my parents were on a vacation in Switzerland. I cabled them with the news. When my father opened and read the cable he gasped and told my mother that we had three half-pound babies. Fortunately my mother read the cable correctly. Agnes had to stay in the hospital for three weeks and the baby girl rapidly grew in the nursery there. She was ready for us to take her home as soon as Agnes was ready to be discharged. My parents opened their house to us. There we stayed while Agnes recovered. My mother was wonderful about helping both with Agnes and her grandchild. As a result my mother became devoted to Catherine, our daughter, and remained so all her life. Later on, whenever we wanted to go away, my mother took care of Catherine who always adored going to stay with Granny and Grandpa.

While all this was going on I was trying to find a job where I would get a good general surgical training so that I could try to return to Great Ormond Street for further pediatric surgical training. I had been recommended to try for a job in Norwich where there was a young and very brilliant surgeon, Mr. Alan Birt. Just before the war he had taken his exams for the FRCS, having trained at St. Thomas's. When he passed the exam he was too young to become a Fellow and had to wait until he was 25 to get the official degree. During the war, while stationed in Italy, he had been one of the pioneers of vascular surgery, repairing severed vessels and thus saving limbs. I went to Norwich for an interview and was lucky enough to get the job as a middle grade surgical Registrar. It entailed working with two of the four consultant surgeons on the staff. I was assigned to Mr. Birt and Mr. Ridley Thomas. Mr. Birt had the busiest practice and was the most progressive of the surgeons. Though he was a relatively slow operator he was most meticulous. His honesty was legendary as was his consideration of his patients.

Having got the job, I found a flat on the ground floor of a four story building not too far from the hospital. The top floor was occupied by the Ob Gyn registrar and his wife. As soon as Agnes and the baby were fit to travel we moved in. The Ob Gyn registrar's wife, who had two little boys and Agnes very soon, became great friends. I found that the hospital was one of the friendliest places I have ever worked. It was run by an administrator who thought that nothing was too good for his doctors, including the resident staff. Though food was still strictly rationed Freddie Gatfield, the administrator, always seemed to be able to provide generously for us. Every evening there was a ham and beer on the sideboard in the dining room for anyone who was working late. On Sundays there was a roast put out for lunch which we could carve ourselves. It was so popular that they had to request that we did not bring our families in to share it.

This was in the very early days of the National Health Service. We found that we were inundated with patients. These patients, except for emergencies, were referred by their local general practitioners. They had appointments to attend the outpatient clinics of a specific surgeon. Though the patients had the right to choose to which surgeon they wished to be referred they rarely chose because they did not know the surgeons. They relied on the choice of their general practitioner. Once they had seen a specific surgeon they always saw the same surgeon every time they came to the hospital unless they specifically requested to be seen by a different one. This allowed excellent continuity of care. There were no specific times given to the patients who attended the clinics. They were merely told which morning or afternoon to attend. They sat around in a large waiting area until their name was called. Then they went into a room where they were interviewed by the surgeon or one of his resident staff. They bought with them the letter from the referring doctor. After they were interviewed and their history taken, they went into an examining room to get undressed while the next patient was interviewed. It must have seemed rather like an assembly line but it worked very well. On a busy day, and most were, between us we could see as many as 50 patients in a session. At the end of each session a letter was dictated to be sent to the referring doctor containing the appropriate recommendation. If surgery was recommended, the patient was told that he or she would be put on the waiting list and sent for as soon as a bed was available. The patients were categorized according to the urgency which we thought that their treatment merited. Patients that had cancer or other urgent conditions were placed at the top of the list and sent for ahead of all others. The patients almost always accepted our recommendations without argument and this speeded things up. They were usually given a few days' notice before they were sent for. If they did not accept their admission date they knew that they would be put back at the bottom of the list. This meant that we rarely had any 'no shows'. At the onset of the Health Service no one had any concept of the enormity of the health problem lurking in the background. As soon as people realized that they could get surgery for their problems without paying for it, they came forward. Patients with hernias, varicose veins, hemorrhoids and similar conditions which they had tolerated for years appeared requesting treatment. Not only could this be done for nothing, so far as the patient was concerned, but their jobs were protected. In the case of women, convalescent homes were provided for their recovery and child-care included where necessary. The work load was stupendous and could never have been coped with at all had it not been for the dedication of so many of the consultant surgeons. Though they were contracted to work a specific number of sessions which were supposed to last only four hours, most of those I worked with devoted much more time. Mr. Birt, for instance, had no time during the week to go round all the patients who were hospitalized under his care. Much of the day-to-day care was delegated to the resident staff whose job was facilitated by the nurses. Without the skill and experience of these ladies the system would not have worked. These individuals worked 12 hour shifts and were paid disgracefully little. In order for Mr. Birt to supervise his service thoroughly, the only time he could find was Sunday morning. Every Sunday morning he would go around his wards with his residents and the Sister in charge of the ward. We saw every patient and discussed each one. It took the whole morning but it was not considered one of the sessions for which he was paid.

As an example of the kind of person he was, one incident is worth recording. On our Sunday morning rounds there was one lady who was to have her gall bladder removed the next day. She asked if Mr. Birt would take her as a private patient as she wanted him to do the surgery himself. (Under the Health Service patients were admitted with the understanding that their surgery would be performed by the Consultant or anyone to whom he delegated the case). Mr. Birt asked the lady what her husband did for a living. She replied that he was a postman. Mr. Birt drew himself up and said; "How dare you ask your husband to pay my private fee? I will not take you as a private patient but I, personally, will remove your gallbladder myself tomorrow morning." He did, and I assisted him.

Though the Government ran the service no one from the Ministry of Health interfered with the actual practice of the physicians. Periodically a memo would be sent round advising, for instance, that too many antibiotics were being used. We took no notice of this and we heard no more about it. We had to sign 'off work' forms for some of our patients. There was a place to insert the diagnosis which merited their being off work. The diagnosis was considered by the doctors to be confidential information and therefore should not to be disclosed publicly. As a result we all wrote either 'inflammation' or 'indisposition' as the diagnosis. To the best of my knowledge, and in my own experience, no one ever dared question these forms.

There is one other law in England which led to a very interesting situation. In order to be cremated it is necessary to have a special death certificate. This had to be signed by two doctors certifying the cause of death. One of these doctors must have been qualified for at least five years. Presumably this law was passed because it is impossible to exhume cremated remains if foul play is subsequently suspected. Since the signing of these special death certificates is not part of the National Health Service, the doctors were allowed to charge the families for them. The standard fee was two guineas for the junior doctor and five for the senior. In order to eliminate any competition Mr. Birt and his residents formed a 'burning fund'. Who ever had the chance to sign the forms contributed to this fund. Most of the requests for this form came to the pathology department who had the bodies in the morgue. The morgue attendant got the forms first. The pathologist could sign the second part as the senior but he was not sufficiently far seeing. A guinea is one pound and one shilling. When he signed the form he kept the whole sum. We found that if we kept the pound and gave the shilling to the morgue attendant he always managed to ask us to sign the forms. In this way we built up quite a sizable sum. Whenever a member of our team left to move on to another job we could have a party. We would pick a fancy restaurant outside Norwich and drive there with our wives for a well-oiled celebration. After a couple of these parties, it was realized that it was dangerous to drive back home through the country roads after we had, as the Irish say, "drink taken". Consequently we decided to rent a bus. This we supplied with liquor and no longer had to worry about the driving. These parties could become quite riotous and Mr. Birt was always very ready to join in the fun. The camaraderie between the chiefs and the residents was very close and these parties did nothing to diminish it. I think the Burning Fund was unique to our group and I doubt that it still exists.

While we were in Norwich, Agnes had a flare-up of her osteomyelitis. She was hospitalized under the chief of the orthopedic service, Mr. Britain. He was a bluff, hard-driving character who had devised an operation for fusing an unstable hip. He was somewhat disapproving of the operation that had been done for Agnes at Johns Hopkins. He was doing his rounds one day with his whole firm, residents, sister and the nurses. He came to Agnes's room, blew in, said Good Morning and was on his way out when Agnes said; "Just a minute Mr. Britain. I am not used to being treated like that. I want to know what you think and what you intend to do." To everyone's surprise he came back into the room, sat down on the bed and chatted with Agnes for about half an hour. The rest of his team had to wait. That he did not resent Agnes's demands was very evident because he invited us to his house for dinner after she recovered. Fortunately Agnes discharged a tiny piece of bone from one of her scars and the whole thing settled down. While she was hospitalized, I got sick and my chief, Mr. Birt, thought that I should be admitted rather than look after myself at home. The hospital was arranged with male and female wards each containing about 30 beds. At the end of each ward was a private room into which patients who needed to be isolated could be put. These rooms had two beds. Agnes had been put into one of these rooms by herself. Mr. Birt suggested that I be put into the room with Agnes. Matron was horrified at the thought of having a male on a female ward and of one sharing a room with a female patient. When she was asked what she thought that we did at home, she capitulated. There I was admitted and stayed for about four days.

During that time there was a by-election for the seat in Parliament representing Norfolk. Mr. Strachey was running as the Labour Party candidate. Mr. Britain, the orthopedic surgeon, was a staunch Conservative. Mr. Strachey was holding a series of meeting around the county speaking to the voters. Mr. Britain decided to do his best to disrupt these speeches. He took his secretary with him in his Rolls Royce to the first meeting. There she took down the speech. They drove on to the next meeting while Mr. Britain memorized the speech. When they got there Mr. Britain proceeded to announce each punch line from the back of the hall before Mr. Strachey got to the point. This totally disrupted the meeting until Mr. Britain was thrown out. He was rather pleased with himself until he saw the write-up in the local paper which said that the meeting had been disrupted by a florid-faced rather disreputable character. This description did not sit well with an internationally renowned Orthopedic Surgeon.

Because the volume of work that we had on the waiting list for non-emergency surgery was long, often more than a year, using the main hospital in Norwich would never get it done. About 15 miles south of Norwich was a small town with a cottage hospital, i.e. a hospital with less sophisticated facilities. This was run by the local doctors who were not qualified to perform surgery. However there was a small operating room adequately equipped to perform minor operations. Mr. Birt decided that we could reduce our waiting list if we sent some of the non-urgent cases to this hospital for their surgery. He arranged for one of his residents to drive there two afternoons a week taking with him an anesthetist. About seven or eight cases were admitted consisting of such things as hernias, hemorrhoids and varicose veins. The operating room staff consisted of a nurse who was the assistant as well as the instrument nurse and a circulating nurse. With this staff we took care of about seven cases twice a week. In the middle of the afternoon the matron of the hospital laid on a fancy tea for us to give us energy to complete the rest of the cases. We left the patients to the care of the local doctors. On one occasion I was operating on a very obese patient with a hernia at his navel. Going through his fat the scalpel became very greasy and slipped out of my hand. As it spun away it landed, blade down, in the patient's groin and sat there quivering. I was terrified that it had hit the femoral artery. I made a rapid inspection. I was relieved to see very little blood. Careful examination revealed that the scalpel had entered beside the femoral artery and damaged neither it nor the vein adjacent. I repaired this second wound and the hernia. I went to the floor to see the patient afterwards to explain what had happened. One of the other patients in the ward said; "That'll teach you to be so fat". I heard no more about this mishap. Malpractice suits were rare in England.

Mr. Birt himself came down to this hospital occasionally to do one of the lists. One day I asked him why he spent some of his valuable time doing this when he had so much more difficult work to do in the main hospital. I was surprised by his reply. He asked if I wanted to deprive him of doing some of what was, in some ways, the most valuable work. It was very satisfying to repair otherwise healthy individuals and to get them back to work. He thought that there was at least as much satisfaction in this as there was in spending several hours removing and reconstructing an esophagus in an elderly patient with cancer. His remark gave me food for thought and has influenced my outlook on surgery ever since. It is not how glamorous the surgery that you are doing is that counts but how much you are really helping the patients from a long-term point of view. Minor surgery is not minor to the patient and the results may be far-reaching. To have a grateful patient is a very satisfying experience, one far exceeding any monetary recompense. In working with children, though they may not be able to express their gratitude at the time, their parents can and do. The fact that what you do may influence the health and happiness of the patient for many years to come, not only increases the reward for good work, but increases the responsibility.

The two years at Norwich were a very happy time. This was made so because of the fact that the other residents were a very congenial group and we had excellent rapport with the consultants. It is hard to single out any of the other residents as they were all so different and each one a special character. One, Raymond Ramsey, who worked for the other surgical firm was older than the rest of us. He had been in Burma with General Wingate's army, the Chindits. There he was captured by the Japanese and had spent a couple of years in a Jap prisoner of war camp. He was fortunate to have survived. When he got out of the army he decided to resume his surgical training and came to Norwich. He turned out to be one of the most fastidious gentlemen I have ever met. His experiences as a Jap prisoner of war must have been devastating for such a sensitive person. At Norwich he was always immaculately dressed including a champagne-colored waistcoat. His boss, Mr. Noon, the senior surgeon on the other firm, was an eccentric character. He was much older than any of the other surgeons, shrewd, but a total nonconformist. One evening when Raymond was performing an emergency prostatectomy, this surgeon came into the operating room to see how things were going. As usual this surgeon was dressed in an overcoat and bowler hat; no gown or mask. Raymond was having a little difficulty. The surgeon demanded that a rubber glove be put on his right hand. Without further ado and without changing his clothes, he put his gloved hand into the wound, fished around with a finger for a moment or two and withdrew his hand with the prostate in it. He then walked out without further comment. Raymond finished the operation. In spite of the onlookers' horror at the breach of all that we youngsters had been taught about proper operating room procedures, the patient made an uneventful recovery. The ward where this surgeon had his patients was on the ground floor and had a tall sash window which went down to the ground. When he came to do his rounds he never used the front door of the hospital but insisted on coming in through this window. He was driven up in his antique Rolls Royce by his chauffeur and the sister in charge of the ward was on the lookout for him. She then threw open the window by raising the bottom half. One day, as he was coming in, he hit his head on the bottom of the raised window. He explained that this was why he always wore a bowler hat. It seems that there were many eccentric characters practicing in the not too distance past. Some of them were surprisingly successful and most very accomplished technicians. They tended to be egotistical and real prima donnas. It was a privilege to have had the opportunity to have met some of them

As for Raymond, his future career illustrates one of the ways that the National Health Service worked. After he had served his time as a Senior Registrar he looked through the advertisements announcing vacancies for Consultant Surgeons. There was one for a hospital just west of London. Raymond found himself on the short list with two other candidates. These others were very well qualified and had been trained in London teaching hospitals and not in provincial hospitals such as Norwich. So far as recommendations were concerned there was not much to choose between the applicants. They were interviewed by the doctors already on the staff of the hospital and the mandatory outside assessor. This latter had to have no relationship, neither with the hospital to which the applicant was applying nor with any of the institutions where they had been trained. There was little to choose between the merits of the candidates, but the outside assessor discovered Raymond's history as a Jap prisoner of war and his war-time record. On this basis he suggested to the election board that this candidate had enough traumas in his life. He thought that he deserved a favorable break. I am glad to say that Raymond got the job.

Since several of the other residents at the hospital had been at Cambridge we decided that it would be fun to go to one of the May Balls. Another old friend of mine from Kings was living just outside Norwich so we all teamed up to make a party. We decided to go to the King's Ball. It necessitated spending the night at Cambridge and having a baby sitter there for our daughter. We arranged all this and arrived in our White Tie and Tails to the Ball which started at 9 PM. The dancing went on all night with a break for a Champagne supper and did not end until 6 am the next morning. Since the college backed onto the Cam there were punts available on the river. I took one of my partners up river a little way for a respite from the dancing. Such a trip could be hazardous as there was a danger that some nefarious character would be on a bridge waiting to pour treacle onto the beautifully dressed lady as the punt went under the bridge. Fortunately we did not encounter this mishap. At the end of the dance, there was a tradition that one punted up the river to the restaurant at Granchester. It is the next village upstream from Cambridge and the trip there is through meadows, and is pleasantly bucolic. We undertook this expedition, still in our evening clothes. Once there we had breakfast before punting back to Cambridge.

Agnes's parents had a friend who lived outside Norwich and we were invited to have dinner with them. They had a large old house in an estate a few miles into the country. We were invited in the dead of winter and the weather was very cold. We were also told that dinner was a black tie affair. Since old English houses are notoriously cold, Agnes decided that she would put on some long-johns under a long black velvet dress. We drove up the long drive to the front of the house and the door was opened by the butler. A waft of heat came out. The house had been modernized and central heating installed. Agnes realized that she was in trouble with her long underwear. She had to retire to the ladies room and remove it, much to her embarrassment. She redeemed herself after dinner. Our host found out that she was interested in art. He had quite a collection of original paintings and he took Agnes round to look at them. They stopped at one and Agnes was asked if she knew who had painted it. She said that it looked like a Gainsborough but she had never seen it before. Our host was delighted because it was an un-cataloged Gainsborough. He had all the documents and the history to prove that it was genuine but he had never published the fact. His reason was that if it was known to be a Gainsborough his son would have to pay exorbitant death duties (inheritance tax) if it's true value was known. We were invited back in the summer and shown around their gardens. They had an old walled garden with a greenhouse in it. In this greenhouse was a peach tree espaliered against the wall and under the glass roof. On it grew the largest and most luscious peaches that I have ever seen. We were each given one and the juice ran all over us as we bit into them. Our host told us that he could sell the fruit for a shilling each in the local market. At that time this was a considerable sum.

 We decided to invite these nice people to have dinner with us at our humble flat. Agnes had everything prepared and was ready, we thought, for their arrival. To our horror they arrived in evening dress. We saw them getting out of the car. How we managed to get changed so quickly I do not remember but we did. It was not an auspicious start but Agnes managed to pull off the dinner successfully.

Outside Norwich were the Norfolk Broads. These are the meandering of the river through the flat lands towards the sea. They are an area where you can sail peacefully. Since the wind was often unpredictable and at times nonexistent, sailing might be little more than drifting. We had one psychiatric resident who was a droll character. On drifting occasions he had an endless supply of 'shaggy dog' stories which whiled away the time. He told us that when he was in the Air Force he had been sent a young airman who hailed from Africa. This poor man was sick enough to be hospitalized and seemed to be steadily deteriorating. No one could understand why as he did not seem to have any specific illness that the doctors could diagnose. He was referred to our friend who started talking to him. It transpired that he had been caught stealing in his local village in Africa. The local witch doctor had cursed him and told him that he would die on a specific day in the future. The patient was busily dying as predicted. Our friend told the poor man that he had magic at least as strong as that of the witch doctor and that, if he followed his instructions, the curse could be lifted. Eagerly the young man asked what he must do. Our friend told him he must go round the fields outside the hospital and find a female grasshopper and drown it in his own blood. When the young man said that he did not know how to recognize a female grasshopper from a male, he was told to collect several and our friend would tell him which was female. The young man did this and brought in a bag full of grasshoppers. Our friend examined them carefully but had to declare that none of them was female. This same scenario was repeated the next day. On the third day tension was mounting for the young airman as the date of his predicted death was upon him. That day our friend, on looking over the collected grasshoppers, said; "There is one". The young man grabbed it and rushed out to cut himself and drown the insect in his blood. He was completely cured and rapidly regained his health. It takes more than book knowledge to be a good doctor.

Norwich, which is the County town of Norfolk, is an interesting city. At that time it still had a market once a week where farm animals were brought in from the country-side for sale. The hospital served the surrounding population. Many of our patients were from the farming community and were the most wonderful people to treat. This area of England had been largely bypassed by the industrial revolution as Norfolk is in the bulge of land to the east of the main route from London to the north and to Scotland. It was a largely agricultural county and had preserved much of its old traditions. The country folk used many words and expressions which were strictly local. Sometimes it was difficult for 'foreigners' such as me to understand what the patient was trying to communicate. The first time a patient told me that she had "bad feelings in the body" I was floored. She seemed very upset when I asked her to be more specific. One of my colleagues explained to me that she was being quite specific. She meant that she had pain in her stomach. Some of the patients lived on farms that their families had possessed for a very long time. We had one old man admitted for surgery. As was our custom, we asked where he lived and with whom. He was 80 years old and we were concerned about who would take care of him when we discharged him. He told us he lived with his mother. He and his mother lived alone we asked? Oh no, he said, he lived with his mother and his son and his son's son and his son as well. There must have been five generations living together on that farm. The beauty of that kind of life was that everyone had a job and therefore felt useful. The old man could bring in the cows for milking even if he could not do anything else (except give advice), and the old lady was indispensable as she knitted clothes for the children. Because they all had their tasks, they felt useful. They tended to be healthy and to live to a ripe old age. They did not travel much. In taking a history from one elderly patient, I asked if he had ever been abroad. He answered; "Oh aye. I came into Norwich once to see a football game". It was the only time he had been out of his village. Another facet of practicing in this area was the farming community's way of dating events. When asking one patient how long she had been having her symptoms, she stated that it would be "nigh on two years cum next muck spreading". This was a very specific time to her. All through the winter the droppings of the cows, which occurred while they were in the barns being milked, were swept out into a pile in the yard. When spring came this pile was put into carts and spread over the fields as manure. The resulting odor which permeated the country side left no one in doubt as to what time of year it was.

I came to be very fond of these country folk. They were tough, plain-spoken and honest, but not too honest. It seemed that a surprising amount of local business was done on the barter system. This did not appeal to the tax officials as they had trouble finding out what was really going on. One farmer bought the farm next to his and paid cash for it. The tax officials were very interested and demanded to know where he got the money. He said that he had been married for nigh on 40 years. He had been giving his wife housekeeping money all that time. Then he said; "Feeding' me the way that she does, if she hasn't saved that much she's not as smart as I think she is. If another farm comes up for sale I bet she has enough saved to buy that too". The tax man gave up.

Agnes and I were going down to my parents for a weekend one time and we decided that we would spend our ration of meat to take with us to help out with the food. We were allowed about two shillings and sixpence worth of meat a week between us. The equivalent of considerably less than a dollar's worth. I went to the local butcher to ask what I could get for this as I wanted to take it to my parents. This butcher supplied the hospital with meat, had been a patient himself and had an excellent relationship with the doctors. He asked me if a leg of lamb would be all right. I was flabbergasted but happily agreed. How he managed this deal I have no idea and did not ask. When we got to my parents home and gave the joint to my mother, she said that she was not sure that she could remember how to cook such a large joint as she had not seen one for almost 10 years.

Married life as a resident is full of conflicting situations. It is impossible to have two equal priorities. As a resident, indeed as a conscientious doctor at all times, one's primary responsibility has to be to one's patients. Either one is available or has to make provision for someone else to be responsible. This is very hard on the wife who has to be tolerant of playing second fiddle to her husband's professional priorities. Perhaps the fact that Agnes had been a patient for so much of her early life had given her great understanding of what she had let herself in for. She never complained when my professional activities clashed with our pleasures. When I came home very late one night because I had been at the hospital operating on an emergency, I found her asleep in bed. I undressed and climbed in beside her. Sleepily she put her arms around me. I asked how she knew it was me. She said that she knew by the smell. I was rather disconcerted until I found out that, coming from the operating room, I reeked of anesthetic gases.

At the end of my two years as a middle grade registrar I had to move on. I was very anxious to get back to Great Ormond Street to continue my training as a pediatric surgeon. Fortunately a vacancy occurred there at about the right time for me. I applied for the job there. They remembered me. I had good recommendations from Norwich and Mr. Denis Browne had approved of me as his house surgeon. I got the job which necessitated our moving to London. There we had to find somewhere to live within easy reach of the hospital. Though I was expected to be available at all times, I did not have to live in the hospital all the time, only when I was on duty for emergencies. This was every other night and every other weekend. By this time we had a very active toddler who was almost more than Agnes could cope with by herself. We decided that she had to have some help. We found that we could employ an au pair girl and so negotiated for one from Denmark. In Norwich the wife of the Ob Gyn resident who had two little boys of comparable age, helped her out when necessary. When our daughter was at the crawling stage Agnes put her on the lawn at the back of our flat. It was obvious that she did not like the tickling of the grass on her stomach so she proceeded to struggle up and start to walk. Very soon she was actively toddling around. To Agnes's horror she found that, walking with a cane and being unable to run, she could not keep up with so active a child. It was another major crisis emotionally. Over the next two or three years we employed a series of au pair girls from Scandinavia. Two of these were memorable and we kept in touch for several years. The first, Kirsten, was very outgoing, speaking fluent but sometimes inaccurate English. Our daughter got along very well with her and they had a wonderful time together. Unfortunately Catherine developed Whooping Cough which she was generous enough to give to Kirsten. She, poor young lady, coughed so vigorously that she fractured a rib. In spite of this she continued to take care of Catherine. Having to employ help for Agnes was an expense that was beyond the means of a surgical resident so it is necessary to admit that Agnes's grandfather had left a small Trust, the interest on which was paid to her. This made a big difference. Leaving Norwich was quite a wrench as we had been so happy there. We had made friends that we would miss, though we kept some for many years. It would have been even sadder had it not been for the fact that I was going to a job which had been my major ambition.

Chapter 10

PEDIATRIC SURGICAL TRAINING 1951

The move to London changed our lives in two different ways. From a semi-rural country town to the big city and from being a middle-grade Registrar to a senior with greatly increased responsibilities.

When we first moved we billeted ourselves with my very tolerant parents. They were happy to have us because my mother had become very attached to our little daughter. They did not live too far out of London and I could commute to the Great Ormond Street Hospital when I did not have to live in. It did not take us too long to find a flat just a block off Baker Street near where Sherlock Holmes was supposed to have had his lodgings. This was in easy distance of Great Ormond Street, so I did not have to live in the hospital as I could be called when needed for an emergency. Just down Baker Street from the flat were Portman Square and the Church in which we had been married. There was also a small Park where Agnes could take our daughter. Our first au pair girl came from Denmark to live with us. After Kirsten left us she returned to Denmark where she got married and had a family of her own. We kept in touch with her. Sadly she died at an early age from kidney failure.

My convertible AC two-seater, though running well, was quite unsuitable for our expanded family. By this time cars were being built again in England but they were not easy to come by. Agnes had her Trust Fund still in the States and her father was the trustee. He assured us that there was enough capital available for him to use to buy us a new car using dollars. The Austin Company had come out with a powerful model, the A 90. Because it was being bought with dollars, we did not have to wait but got one of the first models. We used it to great advantage while we were in Norwich. It was not ideal for driving to and fro to the hospital in London so I acquired a very small motor cycle as well. This was much more convenient for me; though driving a motor cycle in London can, or could be in those days, very hazardous in wet weather. Many of the roads were paved with wooden blocks, originally placed to deaden the noise of the horses and carts. When wet and having a thin coating of somewhat oily slime on them they become exceedingly slippery.

My work at the hospital proved to be every bit as exciting as I had hoped. I had to rotate through the three surgical services there. One was being run by Mr. David Waterston, who had been the senior resident when I was a house surgeon four years before. He had been put on the staff as a consultant to build up a thoracic and cardiac surgical service. This was in the days when cardiac surgery was in its infancy. David was still finding his own way around and it was interesting to work with him. One of the problems which we faced was infants whose esophagi were being damaged by stomach acid regurgitating into them. The problem is now known as GER; (gastro-esophageal reflux). Often this problem was temporary and righted itself as the infant became more mature. We had to decide when this problem was severe enough to require surgical interference to prevent it and, if so, what kind of surgery would best take care of the problem. Many of these infants were admitted to the medical service under Dr .Bonham Carter. He had been a friend of David's since their school days. They decided that it would be good to share a ward and care for the infants as a team. We did ward rounds together and took the infants to the X-ray department when necessary to watch them swallow. This allowed us to observe the extent of the regurgitation. This close cooperation between the pediatrician and the surgeon was, in my experience, unique. We all learned a lot.

Shortly after I arrived the two year term of one of the other senior registrar's term expired. He was Mr. H. H. Nixon, (Nicky), who subsequently became the leading Pediatric Surgeon in England and acquired a world-wide reputation. While we were together before he left he helped me a lot. We became very good friends and we remained so for the rest of his life. Whenever we returned to London we stayed with him and he and his wife stayed with us when they came to the States. After he left Great Ormond Street and was replaced, I had the chance to change to being Mr.

Denis Browne's chief resident. This position was probably the most formative part of all my surgical training.

Mr. Denis Browne, (DB) was a most original character. Being the first surgeon in England to devote himself entirely to the care of children, he took an interest in almost all aspects of their surgery. His work encompassed some problems which have now become subspecialties. Every problem he encountered he approached as if it had never been tackled before. As a result he invented many new techniques some of which were considered outrageous by his more orthodox colleagues. He worked on skeletal deformities such as scoliosis of the spine and club feet. First he thought out how they might have been caused. He decided that most of these deformities were caused by pressure on the fetus while it was developing in the uterus. If this was so it would give an opportunity for some correction if opposite forces were applied while the child was still growing. The sooner these corrective forces were applied the greater the chance of success. He found a way of detecting which infants had the potential for developing scoliosis. He did this by taking the infant and twisting it both right and left while it was lying flat on a table. If it twisted equally both ways there was no need to worry but if it only twisted to a limited extent in one direction, he felt that it had a real chance of developing a permanent curvature of the spine when it started to stand up. He invented a simple splint into which the baby could be put which allowed an arm to protrude through a hole in the curved side of the apparatus while the body was pulled against the curve. The splint was light weight, portable and the infant could be put in it clothed or not and either on its stomach or back. Thus it was easy to nurse and the treatment gave the parents very little trouble. He had a great deal of trouble convincing his colleagues that this was all worthwhile. When one pointed out that only one in ten of the infants that DB considered in danger did, in fact, develop scoliosis, DB's reply was that he thought such a simple and cheap treatment was worthwhile if it spared only one in ten from having a terribly deformed spine. He added that the Roman legions considered 'decimation', where every tenth soldier in a legion was executed, a very severe punishment. Though this is correct, it did not please those who were disagreeing with him. Believe it or not this simple diagnostic technique and treatment is still not widely used. He also developed splints for treating foot deformities such as Club Feet. When the patient was sent early in life, the splints which he developed were extremely successful but when they came late with an established deformity the problem was much more difficult. The foot had to be forcibly manipulated under anesthesia. He invented an apparatus to do this (locally known as the beetle-crusher) and the correction occurred with a loud crunch. Sometimes the onlookers were so shocked that they passed out. After the reduction the patients had to wear a special boot so that every time they took a step they would reinforce the correction and at the same time develop muscles to continue the pull in the right direction. One mother had neglected to apply the splints to her baby as directed so the infant developed a more severe and less malleable deformity. As a result the infant required manipulation under anesthesia. DB, with his usual candor, wrote on the chart "I wish to God it was mother's foot I was going to twist". Most parents were scared of this giant of a man who could be so outspoken but the children seemed to love him. They would run up to sit on his knee. He never turned them away.

Several others of his contributions are worth mentioning. Many have been neglected by modern surgeons but they were great advances all based on careful analysis of the problems to be solved. When thinking about the repair of harelips he realized that noticeably bad results ensued if the nostril was not properly placed and if the lip did not move freely. It was essential to get the muscles that move the lip to work so his operation was designed to do this. It was also essential to make a very straight cut in the edges which were to be sutured together. He decided to watch leather makers at work and noted that they used a chisel of the required length to make their cuts. He had several chisels made and used these to ensure that the cut edges were absolutely straight. He would put a piece of wood under the lip and cut down on it through the lip. He applied the same principles of muscle reconstruction to Cleft Palates. He repaired over a thousand consecutive cases without a breakdown. One case sent to us was a twelve year old girl who, for various reasons during the war, had never been treated. It fell to my lot to perform his operation on her. In spite of the delay she developed perfect speech and was used as an example of the efficacy of his operation. She never had any speech therapy because DB maintained such therapy only made the patients self-conscious. He said that they would learn to copy their parents' speech without help and a Cockney would remain a Cockney.

Another of his interests was hypospadias. This is a condition where the end of the urethra in boys does not reach the end of the penis. He studied this problem for a long time and tried various approaches. I was fortunate enough to be there while he was working on the problem and so could appreciate what he was doing and how he went about it. There were several factors that made the operation that he finally settled on work. First the skin of the penis heals without scarring. Secondly the mucosa of the urinary tract grows very much faster than skin. Using these two facts he was able to repair over a hundred consecutive cases with only eight small leaks which were closed by a further rather minor operation. Unfortunately several plastic surgeons tried to copy his operation, modifying it as they went along. They disregarded the fundamental principles which allowed his operation to work when they instituted their modifications. They decided the operation was no good because their results were not satisfactory. They had not been doing his operation as he had devised it, and had contravened the principles upon which he had based it.

However, one day a Swedish surgeon came to visit to see what DB was doing with these cases. He was offered the opportunity to examine our results. He was so impressed that he returned to Sweden to apply the same principles to adult patients with severe post-infection urethral strictures and had great success.

To work with such a man was a most stimulating experience. Everything that he did seemed to be original yet it was carefully thought out. He did not suffer fools gladly but was always ready to answer questions if he considered them intelligent. Among his colleagues he was considered a very difficult character. A young American doctor had come to study plastic surgery with one of the best known English plastic surgeons. One day he asked this surgeon about Mr. Denis Browne and was told that it would be no good going to see him as he would not talk to him. However the young man decided to come to Great Ormond Street anyway. He arrived unannounced one morning while DB was seeing patients in Out Patients. He spent the whole morning with DB; I was scheduled to go down to the country branch that afternoon to operate on a list of cases. At lunch time DB introduced me to the young man and asked me to take him with me so that he could see some of the results we were getting. During the afternoon the young man told me that DB, during the whole morning, had not ceased to talk with him about the cases, what he was doing and why. When we went round the wards there were several cases with double harelips and associated cleft palates in various stages of repair. He was astonished and said that he had never seen such good results in any of the plastic surgical clinics he had visited. He could not understand why anyone had tried to scare him from seeing DB. One visit was sufficient to convert him.

Another thing that DB tried to achieve was to make his operations as simple as possible. Repairing both harelips and cleft palates is virtually a one-man operation. The assistant can only hold a sucker to keep the field clear. Because we had a three-year waiting list for cleft palates, it was decided that some could be repaired at the country branch. This was to be the residents' duty. When I first got to Great Ormond Street I helped DB with such a repair. The next case he told me to sit down and do the repair myself while he looked over my shoulder. At the end of the case he told me to take as many cases as I could down to the country branch and repair them. In this way I repaired just over 100 in a year. (All this was under the National Health Service. If we had been paid on a fee for service basis we could have become quite rich!).

DB was very well read in many subjects outside medicine and had a very sharp cutting wit. A parent wrote to him to say that he was disgusted with the fact that his child had been so long on the waiting list for repair of the cleft palate. He was writing to the Minister of Health to complain. DB replied that he would be delighted if the letter would get him more beds so that he could reduce the waiting list, but for all the good the letter would do, instead of posting it "he might just as well put it in his pocket or any other similar anatomical cavity that appealed to him". On another occasion the parent of one of his private patients who was being treated for a club foot complained that his child was not doing very well. DB wrote back to agree with the parent saying that he, too, was dissatisfied with the child's progress. Then he added, "The trouble with my method of treatment is that it requires the intelligent cooperation of the parents at home". Not an easy letter to take to a lawyer should one wish to sue!

It was exciting to sit in the next room during our outpatient clinics. There was a communicating door. Every now and then the door would be thrown open and DB would appear either to show me something or to ball me out. On one occasion there was an enormous blasphemous explosion and the door was thrown open. "Come and see this!" In his room were a six year old girl and her mother. I was invited to look in the daughter's mouth where I saw that she had a cleft palate. DB then announced to me that the child's father was a dentist and they had only just noticed the cleft palate.

The patients and parents were shepherded in to see the great man by one of the senior nurses who ran the clinic. One day a mother came out and announced with great pride that she knew what was wrong with her child. She had seen it on the chart. The child had M C B I. Mr. Browne had written it in large letters on the chart. The poor nurse nearly collapsed suppressing her laughter because M C B I stood for "mother a congenital bloody idiot".

A mother brought her small child in with a deformed foot for DB to examine. He looked at the foot. When he asked to see the child's other foot, the mother was horrified. She said "but I only washed one". Such were some of the people that we were caring for. It made no difference as to the patients' social status or income; they all got the same treatment. It was a most satisfying and, in many ways, the ideal way to practice medicine. There was no consideration as to whether the patients or their parents could afford the treatment that was needed. Such was the situation when the National Health Service was in its infancy. Since then, partially because the advances now available for treatment have become so expensive, there have been more problems with the country's ability to pay for this ideal service.

DB's first wife was an authoress who died during the war. He had insisted on living in the hospital so that he would be on the spot if the hospital was damaged during the Blitz. He had nursed his wife in the hospital. After she died he remarried. His second wife, Lady Moira Ponsonby, had been an ambulance driver and was the daughter of a Duke, therefore a Lady in her own right. She was a tall stately lady with a great sense of humor and we found her utterly charming. She had all the character necessary to have won DB's respect and devotion. Not an easy task. Because of her connections DB moved in very sophisticated social circles. One of my great disappointments occurred when DB went on holiday. I knew that he had been using one of his splints on the heir apparent, Prince Charles. I was hoping that it would need to be changed while he was away. In that case I would have been called to Buckingham Palace to perform this task. Unfortunately that never happened. One day the Queen decided to visit the hospital and wished to see DB's cases. DB was late and the Queen was being taken round by Sir James Crooks, known to us, irreverently, as the Royal Tonsil Snatcher. When she came to DB's ward she was being shown around by Sir James and the Sister who ran the ward. The Queen stopped at one cubicle to ask what was wrong with the infant. Sir James did not know as it was not one of his cases. I was trailing around behind. DB still had not arrived. I was pushed forward to explain what we were doing. As luck would have it, the infant in question had been born with an imperforate anus, (i.e. no open end to its gut at the rear). I had to explain to the Queen that we were making a new 'back passage' for its intestine. I found my sole conversation with the Queen rather embarrassing. She is a very sensitive person and seemed to find the experience of going round the hospital to see all the sick children quite a strain. She was very pleasant and understanding but I was glad when DB eventually turned up. He took her to lunch in the hospital dining room and I tagged along.

At the end of my two years there I was in a curious position. The job as a senior registrar is supposed to be for four years but the job at Great Ormond Street was only for two. One had to have served four years before one could apply for an appointment as a consultant. There were very few jobs as pediatric surgeons at that time. The only one coming up was a new appointment in Manchester. I applied for the job without too much hope because the folks in Manchester had sent one of their senior registrars down to Great Ormond Street for training. He and I were both put on the short-list for interviews. When I got to Manchester it was a cold winter day and snowing. The snow was black. The thought of living for the rest of my life in that area was not altogether pleasant. I did not get the job and was glad that I did not. Perhaps my view of the disappointment had an element of sour grapes in it. I was told that I could apply at Great Ormond Street for another two years as an extension of my job. DB encouraged me to do so. When the time came for the appointment I was told that another applicant had been appointed. I was bitterly disappointed. When I next saw DB I told him of my disappointment. He said that he did not know that they had the meeting to appoint anyone for the job and he had not attended. He was very sorry.

This episode caused me to do some very serious thinking about my career. I realized that my progress towards being a consultant in the National Health Service depended too much on who attended a meeting, thus making it very chancy. Also there were very few jobs for pediatric surgeons. It was a specialty that was only just beginning to be recognized. I tried to see where there might be another vacancy coming up. There was going to be one at Great Ormond Street fairly soon. I knew that my friend Nicky Nixon would almost certainly get that appointment and he deserved it. I did not see that there would be another one for sometime unless someone died unexpectedly or the Government changed its policy and expanded the number of pediatric surgeons.

When I had last visited Washington, Dr. John Lyons, who was the senior surgeon at one of the hospitals there, told me that if I ever decided to immigrate to Washington he would welcome me as his associate. Dr. Lyons had taken care of Agnes when she was very sick as a girl and I had met him quite a few times. His reputation in Washington was outstanding, both as a surgeon and as a man utterly devoted to his patients. I knew that if I was going to go to America that was where I would try to go. Agnes and I discussed the matter at length but she refused to help me decide. Such a move would be back to her home town and her old friends but she did not wish to influence my decision. I saw the move as a chance to make my own career on my own merits rather than chancing it on a selection committee. I would have two positive advantages; the professional backing of one of the most highly respected doctors in the town and the circle of friends of Agnes and her parents. I decided to try to make the move.

Chapter 11

PROBLEMS FACING EMIGRATION

Having decided that the prospects of working with Dr. Lyons in Washington might be better than gambling on getting a Consultant job in the near future in England, I set about looking into the problems that I would face. Immigration to the USA would not be a problem as Agnes had retained her American citizenship. As her husband I was entitled to enter her country and work there. However I did not have a license to practice medicine there. When I was at Harvard Medical School I had no intention of returning to the States so I did not take any of the exams that are required to practice there. A medical school degree by itself does not entitle one to practice in any State in the USA. Each State has its own rules and requires an applicant to pass an exam which it sets. While at Medical School it is possible to take a series of exams as one goes along called National Boards. If successful, most States will honor this and grant a license. Not having done so, I had to pass the exam set by any State where I wished to practice. Unfortunately these exams start with basic sciences and I was a long way from having learned these. Dr. Lyons worked in the District of Columbia which, though not a State, had its own licensing authority. Before I could work with Dr. Lyons I had to get a license from this authority. I obtained a copy of their regulations and studied it with great care. I knew that most States granted 'reciprocity' to licensees of other States without further question. This did not apply to immigrants coming with licenses to practice from other countries. But careful reading of the small print in the District of Columbia regulations revealed a possible loop-hole that I could exploit. It said that they would grant a license to anyone coming from a country which would automatically license in that country a licensee of the District of Columbia of similar standing. I figured that England would automatically grant a license to practice there to anyone from the District of Columbia who also had a medical degree from an English medical school. In order to have 'similar standing' to me, a licensee of the District would have to have an English medical school degree as well as my Harvard degree. Realizing that they would require documentation I went to the General Medical Council in England to ask them to give me a statement that they would automatically grant a license to practice to any District of Columbia licensee who had an English medical school degree. They said that it was a waste of their time to write such a letter as it would do no good. I argued that what I was requesting was merely a statement of fact from them and what I requested was accurate. What I did with their statement was my business. They agreed and I got the statement. Armed with this I wrote to the authorities in the District pointing out that in order to be of "similar standing" the applicant would need to have a medical school degree both in America and in England. In that case, the letter showed that any Licensee of the District of Columbia would automatically be licensed to practice in England. They agreed and I got my license. I understand that I am the only person who managed to do this. Thus I overcame the first hurdle.

The next problem was that Dr. Lyons was a general surgeon and not a pediatric surgeon. In making inquiries about the situation in Washington I found that there were no pediatric surgeons in Washington and that the children's hospital there was staffed by general surgeons. Furthermore when a surgeon who had been trained as a Pediatric Surgeon at Johns Hopkins came there to practice he had been denied privileges to practice at the Children's Hospital because Pediatric Surgery was not a specialty. He had moved to another area. It was obvious that I would have to work as a general surgeon and try to build up the idea that children needed special expertise. But in order to do this I had to establish myself as a competent general surgeon. It had been two years since I had done any general surgery and I knew I could use some further experience. My job at Great Ormond Street was ending and I had to find another one. I saw an advertisement for a Senior Registrar at South End on Sea. This is a small town on the north bank of the Thames near its mouth. It is a seaside town which was a resort for east-end Londoners, being only about thirty miles away. The surgical service there was staffed by four Consultants who came from London for 'sessions', both outpatient and operating. In between their sessions their patients were cared for by the Registrars who were also responsible for all the emergencies. Each of these consultants also held appointments at London teaching hospitals and so the standard of surgery could be expected to be high. I decided to apply for the job and was called for an interview. I was taken around by the Senior Registrar who was leaving. While there a lady came into the emergency room complaining that she had a plum stone stuck in her throat. My host confessed that he had never used an esophagascope to look down the esophagus. This would be necessary to remove the foreign body. I told him that I had not used one in an adult but that I had done so in infants and that I thought that an adult would be much easier. If he liked I would see what I could do. He was delighted and set me to work. I slipped the instrument in quite easily and got a good look all the way down to the stomach I found no plum stone but only a slight abrasion where the esophagus had been scratched. We reassured the patient and suggested that she might watch for the exit of the stone at the other end. The patient turned out to be an elderly but famous actress. She was in South End visiting a home she had founded and subsidized. This was a home for retired and pauperized actresses; a charity of hers that very few knew she had formed. She was horrified that we could not charge her for our services. She insisted on giving me a bottle of excellent liquor which I did not refuse.

After the interview I got the job and had to plan to work there. I had to live at the hospital and had one half day a week when I could go up to London to join Agnes in our flat. I could ride my motor cycle, but I discovered that one of the consultants who came on Wednesday hated to drive his car. He was delighted to have me drive him back to London. He even invited Agnes and me out to dinner sometimes. The return journey the next morning was accomplished by getting a ride with the consultant who was due on Thursday morning. I got to his house in time to be picked up in his Bentley for a very comfortable trip. It was not a very satisfactory arrangement for Agnes and me and we looked around to make other plans. I found a little house near the hospital which we could rent quite cheaply. The people at the hospital thought that I should live in the hospital but I argued that it would be as easy to get me at this house as to page me in the hospital and that I could get there as quickly on my motorcycle as from one part of the hospital to another. They agreed to this arrangement, so we sublet the flat in London and moved into the house I had found. The house had a little garden which delighted our dog. We had bought a Wire-haired Dachshund pup that turned out to be a delightful character and a real addition to our family. His kennel name was Tumlow Tweed but we all called him Tweedle. One day when Agnes was shopping in London and had taken him with her he was approached by a rather large dog. Tweedle proceeded to roll onto his back and scream. His screams sounded exactly like those that one would expect from a small child. The traffic came to a screeching halt and the pedestrians rallied round. Then Tweedle got up and shook himself quite unharmed but rather pleased with himself. Agnes was not quite so pleased with the commotion he had caused but, as usual, saw the funny side and had a good laugh afterwards. Tweedle, besides the habit of rolling on his back and screaming when he thought he was in danger, had two other practices which persisted all his life. He loved to bury bones and anything else that he wanted to save. In the corner of Catherine's bedroom in our flat in London was a pile of her toys. One day when Kirsten, our Au Pair girl, was going to clean up the mess there was an enormous fuss from Tweedle. Ultimately we found the cause. Buried under the toys was one of Tweedle's treasures and he was guarding it. After we moved into the house at South End, Tweedle continued his burying habits. We had pancakes and maple syrup for dinner one day. There was a pancake with syrup left over so we gave it to Tweedle. He took it with obvious delight and we thought no more about it. A couple of days later Agnes noticed there was a lump under the rug in the dining room. Inspection revealed that the lump was the syrupy pancake that the damned dog had buried for future consumption. The other regrettable habit of his was a total inability to resist rolling in anything that was really smelly. Decontaminating him was a most unpleasant chore. Once when we had taken him for a walk in Kensington Gardens we were unfortunate enough to find that they had let loose a flock of sheep to 'mow' the grass. Though the sheep were no longer present, they had been smitten with diarrhea while there. Tweedle was delighted with this circumstance and proceeded to roll in every bit he could find. We had to take him back to our flat in the trunk of the car so that we could clean him up.

The experience at the hospital turned out to be very much more significant than I had expected. Being the senior surgeon in residence meant that I had a great deal of responsibility not only for the emergencies but for the day-to-day care of the patients that the consultants had operated on. Except for the times that they were there visiting, I had no one to consult. Since it was a general hospital the patients who were treated fell into many different categories. Some would be considered as presenting problems that now fall under the care of 'specialists'. We had no 'Specialists' on the staff so we had to take care of everything, head injuries and urological problems included. The only exceptions were orthopedic cases and obstetric and gynecologic problems. Because this was under the National Health Service, it was possible to refer cases to 'specialist' hospitals when we were faced with a problem that seemed beyond our ability. There were two categories where I had to call for help. If a patient came with a severe head injury I could call up a hospital outside London which dealt solely with neurosurgical cases. I would contact the surgeon there and explain my problem. That person would either tell me what to do or ask me to send them the case. If the latter I could get the patient into an ambulance and transfer him, or her. This was all covered by the NHS at no cost to the patient. The same applied to difficult urological cases which were out of the ordinary. There were three small hospitals in London which dealt only with urological cases, each of which had ancient antecedents; St Peter's for Stone, St. Phillip's for Fallen Women and St. Paul's. They were known colloquially as the 'pissing apostles'. One of the consultant urologists on the staff of these hospitals was a friend from my days at Great Ormond Street so it was very easy to consult him. The surgeons at these hospitals were very happy to have our referrals as they were likely to be interesting cases that were out of the ordinary.

This situation illustrates one of the better aspects of the National Health Service as it was originally conceived. The average doctor, whether a physician or a surgeon, was expected to deal with ordinary run-of-the-mill cases but have the ability to refer difficult cases to 'specialists'. This had two benefits. Not too many specialists were required because only special cases were referred to them. Their job was particularly interesting as they did not waste their time on routine cases. They became increasingly expert because they had ever increasing experience with the unusual. Since they were salaried by the government they did not have to waste their time with simple routine cases to make a living. It also meant that the generalist, whether physician or surgeon, had to deal with a wide range of cases and this added considerable interest to the work.

The other unexpected benefit of my new job at South End was the excellence of the consultant surgeons for whom I was expected to work. Two were particularly outstanding, Mr. Rodney Maingot and Mr. Donald Barlow. Mr. Maingot (All surgeons in England are entitled to be called Mister since the College of Surgeons was founded in the 16th century when many 'surgeons' were not doctors with medical degrees.) was world renowned as the author of a book on Abdominal Surgery. This was considered a classic and was very widely read and appreciated. He came down to South End every Wednesday to operate and to see some outpatients. I was responsible for arranging the cases that he would operate on. He was quite demanding as he only wanted to operate on two cases. One had to be either a stomach resection or a gall bladder removal and the other a hernia. He had a special technique for repairing hernias using floss silk as a darn. It was very successful and I adopted his darn technique ever afterwards. When it came to resecting stomachs he seemed to know all the methods previously tried and would ask which method I did not know. Then he would demonstrate that method for me to learn. Sometimes he would suggest a method that had not been attempted before. As a result, and by watching the results in follow-up clinics, I decided for myself which methods seemed to give the best results. (I also learnt which ones never to try again.) Mr. Maingot sometimes brought with him visitors from abroad who had come to see him. This was at the time when Sir Anthony Eden had gone to America to have his bile duct reconstructed after it had been damaged when an English surgeon, not Mr. Maingot, had removed his gall bladder. The visitor that day was Dr. Crile from the Cleveland Clinic. He asked Mr. Maingot why he thought that Mr. Eden had needed to go to America to have this reconstruction performed instead of staying in England. The answer was that he thought Mr. Eden was well advised as the Americans had so much more experience with this reconstruction. So many more cases there had their common ducts damaged while it was a very rare occurrence in England. No further comment!

Each of the consultant surgeons had their own cases but they were scattered in the wards. Each surgeon's cases were color-coded on their charts so that when they were making ward rounds they could spot their own cases. By a little bit of sleight of hand I could alter the color code when a particular consultant was visiting. In this way I could show a problem case to more than one consultant and thereby get more than one opinion. It was a somewhat dangerous ploy if I was caught out. Fortunately the second consultant, when he discovered my trick, was flattered that I wanted his opinion and so I was forgiven. But I learned a lot.

Of the three other consultants one was particularly outstanding. Mr. Donald Barlow was the most gifted surgeon I ever met. He was the only surgeon that I worked with who never made a mistake of any kind in the operating room. In spite of his incredible accuracy he was also the fastest operator. As an example, we had a patient with cancer of the rectum and we had to resect his whole rectum and give him a colostomy. This operation requires both an abdominal operation to free the colon from above and make the colostomy and another operation from below to remove the rectum after it has been freed from the abdomen. It is possible to do this operation with two surgeons working together at the same time, one from above and one from below. I suggested to Mr. Barlow that we set the patient up so that I could do the operation from below while he did the abdominal part. He asked why we would want to do that as he could do both parts, one after the other. I said that it would be quicker if we both worked together at the same time. He asked how long I thought it would take if we both worked as I suggested. Having had some experience with this operation before, I said that I thought we could do it my way in little more than an hour and a half. He said that he could do it by himself in an hour and a quarter. I did not believe him but since he was the boss we did it his way. I was his assistant and I timed him. As his assistant all I was allowed to do was to hold things out of his way and stay still. He tied all his own knots on sutures etc. He did this with a single movement tying a square knot each time. (I tried hard to learn this trick but could never master it satisfactorily). While he was doing the abdominal part he demonstrated every detail of the anatomy which he dissected out meticulously. Having finished the abdominal part we turned the patient on his side and he performed the final removal from below. I had never seen the operation performed so well. When we were finished I looked at the time and we had spent an hour and twenty minutes. The patient made a rapid and uneventful recovery. At the end of every operation he performed he would go out to the changing room where he had set up a desk with a red and a blue pen. There he would draw a picture of his operation which was far more graphic than anything he could have written. About the only thing he wrote was that the sponge and instrument count were reported correct at the end of the operation and the name of the person reporting this.

One day he was operating on a patient with a chronic wound in his neck. This patient had been operated on by someone else at another hospital for a problem just below his neck and the wound had never healed. Mr. Barlow reopened the wound and explored it. He appeared to get into some trouble with bleeding and kept calling for more sponges which he stuffed into the wound. Then he began to remove all these sponges very rapidly. One landed on the lap of the anesthetist who received a kick at the same time. Being no dummy the anesthetist covered it up with his gown and said nothing. There being no further bleeding seen Barlow closed the wound which healed uneventfully. The sponge count at the end of this operation was correct and no one else knew about the extra sponge that the anesthetist took out of the operating room with him. Perhaps this maneuver was not quite ethical but the patient did well, no one was sued and no lawyers made any money.

Mr. Barlow had appointments for sessions at three hospitals under the National Health Service. He was a general surgeon both at South End and at Luton but he was a thoracic surgeon at the Chest Hospital in London. He went from one to the other rapidly in his Rolls Royce. He had three sessions at South End, two on Tuesday, i.e. morning and afternoon, and one on Friday afternoon. On Friday morning he operated at the Chest Hospital in London before coming to South End. Since he demanded that I get several major cases in for him to operate on Friday afternoon we were often quite late finishing. When we were finished he insisted on going round the wards to see how his patients were doing. Every dressing had to be removed and each patient examined. I got hell if everything was not exactly to his liking. After all this we had a meal and then I had to operate on any emergencies that had come in during the day. On Tuesday he used to visit a hospital near South End in the early morning to perform a few bronchoscopes before coming to South End for his two sessions. One of these was an outpatient clinic where he would see new patients. He was meticulous in his examinations of each patient even insisting, not only of doing a rectal exam, but also of passing a scope into the rectum. The number of unsuspected problems he discovered was astonishing.

After Agnes and I moved into the little house near the hospital he would, on occasion, come to our house for a glass of sherry and dinner before going home. In this way we got to know him quite well. I discovered that he was a man of independent means. He only practiced surgery because he loved it. At that time taxation in England was at an all time high with a surcharge on incomes over 5000 pounds of 90%. He told us that his accountant had informed him that if he quit practicing and reduced his income by 7500 pounds he would only have 250 pounds less money to take home. I found working for him to be very frustrating. This was not because he was so demanding but because I knew I could never be as good a surgeon as he was. I came to like him as a person as well as admire him professionally. To watch him operate was to watch an artist at work. His results, as demonstrated by the rapid recovery of his patients, showed how much can be achieved by rapid gentle surgery performed with an expert knowledge of anatomy.

Each of the consultants at South End was entitled to two operating rooms during his operating sessions. The second operating room was reserved for one of the residents to use to help with the waiting list. As senior registrar I was responsible for getting the cases in to be operated on the next day. If the consultant had some interesting case that I wanted to assist, I would get in some simpler cases for the other surgical residents to operate on. If I wanted to do some major case myself I would get in more cases than I thought the consultant would do himself so that I would get the leftovers. I had the choice of either helping the consultant or operating in the other room. This arrangement gave me the opportunity to get both teaching and experience.

How it was possible for the consultant surgeons to operate on so many cases in a single morning or afternoon using the limited operating rooms is worth a comment. The change over time between one case and the next was only about 15 minutes. The debris from one case was swept out one way and the complete set-up for the next case which was previously prepared was swept in from the other. It also involved the cooperation of the anesthesiologist who had the patient asleep ready to be wheeled in. The department of anesthesiology was headed by an excellent man. Besides being technically very competent he was always cooperative. He had written a book which was well-known in England and used by young doctors hoping to specialize in this field. In spite of his fame and erudition he was affable and most pleasant to work with. He had an orderly who he had trained as his assistant. When one case was almost finished, he would slip out; leaving the patient to the orderly while he induced the next case. In this way the next case was always ready and the delay between cases was minimal. The ability to change cases this rapidly required great efficiency from the nursing staff. The operating rooms were under the supervision of a 'sister' who was a real tyrant and perfectionist. I think she had come from the West Indies and I learned not only to fear and respect her but to like her as a person.

There was an infant admitted to the pediatric ward that I was asked to see as it could not be fed. It vomited everything it was given and was rapidly going downhill. X-rays showed that it had an obstruction just beyond the outlet of the stomach in the duodenum. Because I was known to have had training at Great Ormond Street I was asked what should be done. I said that the infant required an operation to relieve the obstruction. I was told that the infant was not well enough to survive an anesthetic. I consulted with our anesthesiologist and asked if he would give the infant some oxygen and keep it breathing if I operated using local anesthetic. Being the kind of person he was, he appreciated that it was the only chance to save the infant and he agreed to work with me. Using the technique that I had learned, I opened the patient and found the obstruction that I had expected. I managed to short circuit this by joining the stomach to the nearest part of the small intestine below the obstruction. The patient survived my surgery, and after a rather stormy post-operative period, recovered. The operating room 'sister' that I mentioned before had come in to watch me operate. I was most gratified when she said to me that she thought that I was wasting my time operating on adults.

Another experience that sticks in my mind had little to do with medicine and more to do with the administrative management of personnel. One of the consultant surgeons was doing his rounds and found a glaring error of omission that had been committed by the junior registrar. He started to tear strips off the poor young man until I said; "Just a minute, Sir, I am responsible for what this young man did not do. Please direct your criticism against me". The consultant was obviously surprised and somewhat nonplussed. He said no more. That young registrar never put another foot wrong while he was with us. I gathered that he had somewhat blotted his copy book at the job he had before he came to South End. After I had stood up for him his whole attitude changed and I found he was very bright and a hard worker. When it was time for him to move up a grade, I called my old chief in Norwich to recommend him. He got a job there and I heard that he did very well and was much liked. I like to think that my taking the blame for his mistake helped save his career. It taught me that the responsibility for mistakes made by those under you is your responsibility and if you take the blame, you will always get loyal service from those who work for you. Furthermore most people will see that you were not personally to blame but because you took the responsibility they will respect you for standing up for your workers, right or wrong. There is a reciprocal to this lesson. If you are the victim of some mismanagement do not protest to the minion who may have been directly responsible but go to the head man. Work from the top down not from the bottom up.

By the time I was ready to leave South End to go to Washington, I realized that at the age of 34 I had spent half my life, 17 years since leaving school, learning my trade. Because I had been fortunate enough to have had indulgent parents to help me and had been lucky enough to help them financially by winning some scholarships, I did not owe any money. In retrospect I realize that there were three people who taught me most. They were three very different characters but each was an outstanding surgeon and very caring of their patients. They were not prolific writers because they spent most of their energies taking care of their patients. I noticed that those surgeons who wrote the most were not always the best surgeons. Many of those who contributed most to medical literature have only one or two good ideas which they rehash into numbers of articles. The ability to write does not necessarily equate with being the best medical practitioner. When I had to choose to whom to recommend patients, it was not the famous that I chose but the ones I knew from experience were the most competent and practical. When one is traveling and has a medical emergency in a place where you know none of the medical profession, the best thing to do is to find the chief resident of the hospital where one finds oneself. Ask him to whom he would refer his own family. He has worked with the various chiefs and knows them in a way that no one else does.

The three surgeons who taught me the most were Mr. Alan Birt in Norwich, Mr. Denis Browne (who is now Sir Denis Browne, having been knighted by the Queen) at Great Ormond Street and Mr. Donald Barlow in South End. They were very different characters. Mr. Alan Birt was a relatively slow operator but very precise, open minded and progressive. He worked way beyond the time for which the National Health Service was paying him. After I left he decided that there was a need for a cardiovascular surgeon in the area. He found out who was doing this work elsewhere and getting good results. He went with an anesthetist to study their techniques and started a service in Norwich. His success rate in the early days of this specialty was outstanding. His other memorable quality was his unshakable moral and ethical integrity. He was a good teacher, even-tempered and a delight to work for. The people that it is easiest to learn from are those that you respect the most and Alan Birt fell into this category.

Mr. Denis Browne was a totally different person. He is a most original thinker who studied every problem from its very essence. His ideas were controversial but astonishingly successful. He could be very abrasive and difficult to work for but he was reasonable and would accept new ideas from others. On one occasion he was upset with me because I had allowed one of his cases to be up and around the ward just after we had performed major abdominal surgery on him. He was not much more than a toddler. He was being nursed in a cot with a net over the top to stop him getting out. While I was doing my ward rounds I saw him standing up in his cot and doing belly-flops onto the wound in his stomach. I figured that he would do himself far less harm if he was allowed out of his cot. I explained this to DB who listened and then agreed. Thereafter we changed our policy and our postoperative cases were allowed to dictate their own activities figuring their own pain threshold would guide them. Inactivity does not help healing though some restraint is necessary to prevent strain on a specific area. This policy of allowing activity after surgery was in the process of change throughout the surgical world. When I first started out patients having hernia repairs were kept in bed for three weeks. Now this operation is performed, in many cases, as an outpatient. Not only does this save money but it reduces the incidence of pulmonary embolus which can be fatal.

When I was a house surgeon at Great Ormond street we had a two-year old with Hirschsprung's disease. This is a condition where the patient cannot pass a normal bowel movement though there is no obvious obstruction. The stool accumulates in the large intestine which becomes more and more distended. It was necessary to remove the accumulated feces manually and I spent several Saturday afternoons when I was a House Surgeon doing this for poor little Humpty-Dumpty, as we called him. He was one big belly with little match-sticks for arms and legs sticking out. At this time, though the condition was well recognized, no one knew the cause. Various medicines and some surgical approaches had been tried, all without success. Everyone thought that the problem was in the enormously distended bowel which could not push things along. Shortly after I left to go into the RAF, a surgeon in Boston, Dr. Ovar Swenson, discovered that the problem was in the rectum though this looked grossly normal and was not distended. He found that there was a problem with the nerve supply in the wall of the rectum so that waves of peristalsis did not go through it normally. It was not in the part of the bowel which became so distended but the narrower part at the end which was causing the problem. He devised an operation to remove this piece of bowel but save the anal canal. An Australian surgeon was visiting Boston before coming to Great Ormond Street and he had worked with Swenson. When he got to Great Ormond Street he told DB about this work. Swenson's operation was difficult to perform as he devised it but it was successful. DB was enthusiastic about the idea but figured that there might be a simpler way to perform the operation and achieve the same result. It was too late to save poor little Humpty Dumpy as he had died by this time. There were other similar cases that were under our care and DB started to operate on them. When I returned to Great Ormond Street in 1949 this was a standard procedure and I was able to perform it myself. The operation that DB devised for removing this part of the rectum and preserving the anal function seemed to be suitable for some adults with certain extensive lesions of the rectum. Subsequently I tried it out with success but found doing it on adults was more difficult than in infants. Nowadays, with all the mechanical devices that have been invented for connecting bowel, this operation has been modified and simplified, though the principle remains the same.

The third of the teachers who taught me most was Mr. Donald Barlow. There seemed to be no area of surgery where he was not an expert. His detailed knowledge of anatomy combined with his artistic approach and manual dexterity meant it was a delight to assist him. Though he was extremely demanding, it was obvious that his demands were aimed at seeing that his patients got the best care possible. Before we had flexible lighted instruments to look down the esophagus and into the stomach he invented a straight scope which would allow him to use special instruments through it. He pointed out that if one positioned the patient properly it was easy to pass a straight tube through the mouth into the stomach. Sword swallowers do it all the time. He came to America to demonstrate his instrument and arranged for a sword swallower to accompany him. At the last moment this man had to cancel. Nothing daunted, Barlow decided to demonstrate how easy it was to swallow his tube by standing up in front of the audience and swallowing it himself. He explained to me that gentleness was important when invading other people's anatomy. I had been detailed to run an outpatient clinic where we had to cystoscope (look into the bladder) patients with urinary problems. One day he remarked to me that if one was both gentle and skillful it was possible to do this without any anesthetic. I felt that this was a real challenge to me. Thereafter I performed all these procedures without any anesthetic and found that he was right. There was a simple trick to it which combined knowledge of the anatomy with gentleness. One day Barlow had a private patient that he was about to cystoscope in the operating room. As I watched, he proceeded to instill an anesthetic into the urethra before inserting the instrument. I said that I thought that he had told me this was unnecessary if one did it properly and so I had not been using any. He was horrified and told me he had been talking only about principles rather than practice. However I had become very adept with the cystoscope and this stood me in good stead afterwards. Surprisingly few of the patients that I had scoped without anesthetic protested.

My time at South End terminated my surgical training

Chapter 12

PREPARATION FOR THE MOVE

The decision to move to Washington and to join Dr. Lyons in private practice did not come easily. I liked working for the National Health Service. If I had become a consultant surgeon, I would have been secure for life. Besides being paid by the Government I would have been able to supplement my income with some Private Practice. As a consultant I would have been entitled to six weeks a year vacation, exclusive of 'study leave'. The trouble was that I was out of step with the normal ladder to climb to become a consultant. I had spent two years as a Pediatric Surgical Senior Registrar instead of four years as a senior registrar in general surgery. Furthermore I really wanted to continue to concentrate on pediatric surgery but the prospects of the National Health Service creating more jobs for consultants in this field were uncertain. If I went to Washington, I could join a successful surgical practice with someone who was very highly regarded not only by his patients but also by his colleagues. There was no one doing pediatric surgery there so perhaps I could develop such a practice. I had found out that the other surgeons in Washington did not think that there was any need for special surgeons for children. Dr. Lyons did not agree with the action of the board of the Children's' Hospital though he was a senior member of the staff there. I thought he would be in a position to help me. There was a steadily growing awareness of the value of pediatric surgery in the States at this time and several of the major cities had pediatric surgeons working in their medical schools. There seemed to be growing trend towards the acceptance of this practice. Perhaps I could convert the doctors in Washington to be more accepting. I would start as a general surgeon with Dr. Lyons and try to convince some of the local pediatricians that I was better qualified to treat their patients requiring surgery than anyone else around. It was a gamble but the odds seemed better than hoping that the National Health Service would create more pediatric surgical consultants positions and award one to me.

Such a move meant that I would be leaving my parents and my friends. Being an only child with parents who were so devoted and who had done so much for me made the decision much more difficult. My father was near the age when he would have to retire and so my parents would be able to come to visit us. They were insistent in refusing to influence my plans. On the positive side, we would be joining Agnes's family and friends. Her parents were very supportive of our ideas. They looked forward to having her near them and were delighted that I would be working with Dr. Lyons. They had a tremendous admiration for him and attributed their daughter's very survival when she had been so sick to his devoted care.

Having made the decision there remained the problem of executing it. Agnes had maintained her American citizenship by refusing to vote in the general election in England. Had she voted, she was told that she would have lost that citizenship. It was not easy for her because she knew that I was going to vote as a Conservative and she wanted to support the Labour Party. Because she was a citizen I could obtain a visa to enter the States as her husband. Also she had registered our children at the American Embassy. Thus all the administrative details were taken care of.

During the last years while I was working at South End we had maintained our flat off Baker Street in London. When we rented the house in South End we sublet the Flat to a retired clergyman and his daughter. As I left South End we terminated their lease and returned to spend the last days there while we got everything together to move. Unfortunately the clergyman claimed he was too poor to pay his rent so we forgave it and lost out on that deal.

After Agnes developed acute Toxemia and had to have an emergency Cesarean Section with Catherine, we were warned that she should not become pregnant again in the near future. We waited four years before trying again. This time all seemed to be going well. She was carefully monitored and showed no rise in blood pressure. This time, when she was almost eight months along her waters suddenly broke. A panic call to her obstetrician brought an ambulance which rushed her to the hospital for another cesarean section. We had another girl, Angela, much less premature than had been the case with Catherine. By this time medical practice had changed a little and Agnes was made to get out of bed to eat the same day. She did not particularly like that experience but she made a very speedy recovery and was able to be discharged within a week. Needless to say my parents stepped into the breach to help out. We still had the au pair girl who had come to join us while we were in South End and she was able to help. . Unfortunately she did not wish to come with us to America which was a pity as she was excellent and we were all very fond of her. We had to try to find someone else. We found an English girl who did wish to come and we made arrangements for her to travel with us.

We spent a busy time buying furniture that we thought that we would need when we set up a household in Washington. Because there was still a shortage of basic materials in England, some enterprising cabinet makers were making antique reproductions using old wood from oversized Victorian pieces. There were also some genuine antiques going for very reasonable prices. We acquired a few useful bits of furniture but we had to work out what would fit into a single container. Through Agnes's family in the States we were able to contact a moving and storage company that specialized in moving stage companies. They were very competent and helpful. We managed to get all our possessions safely packed into their container.

We realized that Agnes had not been across the Channel to visit Europe since we had married. It was going to be much more difficult to do this once we were settled in America. She was very anxious to see some of the artistic gems that she had studied in her Art History classes while at college. Having made all the necessary plans for our emigration and booked our passage, we took the opportunity for a vacation on the Continent. My parents agreed to look after our two daughters even though the younger was only five months old. We had not yet sold our car so we took that and drove through parts of France, Switzerland and Italy. It was a fascinating trip as we were looking for very specific things of artistic or historical interest. With Agnes as a guide, we saw many things that are not on the average tour map. I was interested in seeing Switzerland again so we went by Interlaken and Brienz where we stayed at a hotel overlooking the falls where Sherlock Holmes had supposedly fought his arch enemy Moriarty. From there we went by the Jungfrau and over the St Gottard Pass into Northern Italy. We viewed the lakes on our way to Venice. There we stayed a few days, finding paintings that Agnes particularly wished to see in out of-the-way churches. Some of these were rather disappointing as they were so badly lit that it was almost impossible to appreciate their beauty. After we got accustomed to the smell, we found Venice most enjoyable. We stopped at Padua and then on to Ravenna to see the mosaics before the hazardous drive over the mountains to Florence. The scariest part of that drive was the way the heavy trucks came down the mountain roads and through the villages. We noted that they blew their wind horns as they were entering each village. At that sound all the local inhabitants gathered up their children and dashed into the nearest doorway until the monster had passed. In Florence we stayed at a hotel near the center of town. It was the top two stories of an old building which had been converted into shops below, then offices and finally a hotel at the top. There we could have breakfast on the roof overlooking the town and its surroundings. Though I was most impressed by the statues and the buildings, I was somewhat disappointed with the galleries. There were so many magnificent paintings hung on the walls that it was almost impossible to see one without being overwhelmed and distracted by those nearby. From Florence we went to Pisa and then along the Italian Riviera coast and into France as far as Avignon. There we sat on the bridge famous in song before partaking of a most memorable dinner at a five-star restaurant on the other side of the river. It took us two days to recover from that meal, though at the time and since, we agreed that it was the best meal we had ever eaten.

When we got back to England there was just time to pack our personal belongings, sell the car, say Good bye to my parents and catch the Holland America line from Southampton. We were taking our Tweedle with us. We were told that he had to travel in the ship's kennel but we were allowed to take him out for exercise on one of the decks. To start with he was a little sick when we hit some bad weather but he settled down and rapidly made friends with everyone he came in contact with. He was so successful at this that we were soon told that he could stay in the cabin with us, much to his delight. Catherine, who was five at this time, had a great time as she too made friends very easily. The baby, Angela, proved to be a good traveler and the new nanny was a great help. We were met in New York by Agnes's parents who had made arrangements for our journey on to Washington. Her mother took Agnes, the nanny and the children by train while her father and I drove there with Tweedle. My father-in-law took to Tweedle at once because he climbed right into the car and spent the trip lying peacefully at his feet. My in-laws had rented us a suite with its own kitchen in a hotel near the center of town. This was our temporary abode until we could find a house. This we managed to do in little more than a month due to my mother in law' driving Agnes around and since my father in law was a mortgage banker he could raise the money. All in all, the move was accomplished much more easily than I had feared.

Chapter 13

STARTING PRACTICE IN WASHINGTON

As soon as we had unpacked our essentials, I set off to report to Dr. Lyons' office. There I found Dr. Harold Hawfield who was his associate at that time and whose duties and privileges I was to take over. Harold had been with Dr. Lyons for three years and was leaving to merge his practice as a partner with another distinguished surgeon. Harold had agreed to stay on for a couple of months with Dr. Lyons to help me settle in. He proved to be a tireless tutor, showing me around, introducing me to the many people that I would be working with and sparing me from making many mistakes.

In a number of ways surgical practice in Washington at that time was very different from my experiences in England. It seemed to be very much less organized and rather haphazardly arranged. Dr. Lyons, as the senior surgeon at the hospital where we worked, was the only surgeon who had a specific operating time. Everyone else had to call the operating room supervisor and request a time that was vacant when they wanted to arrange to operate on a case. Dr. Lyons had a fairly constant team working with him on all his cases. This was not true of the other surgeons. They worked with whichever of the anesthesiologists that were available and with the nurses assigned by the Operating Room supervisor, i.e. whoever was on duty at that time. The assistant surgeon was one of the residents but they were not assigned to any specific surgeon.

There were two other major differences that I noted at once. Though there were doctors who were anesthesiologists, many patients were anesthetized by nurses under the supervision of a doctor who might be in charge of several cases at the same time. In England the anesthetist was always a doctor though he had an assistant, neither another doctor nor a nurse, but a person who was a technician who he had trained to work with him. The assistant never gave the anesthetic. The other difference which seemed very major was the hierarchy among the nurses in the operating room. In all major cases it is necessary to have at least two nurses in attendance. One is 'scrubbed' and is responsible for handing the instruments to the surgeon. The other, known as the circulating nurse, is responsible for seeing that the scrubbed nurse has the supplies which the surgeon might need, available on the sterile table. In England the scrub nurse was the senior nurse and the circulating nurse was her minion. There the scrub nurse was considered an integral part of the surgical team and most surgeons expected to work with the same scrub nurse for almost all their cases. This had the advantage that the nurse knew what the surgeon usually used, and at what stage in the operation, so that she had the correct instrument or suture ready in hand. In the USA the circulating nurse is the senior nurse in the operating room and the scrub nurse the junior. This nurse does not work consistently with one or two surgeons and so has less chance to develop the anticipatory skills that are so helpful to the surgeon. Some of the better scrub nurses in England considered it shameful if the surgeon had to ask for anything. She thought that she should have anticipated the need. This team-work speeded up the surgery and helped to account for the fact that the English surgeons got through many more cases than their American counterparts. This beneficial use of operating room time was also aided by the fact that English surgeons were assigned time in the operating room on a continuing basis. They were assigned the same time, either morning or afternoon, on the same day every week. This meant that cases could run with very little down time between them because the whole team was ready to go as soon as the case before was finished. The disadvantage was that there was little time to go out to discuss the outcome of the operation with the relatives. This could only be done if the surgeon left the final closure of the wound to his assistant. Since his assistant was a semi-permanent member of his team, the surgeon could trust him or her to use an approved technique. I remember that on one occasion when I was the assistant, the surgeon asked me to use a specific skin closure. I was not familiar with exactly how to achieve what he wanted so I had to invent a way of doing it. A few cases later he came in as I was finishing a case for him. He looked over my shoulder and was kind enough to say that my technique was excellent and a method that he had not thought of using himself. Had he not approved I would have been in real trouble.

The lack of communication with the patients and their relatives was one of the main deficiencies of the National Health Service. It was necessary to enable the medical profession to get through the volume of work that the 'free' service revealed to be necessary. It also high-lighted a major difference between practicing in the USA and England. In England the patients had an almost blind faith that the doctors would do the right thing for them. They did not think that they should argue about the merits of one treatment over another, nor did they want detailed explanations. They had trust in the integrity of the doctors and their skill. Perhaps this trust was sometimes misplaced, but under the NHS, financial considerations did not enter the equation. The doctors were on a salary and were not paid on a fee-for-service basis. This fact led to another great, but less discussed, advantage. There was much less professional jealousy. If a surgeon did not think that he was qualified to take care of a specific problem as competently as one of his colleagues he would have no reluctance in referring the case to the better qualified doctor. As a result, there developed some super-specialists to whom difficult cases could be referred. Because problem cases were referred to them they became increasingly expert through experience.

It soon became apparent to me that I would be working in a totally different environment, both in regard to my relationship with colleagues and with patients and their relatives. It took a little time for me to realize how different the medical environment was.

Quite soon after I arrived I was invited to attend a meeting of the local medical society. Members seemed very interested in my experiences working with the National Health Service in England. One question that I was asked was quite significant as it high-lighted some very real differences. The questioner wanted to know how 'Tissue Committees' worked there. A tissue committee examines specimens removed during a surgical procedure with the idea of determining whether the surgery was justified or not. For instance if an appendix is removed and the pathologist finds it to be perfectly normal, this is recorded. If a surgeon is found to have removed a disproportionate number of normal appendices he is forcefully advised that his practice is not in the best interest of the profession. If he persists, disciplinary action may be taken. I explained that I had not heard of Tissue Committees until I arrived in this country because there were none in England. On further questioning as to how excessive surgery was controlled, I pointed out that surgeons were so busy working through the waiting lists of patients that there was no temptation to do unnecessary work. Furthermore, since we were all working on the basis of a salary rather than a fee-for-service, it was inconceivable that anyone would do anything that he did not consider absolutely necessary. This argument reveals a most important difference between the practices in the two countries.

There was a strong antipathy towards anything that could be considered 'socialist' particularly in the medical profession. This was brought home to me rather clearly. I was invited to talk to a group of the ladies associated with the local, District of Columbia, medical society. Unfortunately they offered me a date when I already had another commitment and I had to refuse. I asked if I could do so at another time as I was anxious to explain some of the good aspects of the National Health Service which did not seem to have been discussed in this country. They promised to call me back to arrange another date. I never did receive that call. Gradually I came to appreciate that there is an inherent fear of government interference with individual enterprise. There remains a conviction that private enterprise is more efficient and avoids much of the micro-management that seems to be practiced by government bureaucrats. When the NHS was first introduced in England there was remarkably little interference with the actual practice of medicine. The doctors were not told how to treat patients and remarkably little paper-work was required of them. In fact the only forms that were required were 'off work' certificates and death certificates. The remainder of the paper work was confined to medical notes about the patients' conditions and their treatments, strictly designed for the use of the doctors themselves.

The specialists became salaried and the General Practitioners were paid on a 'per capita' basis according to the number of patients who signed up with them, thus the whole population had equal access to the medical care available. Employment by the NHS was not compulsory nor did it have to be full-time. Some private practice was allowed and many hospitals were allowed to set up or continue a wing for those patients who opted to pay for their medical services. It was a remarkable compromise and worked very well at its inception. Since those days medical treatments have become much more advanced and far more expensive, resulting in continuing problems. In spite of these problems the service is generally very popular and most people consider that the benefits outweigh the deficiencies. There is a double standard because those who can afford it can get faster and more luxurious treatment though it is not necessarily any better medically.

Having reported to Dr. Lyons' office that first day, Dr. Hawfield (Harold) explained what would be expected of me. He then took me to the hospital where Dr. Lyons admitted all his adult patients. This was a rather old hospital, known as Emergency Hospital, and was situated a couple of blocks from the White House. Though the hospital was old, the most striking feature was the atmosphere. There seemed to be a friendly and cooperative spirit throughout the whole staff. It did not take me long to trace this to the influence of Dr. Lyons. He seemed to know everyone by name, to know about their families and always to speak to them, not only his colleagues and the nurses but even the lowliest of the help. As a result he was respected by everyone and his unselfish attitude pervaded the whole place. It was differently set up from the English hospitals in that there was a much higher percentage of private and semi-private rooms and fewer wards. These latter were for those who could not afford the fees for private accommodation and for totally indigent patients. The patients in these wards were mainly taken care of by the residents under supervision from the Attendings; a title given to qualified doctors who were privileged to admit their own patients and to teach residents.

Harold explained to me that my duties would consist of seeing Dr. Lyons' patients with him when he went on rounds and visiting them every evening to check that they were progressing satisfactorily. I could attend in the operating room with Dr. Lyons but could not assist him. This was the prerogative of the senior resident and an essential part of his education. While I found this a frustrating experience as I was anxious to continue operating or at least helping, I did realize the necessity for the custom. By being Dr. Lyons's associate I was put on the staff of the hospital right away. They were kind enough to accept my Fellowship of the Royal College of Surgeons as a suitable qualification to become one of their Attending surgeons. This meant that I had to take a turn at supervising the residents who took care of the non-paying patients from the wards and the emergencies. I assisted them when they were operating and I might be called at night by the senior surgical resident to be informed that a patient was being admitted who required surgery. After listening to the story, I could give the OK or suggest other possibilities. At first I did not realize how relatively inexperienced the senior surgical residents were. I had been used to being the senior resident (registrar) with nine years post-graduate training. I did not realize that these senior residents were only three to four years out of medical school. My previous American surgical experience had been during my fourth year as a student when I was at Johns Hopkins. There the senior surgical residents were in their fifth or sixth year and had extensive and intensive training. Furthermore they were the cream of the crop having achieved their position through careful selection. As a result of my lack of understanding of the situation, my first reaction was to trust the resident to cope with what seemed to me to be a standard problem. I told the resident to go ahead and went back to sleep. When I was called one night from the hospital with the message that the resident, and therefore the patient, was in trouble, I had to hurriedly get to the hospital to sort out the problem. Fortunately I was able to do this and no harm came to the patient but I learned another lesson.

Besides my duties at the hospital I was given the use of Dr. Lyons office to see any patients that I might have. Dr. Lyons saw patients there every afternoon. I sat in the office while he did this. On rare occasions he would invite me to see a patient with him or to help him with some minor procedure; otherwise I had nothing to do. I found this very boring and tedious. It was a great change from the intensive work I had been used to as a Senior Registrar in England. It was relaxing but too much so. Dr. Lyons' office hours were extensive. He had a busy practice but he never hurried. He always had time for every patient and allowed each to talk as much as they liked. On one occasion, when it was getting late, I asked the secretary what patient he was seeing that was taking so long. She told me that the patient had asked for a late appointment as she wanted to talk to the doctor. There was nothing the matter with her but she wanted to talk. Dr. Lyons tolerated this attitude from his patients and never charged them for his time. Working or perhaps I should say sitting in his office, I learned a lot about this remarkable man from his secretary. She was a most efficient lady and utterly devoted to her boss. Through her I found out many sides of his character that were less well known. He had two charges for his operations, $200, for relatively minor cases and $300 for major cases. Because of his reputation, he had many famous and some very wealthy patients. Some of these felt that they were being undercharged for his services and sent checks well above his fees. One lady who had come down from New York for him to perform major surgery sent a check for $3000 to cover his $300 bill. He took the $300 into the office account but the rest went into his 'needy sick' fund. This is what happened to all the money he received above his standard charges. His generosity and the occasional lack of appreciation of it almost led me to commit murder. One evening I was seeing his patients and came upon a female, I hesitate to call her a lady, in a semiprivate room. She complained bitterly about her accommodation. The next day I reported her complaints to our secretary. She asked if I realized that, not only was he operating on her without charge, but he was also paying for her hospital charges from the 'fund'. I was speechless. I had the greatest difficulty in being even moderately civil to her when I saw her the next night. She was the exception. The vast majority of his patients adored him and respected him, not only as a surgeon, but as a person. He was also respected and even loved by his colleagues. In an atmosphere of somewhat cut-throat competition between the surgeons he stood out because of his honest unselfishness. One patient came to him for a second opinion having had surgery recommended by another surgeon. He agreed with the recommendation of the other surgeon. The patient asked him to take her on and perform the surgery. He told her that she had a very good surgeon and that she should stick with him. When she persisted with her request for him to perform the operation, he still refused but said that he would attend the operation if she would like. This he did and did not charge her for his service. This attitude towards his colleagues helped to explain the high opinion, almost reverence, they had for him.

  I found some of his patients most interesting, not only medically, but as personalities. There was one in particular who was most memorable. On doing my night rounds for him, I entered the room of this patient and found myself fascinated. This patient seemed incredibly well informed about everything and seemed to know everyone of any significance in the political world. She had just had major surgery but did not seem slowed up at all. The political parties were about to have their quadrennial conventions to choose a candidate for the next Presidency. She was worried as to whether she would be able to attend both the Democratic and the Republican Conventions. I sat on the radiator in her room for over an hour most nights listening to her. I had no idea who she was but she was very knowledgeable and interestingly opinionated. When I got home Agnes asked me what had kept me so long. I told her that I had been talking with a most interesting patient but she did not ask me who she was. The next day I was walking from the office with Dr. Lyons to the garage where we kept our cars and said to him that the lady he had in room whatever it was, was a most fascinating character. He said "Don't you know who she is? Mrs. Longworth?" I said that I did not. He explained that she was Teddy Roosevelt's' daughter, brought up in the White House, and had been married to the Speaker of the House. No wonder she was interesting. Perhaps the greatest compliment to her was that I found her so intriguing, even when I had no idea who she was. Many years later, after Dr. Lyons had died, she became my patient. By that time she was in her 80's but was still as sharp as a tack. I had to perform a second mastectomy on her and apologized for having to mutilate her in this way. She replied, "I don't mind at all. I always wanted to go topless ever since I was a girl in the White House". While she was in the hospital after this operation, as I was visiting her, I noticed several books on her bed. One was a textbook on modern physics. I picked it up to check it. She complained that, like most textbooks, it was already out of date. This was a startling comment from an elderly lady with no scientific background. Her age did not seem to have slowed her up very much. It was my practice to make my patients move their arm through a full range the next day after a mastectomy. When I tried to get her to do this, she readily complied, explaining that she was really very supple. To prove this she proceeded to put her foot behind her neck! I was flabbergasted. I had heard that she was often condemned for her biting and sometimes cruel wit. Fortunately I never came across this side of her and came to admire her greatly.

Dr. Lyons garaged his car a block away from the office. He asked the owner if he would let me garage mine there too. Mr. Mayo said he would do so since Dr. Lyons requested him but he did not like Englishmen. I had bought a second hand Ford. I found Mayo to be a very pleasant man. We became good friends quite quickly. He was always doing extra things like tuning the car without charge when he thought it needed it. One day I told him that I thought that it was leaking oil. He looked at it and told me that the main oil seal was the culprit. I would have to have it replaced but that was too big a job for him to do. I had to take the car to one of the Ford dealers. This I did. After I got the car back, it still leaked oil. I told Mayo that he must have made the wrong diagnosis. He took a look and informed me that the garage that I had taken the car to had not replaced the main oil seal. When I asked how he knew, he pointed to a bolt on the engine and told me that it was impossible to replace a main oil seal without removing that bolt. The bolt in question was still covered with caked grim and grease. I took the car back to the Ford garage to tell them the car was still leaking oil. The service manager said there must be some other cause. I asked him how they had managed to change the main oil seal without loosening the bolt that was still covered with grim and grease. He looked startled and was very apologetic. He asked if I would leave the car and he would have it back to me that evening. This he did and there were no more leaks and no further bill. This was the first time I realized what a valuable friend I had acquired in Mayo. He remained a friend long after he closed the garage in Washington and moved to one in Northern Virginia. Whenever I had a problem with a car I always called him and he never failed me. I could call him even on weekends and he would come to the rescue at once. He was utterly honest and generous to a fault. He was equally generous and trustworthy to any of my friends that I recommended to him.

Starting my own practice was a slow and tedious process. I had hoped that Dr. Lyons would refer some of his cases to me when he was particularly busy. This he found difficult to do because all his patients were so devoted to him that they would not accept anyone else. Furthermore the physicians who referred patients to him wanted him and no one else. They did not know me and it took time to win their trust. At the start, the patients that came to me required only very minor procedures. This was somewhat disconcerting as I had been doing very little minor surgery for several years. I felt much better qualified to perform major surgery. I soon learned the importance of treating these minor cases with as much expertise as I could muster. This was driven home to me one day. I had just successfully performed a minor procedure on a lady and was about to discharge her when she asked if I would remove her husband's gallbladder. She confessed that she had been testing me out with the minor procedure before deciding on a surgeon for her husband.

Because I had so few patients I had plenty of time to give to any patients who might come to me. I found that I thoroughly enjoyed talking with patients and finding out as much as I could about them. I was asked to see a gentleman with acute abdominal pain one day. A simple physical examination convinced me that he had acute appendicitis and I recommended immediate surgery. He refused and went home. I was very worried and could not get him out of my mind. That evening, though it was pouring with rain, I drove out to his house to see him again. I found that he was no better, perhaps a little worse. This time he acceded to my demands that he be operated on. I put him in my car and drove him to the hospital where I removed an appendix which was about to rupture. He and his wife were very grateful and I got to know him quite well while he was recovering. I found out that he worked for a radio company and was an expert on such things as amplifiers and radio receivers. By this time we had moved into our house in Washington and I had set up my 'Hi-fi' system. I had this made for me by a friend in England before transistors had replaced vacuum tubes. Also it used 240 volts rather than the 120 current used in American houses. Someone had told me that houses in America had two incoming electric lines and an earth line. If one connected the input of the two incoming power lines one got 240 volts. I had done this connecting the input of my machine with one terminal to each of the incoming lines in the main box. It had worked quite satisfactorily for some time but now it had died. I was at a loss to find someone who could repair it. I asked my recovering patient if he would be able to help me out, since he was an expert in that field. Perhaps out of a sense of gratitude, he agreed to come to my house to see what he could do. When he arrived and saw how I had managed to get an input of 240 volts into the machine I thought that he would have a heart attack. After rapidly disconnecting my brilliant solution, he explained that I needed a transformer to adapt my machine to work on 120 volts and that he could get one for me. I had never really understood much about electricity and always felt lucky that I had learned, rather parrot-wise, enough physics to get into medical school. I am still not quite sure why electricity does not run all over the floor when you pull a plug out of a wall socket. I accept the fact that it does not do so as a merciful act of God. Apparently God was on my side when I did the original wiring as there was no explosion and the house did not burn down. My patient kindly sorted out the whole mess and got my Hi-fi working again. Other than the cost of the transformer he would not charge me. He said that my unexpected zeal in coming to his house that night had saved his life and this, to him, small service scarcely repaid me. I wonder if he realized just how significant a service he had rendered to me.

Besides his work at Emergency Hospital, Dr. Lyons was also a senior attending surgeon at the Children's Hospital. It was there that we admitted all the children that were referred to him. Because I was his associate I was put on the staff there. It was an old hospital and I must confess that I thought that it was very much behind the times professionally. The surgical service was staffed by a variety of general surgeons none of whom had any training in pediatric surgery. The surgeon who had been doing most of the difficult children's work had just developed Parkinson's disease and had to give up this work. I gather he was a charming and very competent person. As a result some of the better pediatricians were looking for someone to take his place. They decided to try me out. There were two or three groups of pediatricians and three or four individuals who soon came to trust me and send me patients. I tried to keep as low a profile as I could as I knew that many of my ideas were foreign to the majority of members of the staff, particularly the other surgeons and also some of the anesthesiologists. Though my pediatric practice grew slowly it was not going to be large enough to bring in an adequate income, so I continued with the adult practice as well. As far as the indigent children were concerned and children without referring pediatricians, they were taken care of by a rotating roster of surgeons consisting of one senior attending and two junior attendings'. Harold and I were the two junior attendings on one team. I found he was very happy to listen to my opinions and seek my advice. There was not an ounce of jealousy or any other vice in his whole character. We always got along in every way. Because some of the patients coming in through the emergency room or the clinics had insurance, there was a financial incentive to take care of them. This led to the reluctance of some of the surgeons to give up their prerogatives with regard to these patients. When, later on, the lay board of the hospital came to realize that children did merit specially trained surgeons and they decided to appoint a full-time pediatric surgeon, this led to some very awkward disagreements.

Before this appointment was made, I became involved in a situation which was very revealing and, to me, rather unhappy. . One of the senior pediatricians asked me to see a small child with intractable constipation. I examined the child, found that I needed to evacuate the impacted stool from high in the intestine and did so with the aid of an anesthetic. My examination convinced me that the child had Hirschsprung's disease. This is a condition where the nerves in the lowest part of the intestine have not developed properly. As a result the contents of the intestine are propelled only so far. They cannot be pushed though the area which has the deficient nerve supply. Though the condition had been known for many years, its true cause was only discovered in the late 40's by the group at Boston Children's hospital. At Great Ormond Street in London we had learned about their work and copied them. The cure was to remove the malfunctioning part of the distal bowel and connect the remainder to the anal canal. This is a somewhat tricky operation but pediatric surgeons were performing it with great success. Having seen this particular child, I wrote a note on the chart suggesting the diagnosis and recommending an X-ray which would confirm my opinion. I also called the referring physician. Most apologetically he informed me that he had only seen the child because the child's own pediatrician was out of town. This pediatrician had returned and did not wish me to see the patient any more. He had his own surgeon. This surgeon did not believe in Hirschsprung's disease. He had the child transferred to another hospital where he performed several misguided operations without improving the situation. I was very frustrated but did not see what I could do. A couple of years later a baby was admitted to the 'staff' service and was seen by Dr. Hawfield. He called me and said that he had a baby that he would like me to see with him. I went to the ward with him. Before he could tell me anything about the problem I noticed the name of the baby. It was the same last name as the child mentioned above. I said; "Are you suspecting Hirschsprung's?" He said he was but how did I know. I told him the sad story of the other child who turned out to be the older sister of the current patient. It turned out that the older sister was still in trouble. The parents had spent all their money on the medical expenses of the older child and had to send the second child to the hospital for free care. We confirmed the diagnosis on the baby and Harold asked me to operate as he was not familiar with the procedure. I made the necessary plans and arranged for one of the anesthesiologists with whom I had developed a very satisfactory relationship to give the anesthetic. The night before the operation I went to the hospital to check that everything I would need would be ready. There I met the Chief of Anesthesia. He said to me; "Why are you going to kill that baby tomorrow?" I spent a miserable night appreciating how much depended on the next day. Besides the life of the baby, my whole reputation hung in the balance. I went ahead and performed the operation as I had done before under the tutelage of Denis Browne. Actually the baby was only 3 months old and the standard recommendation was to wait until the baby was at least 6 months of age. The procedure went very smoothly and the baby had a normal bowel movement on the way to the recovery room. She never looked back and was discharged within a week. This is not the end of the story. The parents, who were very grateful to me, were working for an embassy in Washington at that time. They were subsequently transferred to New York. A couple of years later they called me up from New York to tell me that their older daughter was still suffering from her original problem. Since their younger daughter was now completely healthy, they asked if they could they bring the older one down for me to cure. I told them that should not be necessary because there were excellent pediatric surgeons in New York. I would contact the one I knew on their behalf. I rang up Dr. Santulli and explained the situation to him. He agreed to take on the child which he did. He found that she was nearly moribund but he revived her and then cured her. I went over the hospital records of this child when I had first seen her. To my amazement and utter disgust I found that my notes, consultation and recommendations had been removed in total. This made clear to me the difficulty I would have in establishing a purely pediatric surgical practice in Washington at that time. Perhaps I could sow the seed for others to follow. This was my thinking at that time but with hindsight I realize that I might have done much more if I had pursued the issue of the original ignorant mistreatment of the older daughter or I had brought up the deletions to her chart when I discovered them. I was too acutely conscious of my foreign back ground and surgical training to face the repercussions that almost certainly would have ensued. Maybe if I had done so at that time the upgrading of the surgical care of children in Washington would not have had to await the arrival of Judson Randolph as the full-time surgical chief.

Because of the training I had in the treatment of congenital deformities including those of infants' limbs, particularly club feet, I was anxious to prove how good Denis Browne's methods were. All these cases were treated by orthopedic surgeons. I suggested that we could divide those cases coming to the free clinics into two groups. I would be allowed to treat one of the groups and the arthropods' the other. Since they would all be free patients there would be no financial considerations. This suggestion was refused! I did deal with one case that was referred to me by a non-medical friend who knew of my training, but only one. Cleft palates were the province of the plastic surgeons. Though I had successfully operated on over 120 in one year at Great Ormond Street I only dealt with two in Washington. The first was a 12 year old boy from the clinic that had been inadequately repaired years before. No one else wanted to correct the problem. The other was referred to me by the patient's aunt who knew my history and trusted my competence.

Another major difference in practice which I discovered was that of specialization. In England general surgeons steered clear of gynecology and orthopedics but not urology. In Washington I found that the general surgeons did everything else but urology. Thoracic surgery was another field which was different. General surgeons were not expected to open chests and when I did so to get at the upper stomach or esophagus there were some raised eyebrows. On one occasion when I was going through the chest I noticed that one of the thoracic surgeons was looking over my shoulder. He never said anything at the time but I subsequently discovered that he reported that I obviously knew what I was doing and should be allowed to continue. I was chagrined to find that I was barred from urology even though I had extensive experience in the field. I went to see how some of the local urologists were performing a prostatectomy and thought that their methods were way behind the times. I managed to keep my opinion to myself. A patient was admitted to another hospital in acute abdominal pain with suspected appendicitis. I was asked to see the patient. I thought that he had renal colic due to a stone in the ureter and not appendicitis. An X-ray seemed to confirm this diagnosis. I thought that by placing a tube in the ureter I could confirm the diagnosis and probably cure the patient. I scheduled this procedure in the operating room. When I got there, with the patient anesthetized, the nurse asked me where my cystoscope was. To my horror I found that the hospital did not supply a cystoscope and each urologist had his own. I rang up the chief of urology at that hospital to ask if I could borrow his. Fortunately he was a friend of Dr. Lyons. After I had explained my predicament, he laughed and gave permission for me to use his scope. This I did and rapidly inserted the tubes into the ureters. I then asked the nurse to call for the X-ray department to take the necessary pictures. Her immediate comment was; "but you haven't got them in place already have you?" She meant had I already inserted the ureteric tubes through the bladder into the ureters, (tubes between the kidney and the bladder where I thought the stone causing the colic was). I had the X-rays taken and they were satisfactory and the patient cured. It was another lesson learned and in the future I steered clear of similar situations as much as I could, though I knew that I was fully trained and completely competent to deal with them.

While these various episodes reveal some of the petty jealousies that can occur in the competitive fee-for-service environment, they also highlight the problem that can be encountered when an attempt is made to transfer post-graduate training from one country to another. It is not a criticism of either but shows that adaptation from one to the other can be difficult and frustrating.

Chapter 14

UNIVERSITY TEACHING APPOINTMENT

During the first couple of years as Dr. Lyons' associate I found that I had a lot of time on my hands. Frankly I was bored. The contrast from being overworked as a Senior Surgical Registrar in England to sitting around every afternoon in Dr. Lyons office was hard to accept. He was the person that all his patients wanted to see and only him. He seemed to be quite unable to direct any of them to me though he did nothing to discourage any who were referred to me. I decided that I had to do something more active. The idea of approaching one of the Medical Schools locally occurred to me. Perhaps I could do some undergraduate surgical teaching. There were three Medical Schools in the District of Columbia, George Washington University, Georgetown University and Howard University. Dr. Lyons was a Clinical Professor at George Washington though he rarely went there. I made inquiries both at George Washington and at Georgetown. At Georgetown the professor of surgery seemed to be very pleased to have me come on the staff there and to do some teaching. He wanted to know how much time I could give them. With Dr. Lyons' blessing, I said that I could give part of every afternoon. I soon found that I was teaching the fourth year students in the outpatient surgical clinics. I was also given the privilege of admitting my private patients to the hospital for surgery.

The teaching was an experience that I enjoyed. It appeared that I had a rather different approach to the previous teachers. At these clinics patients would come in and be allocated to a student. This student would interview the patient and examine him or her. Then he would come to present his findings to the other students and to me. I would ask what he thought was the matter with the patient. He usually gave me a long list of possible diagnoses. The students seemed disconcerted when I asked what they thought the diagnosis really was, not what all the possibilities might be. I pointed out that it was necessary to have the latter in mind in order to plan further investigations on a rational and economic basis. If it was a straight forward problem, exactly what they were going to recommend to the patient in order to deal with the situation. If the diagnosis was not clear, what should be the next step to make a definitive diagnosis? I explained that they were likely to be out in practice in another year and their patients would not want a long list of possibilities but a definite recommendation. Most of the students seemed to enjoy this practical approach.

I was still rather new to the medical environment in which I had found myself. I was brash, self-confident and proud of being somewhat nonconformist. On one occasion a lady appeared with a large abscess under her arm which needed to be drained. It was as big as a grapefruit and exquisitely tender. The standard procedure was to send such a patient to the surgical staff to have this drained under general anesthesia as an injection of local anesthetic is a very painful procedure when the area involved is large. I decided that I would show them a different method; swift and cheap painless and efficient. I asked for a spray bottle of Ethyl Chloride and a scalpel. Ethyl Chloride when sprayed on the skin numbs the area and allows an incision to be made painlessly. At least that is the idea, but it is not very efficient if the area is large and the abscess deep. The anesthetized area is only superficial and the abscess itself remains very tender. Ethyl Chloride also is a very fast acting general anesthetic if inhaled. We had used it in London to induce general anesthesia in children undergoing outpatient surgery before we switched over to ether. I decided to show the students what could be done with it. I soaked a sponge with the Ethyl Chloride and held it to the patient's nose and mouth. She became unconscious almost immediately and I opened the abscess, draining it thoroughly. The patient awoke very rapidly as Ethyl Chloride is very short-acting. She had no idea that anything had been done until she realized that her pain had lessened markedly, much to her delight. It was an impressive demonstration. It was not until afterwards that I realized what a risk I had taken. Using Ethyl Chloride as a general anesthetic can, on rare occasions, cause immediate cardiac arrest. Had this happened to this patient, I had no facilities immediately at hand to correct it. In my enthusiasm to teach what could be done, I had exposed the patient to an unwarranted, though very small risk and myself to a result that could have ruined my career.

Two other episodes remain clear in my mind. A lady came in with a lump in her breast which was very suspicious for cancer. We referred her to the surgical department for further care. After a biopsy, which was reported to be malignant, her breast was removed. She came back to our clinic for follow-up. Subsequent pathological examination had revealed that the diagnosis of a malignancy was wrong and her lump had been benign. We tried to explain this to the patient, admitting the error and assuring her that she had nothing further to worry about. She steadfastly refused to believe us, stating that we would never have removed the breast if it had not been cancerous. We never did convince her.

The other memorable experience occurred just at the end of the academic year. When I was slightly late getting to the clinic and there were no patients to be seen, I found the students sitting around playing pinochle. One of the students was a Nun who was going through Medical School with a view to becoming a medical missionary. I found her playing enthusiastically with the other students and holding her cards very close to her habit! I was sorry that I did not have a camera at hand as it would have made a memorable picture.

After I had been working at Georgetown for a while, I was asked if I would take on the responsibility of their Home Service Program. This was a charitable program where impecunious cancer patients were visited at home. They were taken medicine, and their families given help and advice about taking care of them. These were patients who were dying because of their disease and the only treatment available was palliative, designed to minimize their misery. A team had been formed consisting of a nurse, a social worker and a doctor who drove around once a week to visit these patients. The two main problems were controlling the patients' pain and advising the family as to the best way to nurse them and maintain their nutrition. Controlling their pain became my chief responsibility. Instructing the family as to how to give injections of narcotics was not a very reliable solution and had the disadvantage of having to leave considerable supplies of addictive injectables in the homes. I remembered that I had heard that a hospital in London had formulated a mixture that could be taken by mouth and that it was very effective. I managed to get hold of the formula, known as the Brompton Cocktail. After talking with the chief pharmacist at Georgetown Hospital, we managed to make up a very similar mixture. It consisted of large doses of morphine (substituted for heroin which was available in England at that time) and some other ingredients in an alcohol base, flavored to be palatable. Morphine taken by mouth is an effective pain killer but has to be given in much larger doses than when it is injected.

We decided to try it and found it most effective. Because it could be taken by mouth it was much appreciated by the patients and their families. It was put up in large bottles and the patients could take an ounce as they needed it. Once we dropped a bottle in the street where it smashed and the contents, full of narcotics, ran into the drain. Who benefited I do not know but our patient lost out that time. With me on these trips were two very devoted ladies, the nurse and the social worker. Sometimes we had a chauffeur but on other occasions I drove them in my car. At this time I was driving a Morris Minor convertible which, though cramped, was fun except when it rained! Our trips took us to some of the most dangerous slums in the city and areas which I had very little idea existed. The nurse occasionally had to go out to visit one of the patients in an emergency at night. She went alone. After visiting one patient in a particularly bad neighborhood I made her promise not to make an emergency visit there without a police escort, which she reluctantly did. Both she and the social worker were devout Roman Catholics and they knew that I was a renegade Anglican but they tolerated me with genuine affection. As we were going past the Shrine of the Immaculate Conception in North West Washington one afternoon they asked if I had ever been in the building. I had not. We stopped and went in. It is a modern, very impressive building. I expressed my appreciation. I asked if they had ever been in the National Cathedral which, though officially inter-denominational, is really an Anglican Cathedral. Since they had never been there we decided that we would visit it another day. This we did. They were awe-struck and I was amused by their comment; 'This is what a Catholic Cathedral should look like'. I pointed out that it was built after the plans of European Cathedrals almost all of which were Roman Catholic before Henry the Eighth broke with Rome and established the Church of England.

One day I found that I had been replaced as the doctor for this program because someone else was doing it and getting the small salary that I was being paid. I was given no warning and no notice of the change nor any reason. The administration of Georgetown Hospital and Medical School seemed to be, at this time, chaotic and untrustworthy. The latter I found out to my cost a few years later. This seemingly haphazard administrative detail astonished me because I knew that it was a Jesuit institution. I thought that the Jesuits were efficient almost to the point of being fanatical.

After I had been working with Dr. Lyons for a little more than a year I found that he was giving me a check every month for more than the share of the practice income that we had initially agreed upon. Instead of getting 10% he was giving me 15% of our gross income. As soon as I realized what was happening I discussed the matter with him. I told him that I had agreed to 10% for three years and this is what I expected. We had no written agreement because when I came originally and asked him if he wanted me to sign anything, he said certainly not. If our verbal agreement was not sufficient it would suggest that we did not have trust in each other, so the whole arrangement would not work. He explained to me that I was doing more work than he had expected and bringing in more money. I protested that I had made a verbal agreement with him but he insisted that he had to live with himself and that I deserved the increase. That was the way it remained until he sent me off on my own. No one could have been associated with a finer character, more unselfish and devoted. No wonder he was admired by his colleagues and loved by his patients.

When my three years were up I had to leave Dr .Lyons to start my own practice. Dr. Lyons insisted that if I stayed with him it would inhibit my developing a reputation of my own. I was not too happy about having to let go of my security blanket as I was worried about starting on my own with the associated expenses of establishing my own office .I found that there was a Gynecologist who had an office in the same building and he was willing for me to share his office with him. He had a very reputable practice and also worked with many of the same referring doctors that I had been associating with. It seemed like a heaven-sent opportunity and I moved in with him, sharing expenses. During this time I worked increasingly at Georgetown Hospital where I found myself largely responsible for the surgery of their pediatric service while still continuing with adult patients.

One day the professor of surgery asked me if I would be interested in joining the professional surgical staff of the University as a full-time member. At this time the Children's Hospital had no University connection and I saw an opportunity for enlarging my Pediatric practice and perhaps joining the Children's Hospital to the University. I also liked the idea of being able to teach and having a secure income, though it might be smaller than I could achieve on my own. I agreed to accept the professor's offer. He introduced me at a party as a new member of the surgical team. I decided to take a short break before joining up. I resigned my office arrangements and booked to visit England. Two days before I was due to leave with my family, I was going round the department of surgery at Georgetown and noticed that they were doing some building and redecorating there. I asked if they were building an office where I could work. I was told that they knew nothing about that and did not know that I was to join them. I rang up the Dean and asked him what was going on. He said that he had heard nothing about an appointment for me and the professor had not made any mention of it to him. This was a horrendous shock as I had made all my plans based on what I had been told by the professor. I found myself leaving for an overseas vacation with no office to return to. A hurried phone call to the gynecologist I had been sharing with confirmed that I could continue with him when I got back, until I could make more permanent plans. This experience with Georgetown added to my distrust with the administration. I have found that my experience was not unique. One of my Harvard classmates, who was a very well qualified pathologist and bacteriologist, was interviewed for the position of head of the department of Pathology. At the end of the interview he was asked not to take any other job until he heard from them. He is still waiting to hear some thirty years later! They lost other good candidates for important teaching positions because they failed to support them adequately. It is a great pity as the school attracts many excellent students and could have been much better than it was. Since that time much has changed for the better.

As I think back on the things that motivated me to make some of the decisions that have influenced my career, I realize that a few of them were more subconscious than carefully thought out. One of these was the attempt to join the University as a full-time employee on a salary rather than a freelance practitioner. The idea of being my own master and planning my own activities was very appealing, but I hated having to send bills to my patients. Up to the time when I applied to work for the surgical service at the University, I had been exposed to two different practice environments. I had worked under the National Health Service in England and I had worked with Dr. Lyons in Washington. Under the NHS I had been paid as a resident and the cost of the medical care that I participated in did not impact on me in any way. At that time the Government had a very 'hands-off' attitude towards how the medical profession practiced its art. The chiefs, Consultants, who were my bosses, were also paid a salary and the individual services they performed did not influence this. They were paid according to the time they devoted to the service. They did not have to devote all their time to the service and were allowed to take care of patients outside the Service if patients wished to contract individually with them. This they did on a fee-for-service basis. I was not involved with this activity except in a very peripheral way. When I started working with Dr. Lyons in Washington everything was on a fee-for-service basis. Dr. Lyons billed his own patients and I had to bill those who came to me. Since Dr. Lyons had only two charges, one for minor surgery and one for major surgery, and did not hesitate to operate without fee on any patient that he thought could not afford a fee, I thought that this was a very wonderful way to practice. Because of his background as a surgeon, his reputation and his obvious devotion to all his patients, his practice was very busy. His income, though not excessive, was very adequate for all his needs. When I first joined him I was at a total loss to know what to charge the patients that came to me. As a resident in England I had been very busy and had been performing a large number of operations, many of them major. I figured that if I performed the same number here and was being paid at Dr. Lyons' minimal rate I would be making over $1000 a day! I did not realize how impossible it would be to achieve anything like that volume of work in the free-for-all cut-throat environment that I had entered. My idea that I should charge what I thought my services were worth was influenced by what the referring physician thought that I ought to charge. This was brought home to me very clearly on one occasion quite early in my practice. I was called to the Emergency room at the hospital at the request of a referring physician. I found a patient who had caught his hand in a circular saw. It was quite badly damaged so it took me couple of hours to put it all together again. Fortunately it healed very well and the patient had good function with his hand. After it had healed, the patient came to the office to pay his bill. He told me that he did not understand why my bill was so much smaller than the fee that his physician had sent him for referring him to me. I had a very satisfied patient but a very disgruntled referring physician. I never got another patient from that physician. Though the patient was very happy, it did my practice relatively little good. One cannot live on self-satisfaction no matter how good it feels especially if no more patients are referred to you.

This brings up the whole question of 'fee-for-service'. The practice of medicine is unique in this respect. In some professions it is relatively easy to assess what a service is worth but it is much harder to put a monetary value on health. What is the saving of a persons' life worth? If a doctor renders such a service what should he charge? If he relieves suffering, does it have a measurable monetary value? If he prevents severe disfigurement what is that worth? Of course it depends on the patients' situation.

An almost invisible scar is worth far more to someone in the entertainment industry than to a manual worker, though the amount of work required to achieve the best possible result is the same. Any reputable doctor will do his best to achieve the best possible result for every one of his patients regardless of what he may be paid. Should he play the 'Robin Hood' game and charge the wealthy patient a great deal more than an impecunious one? This was the practice that was prevalent when I first came to this country but things have changed since health insurance has become so wide-spread. Now it does not seem to matter what a doctor charges a patient because the patient only pays a fixed percentage above the standard fee set by the insurance company. The insurance company pays according to a fixed scale depending on the exact service rendered. Amazing as it may seem, this set fee is not really set at all. It depends on many little details of the service such as whether an injection was given or an X-ray ordered and interpreted. Because of this microscopic breakdown of the service rendered, a great deal of paper-work is required. Now courses are given to doctors advising them how to describe their service so as to get the most money from the companies. If they were paid a specific fee for treating say a patient with pneumonia or appendicitis, it would save the doctor time and the insurance company considerable amounts in administrative costs. Maybe the doctors would be overpaid for some services but they would also be underpaid for others. In the long run it would even out.

In my considered opinion the Fee for Service concept is the single most important factor that is responsible for all that is wrong with the delivery of medical services in this country.

When I started out there were many fewer of these regulations to contend with. If I wished to reduce a patients' bill, I could do so. If their insurance paid a percentage of my bill I could forgive the patient the remaining percentage if I chose. Now if the patient has Medicare or Medicaid coverage which pays about 80% of the fee that they think is fair, it is a criminal offense to write off the 20% that is not paid. With all these restrictions and regulations it is no wonder that the patient-doctor relationship has suffered.

There was another factor that influenced my considering a full-time university appointment and that was the security of an income with a pension after retiring. When one has a paid job with retirement benefits it is not so necessary to put by enough money to live on when one can no longer continue practicing. It is interesting to note that an increasing number of doctors are joining HMOs (Health Maintenance Organization) or other forms of group practices where they are salaried. Now some of these doctors are beginning to flee these salaried environments as they have found that the atmosphere in which they have to practice is inimical to the practice of first-class medicine. The organizations running these practices are more interested in making money than practicing good medicine. They tend to try to run these group practices as businesses. They try to get as many patents seen as possible as quickly as possible with scant regard for the standard of medical practice. No time is allowed for empathy as this does not have a monetary value. I did not get a university appointment and continued in private practice. This gave me the ability to treat my patients to the best of my ability without interference and without regard to whether they could pay for my services. It may not have been financially beneficial in the long run but it allowed me to have the satisfaction of a clear conscience and the genuine affection of many of my patients.

Chapter 15

PRIVATE PRACTICE

After my disappointment at not becoming a full-time part of the faculty at Georgetown University, I had to determine how I was going to shape my career. To start with I continued my surgical practice on my own, sharing an office with a Gynecologist. He was a most pleasant person but had one serious problem. I found that he was a binge drinker. The majority of the time he was sober and an excellent gynecologist with a fine reputation and a very successful practice. Occasionally he would shut himself up for a day or two and drink. Ultimately this was the death of him. During this time I had retained my friendship with Dr. Harold Hawfield who had been my predecessor with Dr. Lyons. After he left Dr. Lyons he joined practice with a Dr. Crenshaw Briggs who was older than either of us. Dr. Briggs was an excellent and most conscientious surgeon. They worked happily together until Dr. Briggs became sick and had to retire. I discussed the situation with Harold who was obligated to pay Dr. Briggs as he took over his practice. We decided to join together and that I would share his responsibility for paying off Dr. Briggs. I moved into their office and shared everything with him. This allowed each of us to have a little time off. Otherwise we were either working or on call 24 hours a day, seven days a week. We shared our patients, each seeing the others as well as our own, except that I was responsible for most of the pediatric surgical cases. After a while we decided to take another surgeon in with us. He was a German who had fled to this country immediately after World War II and had post-graduate training here. Prior to leaving Germany he had graduated from medical school there and done some postgraduate work in gynecology. I found him a great addition as I admitted I had little training in gynecology. I was happy to turn over those cases to him whenever I could. Naturally all was not always smooth sailing as we were very different characters, an American, an Englishman and a German. The glue that held us together was the fact that each of us cared more about our patients than anything else. Each was always ready to help the other whenever we ran into any difficulties.

We were working primarily at the Washington Hospital Center. I must admit that they rather resented the fact that, when I had some patients at Georgetown and at Children's' Hospital, the other two had to make rounds there when I was unavailable. This led to my doing less and less work at Georgetown. We became senior surgeons at the Washington Hospital Center where Hawfield became President of the Medical Staff. Later I also was elected President. Until this time this position was honorary but it was becoming more time consuming. A small honorarium was voted. As the administrative duties increased, the hospital decided that they needed a full time medical administrator. Hawfield was offered the job and took it. I found that this was a great loss to our partnership as he was a very level headed person and a very calming influence when we had disagreements.

Sometime before Harold left our practice I was asked by a patient if I would consider operating on her under acupuncture! She required having her gallbladder removed. I had read a lot about acupuncture and had a respect for the ideas of hypnotism. We had a member of the anesthesia staff who had studied acupuncture and was very interested in trying it out on a patient undergoing major surgery. We discussed the situation with the patient and came to an agreement that we would try out the operation with acupuncture but if any of us saw that it was not working we would switch to general anesthesia at once. With these conditions established we proceeded and the anesthetist placed the acupuncture needles and I was told to proceed with the operation. With much trepidation I made a tentative abdominal skin incision. There was no response from the patient. I proceeded to make a definitive abdominal incision, again with no response from the patient. I opened the abdominal cavity. At this point I had to insert retractors to obtain a view of the abdominal contents and the gallbladder. As I started to do this the patient indicated that she was feeling pain so we instituted general anesthesia at once. As soon as I got a good view of the area of the liver and gallbladder I saw to my horror that the patient had a very large thin walled hemangioma occupying the left half of her liver. If the patient had sustained a severe blow to her upper abdomen at any time this hemangioma could easily have ruptured. This would have led to a lethal hemorrhage. It was obvious that this lesion had to be removed and this was a dangerous unanticipated complication. I was very glad that the patient was asleep. We organized some blood to be ready and I sent for my partner, Dr. Hawfield, to help me. Sure enough, as I started to remove the offending and life threatening lesion we got into some severe bleeding. With the help of my partner, we managed to get the bleeding under control and the lesion out of the liver and then the gallbladder removed. Fortunately the patient made an uneventful recovery. It is hard to explain what a surgeon goes through when such an unexpected complication occurs in what is expected to be a straight forward and somewhat routine operation. The patient's life is at risk. To do nothing leaves the patient at risk for a future lethal accident while to attempt a dangerous operative procedure is not without risk. Such an experience is both mentally and physically exhausting.

While we were working together as a threesome I had my first, and I am glad to say only, experience with a malpractice suit. It is worth recording as it illustrates some of the unexpected hazards of medical practice. Hospitals require doctors to carry adequate malpractice insurance before they can become members of the staff and admit patients. Such insurance is also necessary as protection from the devastation of a major adverse monetary decision which could wipe out all one's assets. While we felt that the premiums were exorbitant and took an unwarranted bite out of our income, we accepted its necessity. Because we were proud of our standard of practice we never thought that we would need it. Our naiveté did not take into consideration the vagaries of the legal tort system. My experience gave me a bitter lesson about this and brought home the necessity of having such insurance.

It all started, as far as I was concerned, when I was the duty surgeon responsible for 'Staff' cases. These were cases who were admitted without having a private doctor of their own. One day I was called in consultation to see a patient who was under the Gynecology service. This patient had been seen in the gynecology clinic, having been referred there by her own family physician. It was determined that she needed a hysterectomy and she was admitted to have this done. The operation was performed by a resident in training under the supervision of Gynecologist A. Postoperatively the wound broke down and the patient had to be taken back to the operating room to have the wound repaired. This was done under the supervision of Gynecologist B as Gynecologist A was not available. It was a difficult operation as the patient had become very much distended. In doing this repair a piece of small bowel was caught in the wound. The patient developed intestinal obstruction and the bowel which had been caught in the wound broke down. This formed a fistula between the bowel and the skin through which the intestinal contents emptied. It was at this point that I was called in and asked to take over the case. I found a very sick patient becoming dehydrated and malnourished. With the help of my two colleagues we re-hydrated her and fed her intravenously. Once we had improved her general condition we set about trying to discover why she was in the condition that we found. Usually a small fistula from the intestine to the skin will close down of its own accord unless there is an obstruction in the bowel beyond the site of the fistula. With the aid of the X-ray department we demonstrated that there was indeed an obstruction beyond the site of the fistula. Obviously further surgery was necessary to deal with this problem before the fistula could be closed. She was taken back to the operating room and I worked with the senior surgical resident to put things right. We found the obstruction where the bowel had kinked at the site where the uterus had been removed. We resected both the site of the obstruction and the site of the fistula and repaired the continuity of the bowel. Postoperatively the patient did very well except for a minor wound infection. The resident felt that she should remain in hospital until this infection in the wound resolved. I disagreed as the infection was minor and the patient had been hospitalized for a considerable period of time. I felt that getting home would be most beneficial for her. I had her discharged to be followed up in my office as I felt a personal sense of responsibility for her full recovery. I saw her in my office and easily drained the small infection in her wound and discharged her. I assumed that she would return to her family doctor for any other problems though I assured her that I would be happy to see her if she thought that there was anything more I could do for her. The three of us were rather pleased with ourselves for having saved her life. About a couple of years later I was devastated to receive a summons from a malpractice lawyer on behalf of this patient. He was accusing me, my resident, Gynecologist B and the hospital of malpractice and demanding 2.5 million dollars. I found out that we three doctors, Gynecologist B, my resident and I were the ones accused as we were the only ones whose names the lawyer had time to read from the hospital charts before the statute of limitations ran out. My resident was panic-stricken and, after he had given a deposition about the case, went to the lawyer offering to give expert witness against me. Although he had already been 'deposed' he was deposed again in his new capacity. I obtained copies of both depositions which revealed some startling alterations between the two sworn depositions that he had given. I was being advised by a lawyer supplied by my insurance company. I had to go to be deposed by the plaintiff's lawyer. I was not very happy and was somewhat scared as that lawyer had the reputation of being the smartest malpractice lawyer in town, though not necessarily the most scrupulous one. He asked me why I thought the patient had gotten into the trouble that I found her in. I replied that I was a defendant and not an expert witness and that it would be improper for me to answer that question. He said; "Surely you must have read the chart of the patient when you took over the case." I agreed that I had done so but that the chart was really all 'hear say' as it contained opinion rather than proven facts. When he asked what I meant, I suggested that we look at the chart when I was in charge of the patient. We turned to a page which referred to the time between the second and third operation that the patient had been subjected to. Written there was a note that said; "Patient doing well" signed by a resident. Immediately underneath was; "I totally disagree with you. Go back and reexamine the patient." and my signature. I pointed out that one statement was the resident's opinion and the other mine. Without further evidence neither could be considered facts. After that exchange, the rest of the deposition went very easily. I was rather proud that I had scored a point against such an astute lawyer. The next thing I heard was that this lawyer had offered to settle the case for $12,000. The lawyer who had been assigned to me by the insurance company wanted to settle the case out of court. I would be responsible for $3,000, the Gynecologist $3,000 and the hospital the other $6,000. I was very reluctant to settle as I thought that all I had done was save the patient's life. However my lawyer explained to me that it would cost the insurance company more than $3,000 to defend me in court even if we won! Furthermore the case would be heard in the District of Columbia. He had found that the juries in the District Courts were unpredictable. Ultimately I agreed to go along with this settlement provided my insurance company wrote me a letter that stated that, in their opinion, I was not involved in any malpractice. This they did. It was a very traumatic experience for me. I was surprised that I would not even have my expenses paid if I won acquittal let alone any compensation for lost time and derogation of my surgical and professional reputation. The plaintiff's lawyer pursued the case even though he must have realized that it was unjustified or he would not have advised his client to offer to settle for $12,000 rather than 2.5 million originally claimed. It is this type of unscrupulous lawyer that causes so many malpractice suits and is a major factor causing 'defensive medical practice'. The latter is a very real factor in the escalating cost of medical care. Since the lawyer had taken the case on a contingency basis, he took at least a third of the award without the risk of any monetary loss if the case had gone against him. So far as I was concerned it was an unpleasant but educational experience. Subsequently this same lawyer came to the hospital with a 'panel' to explain about malpractice and how to avoid it. He explained that he only took cases which he considered had real merit and was most scrupulous in collecting evidence. I was tempted to ask him if allowing a witness to forswear his sworn deposition was included in his definition of scrupulosity. However I sat back and bit my tongue.

During all this time I remained wedded to the idea that Washington required a real pediatric surgical service. When I first arrived quite a few of the local general surgeons were on the staff of Children's Hospital and they took turns being responsible for patients who came in without a pre-allocated surgeon. None of these surgeons had any specific pediatric surgical training. I found that several of the pediatricians were very happy to find someone knowledgeable to whom they could refer their patients. Fortunately most of these were excellent pediatricians with very busy practices. This helped my practice though not my rapport with some of the other general surgeons. I was determined to try to improve the general standard of pediatric surgery and thought that this could not be done unless the hospital appointed a full-time surgeon to run the service. I got myself appointed to the medical board of the hospital where I could voice my ideas but realized that this was not the only or the best approach. I was lucky enough to become friends socially with some of the members of the lay board. I lobbied them mercilessly. They had a great influence as they were responsible for raising the money that the hospital always needed. Some of the pediatricians who referred patients to me were also social friends of members of the lay board and they were sympathetic. This approach paid off and the hospital was persuaded to appoint a full-time pediatric surgeon. I would have liked the job and even went so far as to approach Dr. Hufnagel, the cardiac and thoracic surgeon at Georgetown, to ask if he would take over being responsible for that aspect if I got the job. Dr. Hufnagel, besides being a charming gentleman, had an international reputation, having been the first person to replace an aortic valve in a human heart. I realized that I was not very likely to get the job at Children's as I had been out of the academic pediatric surgical circles for some time. I had become a surgical Fellow of the American Academy of Pediatrics and was a founding member of the British Association of Pediatric Surgeons but I was not associated with the Boston group centered at their Children's hospital. This was where Pediatric Surgery started in this country and it maintained leadership in the field for some time.

The board at Children's' Hospital made a great effort to find the best candidate to become the full-time surgeon. They chose Dr. Randolph who had recently finished his training in Boston with Dr. Gross, at that time the leading pediatric surgeon in America. I wrote to him to explain how much he was needed here and expressed my encouragement for him to take the job. This he did. He had a rather rough time to start with as the local surgeons resented the fact that he thought that all cases not referred to a specific surgeon should be part of the service which he would run. He would take these cases and operate on them when necessary. This deprived the local surgeons of a small but real source of income. Some felt that his attitude implied that they were not competent to take care of all these cases. However he was supported by the board and I appreciated the fact that he was raising the standards of practice. He persuaded the board to appoint a senior resident as a pediatric surgical trainee. Gradually he built up a pediatric surgical training program which was recognized as one of the best in the country. To do this he had to exclude the general surgeons and I was one of the very few who remained. I happened to be both a general and a pediatric surgeon with two and a half years training as the latter.

During the next few years Children's Hospital engaged more and more full-time physicians, both as general pediatricians and in a number of specialties. It associated itself with George Washington University, a move which gave it academic standing. Thus it changed from being a local hospital devoted to children where local doctors could admit their patients, to being a true specialist teaching hospital and research center. When local pediatricians sent patients for admission they were taken over by the full-time staff. The communication between the referring pediatrician and the hospital staff was not always of the best. I found that a patient from one of the pediatricians who had been in the habit of referring his surgical patients to me was being operated on by one of the full-time staff. Since this pediatrician was a personal friend of mine, I asked him about the case. He was surprised as he did not know that the child was being operated upon. He had referred a problem case to the hospital where it was being taken care of by the full-time pediatricians on the hospital staff. They decided that the patient required surgery and called in the full-time pediatric surgeons; all this without informing the referring pediatrician of the patients progress or of their plans. I came to realize that my practice was doomed as I would get fewer and fewer cases if the private pediatricians were being bypassed in this way. Fortunately I still had my adult practice which I shared with my partners. By this time Dr. Randolph had enlarged his staff with several more full-time surgeons, one of whom was an exceptionally brilliant young lady. She was outstanding in several respects, technically very deft, very caring of her patients and an excellent teacher. When Dr. Randolph resigned, she applied for his position but, for reasons which I do not understand, she was not appointed. The surgeon appointed instead only lasted for a year before he had to be replaced. The lady in question was not prepared to work as second fiddle to a less experienced 'boss'. When she was offered the post as chief of the Pediatric Surgical service in Los Angeles Children's' Hospital she took this appointment. There she has became nationally well known because she ran an outstanding clinical and teaching service. George Washington University and Washington Children's' Hospital made a very serious mistake in not making her their chief of pediatric surgery.

As Pediatric Surgery became an increasingly recognized specialty, a group was formed called the American Pediatric Surgical Association. I applied to become a member but was turned down because I did adult surgery as well. In fact when the American College of Surgeons instituted an examination for special competency in pediatric surgery I was refused admission for the test the first year. I was allowed to take it the second year and passed it. I was still not eligible for membership in American Pediatric Surgical Association. One episode I found particularly galling was when one of Dr .Randolph's graduated trainees decided that he would like to become a member of the British Association of Pediatric Surgeons. He asked me, since I was a founding member, if I would sponsor him. This I did.

Chapter 16

LIVING IN WASHINGTON

During our first few years in Washington we continued to live in the first house which we found with the help of my mother-in-law. It was very convenient since it was on a main road with easy access to the hospitals and my office. It backed onto the road and faced a semicircular drive. This drive just went round three houses of which ours was the middle. Across this drive was quite a large open space where we could allow our children to play. The nanny we had brought over with us from England did not work out and we had to let her return to her home. Since it was quite impossible for Agnes to take care of two active children and a four storey house, we had to find help for her. By great good fortune we heard of some State Department people who had returned from Panama with a cook but had then been posted abroad again. They did not wish to take this person with them and she did not wish to return to Panama. We made the necessary contact and she came to work with us. She stated that she was afraid of dogs. However within a very few days she became, not only tolerant of our Tweedle, but very fond of him. She proved to be a wonderful addition to our family. She was a superb cook and our children came to love her.

Our front lawn, which was facing the drive, had a marked drop off to where there was an entrance to our garage. One day I decided that it would be much better if I built a wall around this bit so that we could level the lawn. I dug a shallow ditch and filled it with concrete, getting it ready to build the wall the next Saturday. I got everything prepared and mixed up a mess of cement. After I started to lay the bricks a neighbor came up to ask if I would like him to help. I readily agreed and we were going great guns when my telephone rang. I was wanted for an emergency at Children's' Hospital. I had to stop work and go. Rather than waste the cement, my helpful neighbor offered to continue until I could return. When I got back he was just laying the last brick. This was the start of a wonderful friendship, cemented, as it were, with hot buttered rum and good food! Colonel Batte was an Army officer and his wife, Elenita, was a very attractive lady who became great friends with Agnes. This couple became very attached to Tweedle and was happy to take care of him if we went away. Tweedle always knew what he wanted and just how to get it. When he wished to visit the Battes he would sit outside their fence and woof gently until he was let in. He used the same trick with our neighbors, the Millers, on the other side. They were lobbyists for Texas and had to attend numerous cocktail parties. They did not drink at these parties but ate a steak which they grilled outside before they went. It was not long before Tweedle understood what they were doing. He would sit on our side of the fence and when he thought that they were through eating he would woof gently to let them know he was ready to clear up their bones. They too became quite fond of him. Other than the fact that he was a terrible flea bag and he adored rolling in the foulest smelling dirt he could find, he was a wonderful dog. Talking of fleas, we went away for several days one summer taking Tweedle with us. When I went down to the basement on our return I was astonished that a cloud of dust arose every time I put a foot down. Suddenly I realized that it was not dust but fleas that I was stirring up. We had to have the area fumigated but we realized that Tweedle had been busily absorbing them when he was present.

We found that there was a real problem with the drive in the semicircle in front of our house. It sloped down to a central point outside the middle of our house. When we had a heavy rain it filled up with water forming quite a pond which took a long time to disperse. One day, after such a rain, we looked out of the window to see a couple of ducks happily swimming there. Not only did the rain form the pond but it also flooded our basement which was at ground level on one side. We had furnished this basement as a recreation room. In it we had a couple of Persian rugs which my father had acquired when he was stationed in Baghdad in the 1920's. These got well soaked one day. They proceeded to emit a remarkable and undesirable odor. It seemed to confirm the story that I had heard about antique Persian rugs. They were woven in remote villages and brought out over the mountains on camels. Camels, I was told, will not urinate on hard ground so the drivers put the carpets under their feet so that they could relieve themselves. Not only did this habit enhance the colors in the carpets but it left the potential for a characteristic odor when wet. Our experience seemed to verify this somewhat apocryphal story.

In trying to solve the problem of this occasional flooding we discovered that there was a drain which was supposed to allow the water to enter a sewer system. This was not working. After a lot of investigation and some digging we found that there was a large tree trunk which had been allowed to block this drain, probably before the houses were built. Once we had managed to get this obstruction removed we had no more flooding.

One day we found Tweedle dead in our garden. We never found out exactly what happened but wondered if he had eaten some poison. Our children were devastated and we decided that we must get another dog. The children wanted a dog that could run. Tweedle, with his short legs, was less satisfactory for them. By this time I had become quite interested in hunting and I thought that I could combine their interest with having a longer-legged dog with my interests by acquiring a Labrador retriever. We found an advertisement for some puppies and went to look at them. The lady who owned them bred them as show dogs. She recommended a little bitch. We took her advice and this led to another and totally unexpected turn in my life.

It was obvious from the first that this was a very intelligent dog, very active and full of potential. I got a book on how to train retrievers. In it, it explained some of the commands that one should teach such a dog. Among these was the advice that it was necessary to use commands that sound very different, so that the dog can easily distinguish them. One such command that was recommended was Charge when we wanted the dog to lie down. We dutifully tried to teach this to Sheba, the name we had chosen. This led to a near disaster. One day when Sheba was a few months old, the door bell rang. Agnes went to the door and Sheba joined her. Agnes told Sheba to sit while she opened the door. Sheba was much too excited to obey and Agnes in desperation shouted 'Charge' at her as she opened the door. Sheba obeyed, but the delivery man dropped his package in terror and was last seen in a cloud of dust disappearing into the distance.

For our vacations in the summer we often went up to Agnes's family summer lodge in North Wisconsin. At that time the family did not welcome dogs so we had to leave Sheba. A friend recommended that we leave her with a retriever trainer, Jay Sweezey, on the Eastern Shore on the other side of the Chesapeake Bay. There we deposited her while we went away. On our return I went with the children to pick her up. The trainer was upset that we were going to take her back. He said that she was one of the best dogs that he had tried to train. I told him that she was the children's pet and we wanted her back. He wanted to give us a demonstration of how good she was and invited us out onto a pier so that he could show us what she would do. He said that she had never retrieved a live bird before but we could watch her first attempt. He tossed a duck into the water. The duck had its wings and legs tied so that it could not fly or swim very fast. Sheba sat by the trainer, all of a quiver, until the trainer said Fetch. She immediately launched herself off the pier and swam to the duck which she picked up in her mouth. Not being able to climb up onto the pier she swam with the duck to the shore. When she got there the duck swung its head around and pecked her. She dropped the duck, looked at it, and picked it up by the tail. She then proceeded to bring it back to the trainer and deliver it to him. The trainer was so convulsed with laughter that he nearly fell into the water. I was amazed at the dog's ingenuity. Nevertheless we took Sheba home with us, but I determined to try to continue her retrieving training. This I did by getting up early and by using any spare time I had, to teach her to take hand signals. One way to do this was to use a baseball diamond. By placing a number of 'bumpers' (canvass bags filled with kapok normally used as fenders for small boats) on first, second and third bases, making Sheba sit on the pitchers' mound and standing myself on home base, I tried to get her to retrieve a bumper from the base that I pointed to. It takes a bit of patience but she was very anxious to please. It was obvious that she was a natural, determined and enthusiastic retriever. The next summer we were to go to Wisconsin again so I asked Sweezey, the trainer that she had been with the summer before, to take her again. He said that he could not do this as he was taking some of his other dogs around the country to run them in field trials. After some discussion he said that he would consider taking Sheba with him but did not think she would work for him. I took her down to him and we decided to try her out. We went into a field and he called Sheba who went to him and sat beside him. He then released a pigeon which I shot. Sheba waited for his command and then immediately retrieved the bird and brought it back to him. He agreed to take her with him and we agreed that he could run her in a field trial. When I asked where he was going, he said that the first trial was an International trial in Duluth. It would occur while we were in Wisconsin and would be only 40 miles from where we would be.

In these trials they have a special class for what they call Derby dogs. These are dogs under two years old. Sheba was about 18 months old at this time and so would qualify. We decided to go to watch this trial and to see what our dog could do in a real competition. The trial was supposed to start at 8 am but we were a little late. When we found our trainer we asked what had happened. He told us that Sheba had been called back. We discovered that they run a series of tests and any dog that does well is called back for the next test. We watched the next tests and Sheba kept doing well and kept being called back. Late in the afternoon she was still being called back, so I asked one of the officials how long this would go on. He said that the judges could not decide the winner between two dogs and that Sheba was one of them. She finished up in second place much to my pride as I had done most of the training. This was the first of many happy experiences with this dog. In spite of being an excellent hunting dog both in the field and over water she was a delightful pet at home. She was by no means perfect but she was a constant source of pleasure and adventure.

One day I was to go duck hunting with Colonel Batte, the erstwhile neighbor who had helped me with building the wall. He had been made commander of an Army station on the shore of the Chesapeake Bay. He was going with some fellow hunters on this station. These hunters had never had a dog with them before and were somewhat skeptical about my bringing Sheba with us. We went out before dawn to set some decoys in front of the blind that we were going to use. We got into the boat with the decoys and Sheba. When we got just off the blind, the others started to toss the decoys into the water. As soon as the first decoy hit the water Sheba was over the side to retrieve it. I spoke somewhat sharply to her and tried to avoid the dirty looks that the others were giving me. Fortunately Sheba understood her mistake and did not repeat it. After that we had some quite good hunting and Sheba behaved. In the middle of the day we shot a duck which dropped into the water beyond our decoys. The others said that they would retrieve it in the boat later. I said that, if they would let me,

I would get Sheba to retrieve it for them right away. They acquiesced so I sent Sheba. She swam through the decoys without bothering them and then started to look around. She seemed a little lost but looked back to me. I gave her a hand signal to go back further. She immediately turned and went further out where she could see the duck. In no time she had it and brought it back to us. My companions were converted to the usefulness of a well-trained dog and her initial goof was forgiven.

That dog had a remarkable memory. I had trained her to look for hidden objects as part of my trying to teach her to take hand signals. Sometimes I would drop an object and walk on for a considerable distance. Then I would tell her to go fetch. She always knew where to go to fetch what I had left. One day I was hunting by myself on a friend's farm. In the morning I flushed a quail and shot it. I was sure that I had hit it but it dropped into a hedge row. Sheba was with me and she went to look for it but could not find it. I went on and as I was returning late in the day I went through the same field. Sheba disappeared into the hedge row where we thought the original bird had dropped. After a few minutes she emerged with the bird in her mouth and delivered it to me. Somehow she had remembered all day where that bird should have been.

After I had left Dr. Lyons and was practicing on my own I acquired a secretary, Mrs. B. What she lacked in expertise in some aspects she more than made up in devotion and loyalty. She had some trouble with dictation as I used words and phrases to which she was unaccustomed. One time, when I was going on holiday, I asked her to send some 'Billets Doux' to patients who owed me money. I received a letter from her to say that she had sent 'Bill is Due' notices and had some success!

Mrs. B. knew about my interest in hunting and told me that she had a nephew who had a farm in Pennsylvania just over the Maryland border. He loved to hunt so we were introduced. He and I became very good friends and spent many happy days together, both on his farm and in duck blinds on the Chesapeake Bay. Being an inveterate pipe smoker I nearly caused a major disaster one day. We were sitting quietly in a duck blind which was well hidden with brush in front of us. Nothing much was happening so I decided to smoke my pipe. This blind was right on the water and was partly flooded when the tide was in. We had our guns and the ammunition on the seat to keep them dry. It was a 'blue bird' day, clear, sunny and not too cold. As I started to light my pipe there was a slight breeze; just enough to waft some of the camouflaging dry brush onto my burning lighter. Instantly there was a magnificent blaze. We grabbed guns, ammunition and our lunch as we fled the blind. Being situated partly in the water it was possible to scoop enough water onto the fire to put it out before too much damage was done. My hunting companions were surprisingly kind to me, even going so far as to say that they thought that we had too much brush on the blind, making it difficult to see what was going on. It is most important to hunt with real gentlemen!

Shortly after we arrived in Washington to live, my father-in-law arranged for us to be elected to the Chevy Chase Country Club which was close in to the city but had beautiful grounds and many other amenities including a very satisfactory golf course. I decided that I had better learn to play golf. This I did with moderate success but great enjoyment. It was also an asset to developing my surgical practice as I met both referring doctors and patients there.

In the meantime Agnes had developed an interest in antiques and used to attend many of the auction sales. Her background in the history of art which she had acquired at college was a great help. In this way we accumulated quite a few beautiful pieces which we have enjoyed over the years. I tried to interest her in becoming a docent at one of the art museums but she was too shy to do this. It was a pity because she had the ability to be a great teacher. Great teachers are those with enthusiastic love of their subjects; an enthusiasm which they are able to impart to their hearers.

I was only able to take about two weeks vacation a year after I left Dr. Lyons. This was partly because of my responsibility to my current patients and partly because I was afraid that I would be forgotten by my referring doctors if I was not readily available. Most summers we were able to go to the family lodge on the Brule River in north Wisconsin. We would go there with our family and join the rest of our immediate family. After a couple of weeks I would fly back to Washington and the others would join me at the end of the month. In order to get there we had to fly, changing planes either in Minneapolis or Chicago, Then take another plane on to Duluth which was the nearest airport to the Brule. On one occasion we were flying, en famille, i.e. Agnes, two daughters, a nanny and myself, via Chicago. I had been very careful to arrange that we would have plenty of time to change planes at O'Hare airport in Chicago as we were to be met in Duluth by my father-in-law who would drive us the 40 miles to the lodge. To make this connection we decided to fly from Baltimore. When we got to Baltimore we found that the plane was being delayed for an hour. This meant that we would have trouble making the connection in Chicago. When we did get to Chicago we found that we had less than 20 minutes to catch the plane to Duluth. It was due to depart from the other end of O'Hare airport. It was quite a problem for Agnes to walk that far swiftly. However we made it just in time and we were the last people to climb the ramp to the plane which was sitting on the tarmac. I got on with the children and Agnes was the last of the party. She asked if they had transferred our baggage. This was essential to us as we could not arrive at the lodge without the baggage which my father-in-law was to pick up with us in Duluth. This was why I had taken the trouble to arrange for us to have plenty of time to catch our connecting flight. She was assured that they had not had time to transfer our bags. When Agnes got half-way up the loading steps to the plane she sat down and announced firmly that she was not moving until they put our bags on the plane. Since the steps were attached to the plane it could not be moved until Agnes was off it! They did not dare move a 'handicapped' person forcibly. A number of men with walkie-talkies were seen dashing around and after about five minutes a truck was seen driving up with our bags on it. After this Agnes climbed on to the plane to join us. My daughter, Catherine, was mortified by her mother's behavior though it was most effective. But that was not quite the end of the story. I had flown back early but Agnes and the girls were flying back at the end of the month. As their plane was about to land in Chicago, Agnes was paged. They had a car waiting to drive the family and their luggage to their connecting plane for Washington. We had not arranged for this but I figured they wanted to get that awful woman out of the way as smoothly as possible.

The family lodge on the Brule River was a very satisfactory place for us as there was something there for all the family. The children had other children who were staying at other lodges on the river to play with. Agnes loved the river and was very competent in a canoe, even poling sitting down. I enjoyed the river, fishing and canoeing. We shared the lodge with my in-laws so there never were any dull moments. Jim, my brother-in-law, became a good friend as we seemed to enjoy the same things. He taught me a lot about fly fishing and we often went out together. My father-in-law seemed pleased that I had become interested in fly fishing so he, very generously, gave me a beautiful Orvis split bamboo fishing rod. One experience I especially enjoyed was night fishing. The large brown trout tend to feed at night. We would go up river in the evening, have supper at a camp ground and then set out down river at dark, hopefully when there was little or no moonlight.

On one occasion we decided to explore the upper reaches of the river. Jim knew that we could put the canoe in well up the river near its source at a place called The Chimneys. He had been given a relatively light canoe so we decided to put in there and try to come down stream. We drove up to the chimneys and set out towards the river, carrying the canoe, our fishing gear and food. We did not realize that it was over half a mile to the river and much of it was bog. By the time we got to the river we were exhausted. The river was very narrow as it ran between alder bushes. It was also blocked by beaver dams over which we had to work the canoe. The fishing was non-existent although the water was crystal clear. We did not see any signs of trout and, if we had, casting would have been impossible. It was an interesting adventure but exhausting.

Fishing was not our only activity. We did a lot of work around the lodge; rebuilding part of the dock, repairing and refinishing some of the furniture and mending the screens on the porch where necessary. We liked to have a drink before lunch but we made a rule that we could not have one unless we had done something useful during the morning.

There was a small lake near the entrance from the main road to the various lodges. It was owned by a classmate of mine from medical school. As my father-in-law had stocked it with trout some time before, I got permission to fish it. Since it was set in bog we had to fish from a canoe. Jim and I would go there very early in the morning to catch a few tasty small trout for breakfast. I also went there occasionally with Agnes during the afternoon as it was a pretty spot and sometimes teeming with goldfinches. Furthermore the fishing was challenging and Agnes, who was an excellent guide, enjoyed the peace and watching the birds.

For other vacations I took time off to make a couple of trips to the Caribbean Islands. The first time I went was to take Agnes to convalesce after a nasty bout of pneumonia. We went to Jamaica. We flew via Miami where we had to change planes. When we arrived at the Jamaican airport there was no sign of Agnes's luggage. After a long delay we were informed that it had gone on to another island and it would be a couple of days before it could be retrieved. While we were waiting for this news they supplied us with Rum and Coconut Water to drink. This did ease the wait considerably. Then we had to go to the local shops to get the necessary supplies for Agnes which included suitable clothes for the beach and toilet accessories. After we returned home the Pan Am. Airline refunded us for all our extra expenses! The vacation did us both a lot of good and Agnes came home completely restored.

Our second trip was entirely different. A classmate of mine, Ed Wallace, suggested that we might like to join him, his wife and another couple, to charter a sailing boat and sail around some of the Lesser Antilles Islands. They were to go in January. We agreed to join them in New York and fly via Martinique to St. Lucia Though Ed was an accomplished sailor, he knew that sailing in these waters was treacherous and we all agreed that we should charter a boat with captain and crew. We subsequently came to appreciate the wisdom of this decision. The boat we chartered was a 65ft steel schooner which had been built in Europe and sailed across the Atlantic. It was manned by the Captain, Jan; the cook, Jan from Sweden; and Jan, from South Africa. The fact that they were all Jan was confusing but we sorted it all out. After we got to Martinique we had to transfer to a local plane to get to St .Lucia. It was, indeed, a local plane as it was filled with locals. It was beginning to get dark when we arrived and we had to find the dock where our boat was tied up. Either our directions were not too good or the taxi driver was not too bright, so it took us some time to find the right place. It was dark when we got there and we were not exactly warmly welcomed by the skipper. The first thing he said was that we could not come aboard with our shoes on! We took them off and were shown to our sleeping accommodation. After that we were given a drink and a very adequate dinner. We had hoped to set sail right away but the skipper said that he was not going to take the boat out that night. We resigned ourselves to spend the first night tied up at the dock. It was a miserable night as it was very hot and stuffy below the deck but we got through it, wondering if the rest of the trip was going to continue in this way. Next morning it seemed to take forever to get going. We had said that we wanted to put in at a small harbor called Cumberland Bay. The skipper admitted that he had never been there but was game to try. Cumberland Bay was further than we had estimated and we had made a rather late start. It was quite dark when we got to where we thought the bay should be. We were sailing along the west side of a black and ominous cliff with no lights visible anywhere. Then Janny P, the crew man, said that the entrance was exactly opposite the tree which we could see, outlined against the night sky. He must have been there before and was obviously a most experienced sailor. We headed towards the cliff, having put out a stern anchor in case we had to kedge off. We sailed right into the cliff without hitting anything until Janny P. said that he thought that we were there. He told the skipper to hold the boat and he would swim over to see if he could find something to which to make fast the bow line. This he did and returned to say all was well. Then we all relaxed with a drink before dinner. It was pitch black and we had no idea where we were. We all had an excellent sleep that night as it was cool enough and the air was wonderful. When we awoke the next morning we could hardly believe our eyes. We were in a tiny bay surrounded by cliffs with only just about enough room to swing the boat around. There was no sign of habitation and our bow was tied up to a palm tree. Running down into the middle of the bay was clear stream. We decided to take a swim before breakfast and dove over the side. As we entered the water it was pleasantly warm but as we came up we went through where the stream was coming in and it was icy cold. While we were having breakfast a couple of local inhabitants came up to us in a rowing boat offering some limes. Where they came from we could not imagine but we bought the limes. They were tiny but full of sweet juice and we decided we had made a very good buy. From then on the trip became a truly magnificent and memorable holiday. We anchored in often virtually uninhabited places, where we could snorkel off unspoiled reefs. We had fun teaching Agnes to snorkel which we did in some very shallow water. She found that it is impossible to giggle when snorkeling, but she soon became quite accomplished at it and thoroughly enjoyed watching the under-water life. The skipper was surprised to find that we really wanted to sail and not just sit around and drink. Apparently his previous charterers' were far less willing to help with the actual sailing. During the course of the trip it was clear that we had made a wise decision to have a professional skipper and crew as it was not easy to avoid hidden reefs in waters so poorly charted. We finished up sailing down the west coast of Granada with an offshore breeze wafting the intoxicating aroma of spices. We had become good friends with the skipper and crew and kept in touch. I found that the skipper subsequently sold the boat to a relative of the chairman of the Dept. of Dermatology where I was working. The latter made some alterations to it and then sold it. The last we heard was that the new owners had been arrested and the boat confiscated by the Coast Guard for running drugs from South America. We were all very sad about the subsequent unsavory history of a boat which had given us so much pleasure.

A few years after we had become members of Chevy Chase club, the board decided to build an outdoor skating rink. This was a great place to get some winter exercise and my previous skating experience at Cambridge provided me with a background. This rink was used enthusiastically by the young sons of members to play hockey. But time was also set aside for the adults. I helped form a group which decided to try to learn to dance on skates. None of us became very proficient but we had a lot of fun. There were two skating clubs in town, an ice dance club and a figure skating club. We decided to invite them to a dance party. I was acting as a sort of host for the club. I had noticed that one of our guests was a very attractive lady who was obviously an excellent skater. As they started to play a fox-trot I noticed that she was going out without a partner. Since I had some knowledge of the dance, though no expertise, I asked her if she would like to dance. In slightly broken English she said that she would. As we took the first preliminary steps I realized that I was totally outclassed. However she was so good that I performed better than I had ever done. She had me in the right place for every step and turn. I never enjoyed a dance as much. When I got back to the club house I asked our professional who the lady was. He informed me that she was Czechoslovakian and had just defected from their Olympic dance team! No wonder I found her such an excellent partner. At other times I found a very enthusiastic lady who was always ready to try something new. She did not seem to mind too much when we got skates caught and came crashing down. As a matter of fact, though ice is very hard, falls on it rarely do much harm as one tends to slide because it is so slippery. The faster one was going the less the damage, usually!

There was one other memorable activity which occurred every Sunday afternoon when I first arrived in Washington. It was a Volley Ball game played in the Glovers' garden. Mr. Glover had been a partner with my father-in-law and owned a considerable area of land not far from where Massachusetts Avenue crosses into Maryland. The game had been going on for many years amongst the Glovers' friends. Agnes and I with our girls were invited to join in. They were pickup games and those playing varied from Sunday to Sunday. Some of the players were quite eminent persons, including on occasions, a Supreme Court Justice, 'Whizzer' White, an ex-ambassador to Ireland, Bill Taft (a relative of the late president Taft) and several prominent members of the government. When the Glovers sold their property where we used to play, this Sunday game folded. It was like the end of an era as all the players were either getting old, had died or moved away. The property where we played, after being sold, became a housing development.

Over the years I watched the development of Washington DC and its suburbs. The house which my father-in-law built 'out in the country' and where Agnes grew up was sold. When she was a child she could look west in the evening and see nothing but one light from a farm house a couple of miles away. Now it is completely built up as far as the eye can see. Her father sold the house just before we came to live in this country. He had about12 acres in the western part of the District of Columbia. Over the last 50 years that property has been sold several times. The last time it was sold to the Japanese as a residency for their ambassador. They paid about 50 times the amount that my father-in-law sold it for in the late 1940's. This illustrates the incredible increase in the value of property in the north west of the District of Columbia and its neighboring suburbs.

After we had been living in that first house in Washington for several years it became apparent that a four storey house was not a long-term solution for Agnes. Going up and down stairs was becoming more of a strain for her and would obviously become even more so as time went on. We decided to look for a house where stairs would not be a limiting factor. After various plans such as buying a plot and building, we found a house that seemed ideal. It was in Maryland but so close to the District of Columbia line that the back garden actually abutted onto the dividing line. It was also less than a block away from a main road into the center of town. It was very convenient for me to drive both to my office and to the hospitals. We built a master bedroom suite out into the garden from the back of the house and, over the next few years, rebuilt the kitchen. The garden had been well planted and maintained by the previous owners and Agnes had a great time not only maintaining it but improving it.

Our Home in Washington with Agnes rose garden

She added a rose garden which was very successful and we tried to preserve the variety of azaleas and camellias that were already there. This garden gave Agnes a great deal of interest and pleasure. When our younger daughter was married we put up a tent in the garden for the wedding reception and it had live roses growing in the midst of it. We lived in this house for almost thirty years. Over the last few years there, Agnes' health gradually deteriorated and she had more difficulty getting around. She never would give in but the effort she made was heart-rending. Fortunately I was able to get some help looking after her and was able to keep her at home until she died peacefully one night. She had been a wonderful wife and we had a great life together. I loved her very much and continue to remember all we went through from our transatlantic courtship, my post-graduate training, our life in England to our emigration to the USA and all that ensued from that move. Her unstinted love made me a better person and a better doctor.

Chapter 17

RETIREMENT FROM PRACTICE

When I retired from practice, I felt a personal disappointment that my ambition to become a recognized pediatric surgeon had come to naught but I do feel that I made a significant contribution to the establishment of pediatric surgery in Washington. However I find retirement leaves a lot to be desired. I miss the contact with patients though some of them occasionally call me to ask for advice or recommendations to those still practicing. When I run into some of my old patients socially they remember me and seem pleased to see me. One, upon whom I had performed major reparative surgery for congenital malformations, has called to express gratitude. This is a great sense of satisfaction. It is surprising how few bother to write a note of thanks. Patients seldom realize that a note expressing gratitude can mean much more than any monetary payment.

After Agnes died I married Jocelyn. I had known her for many years. I met her when I was called to take care of a sweet little boy with a lump on his leg. Unfortunately this turned out to be rhabdomyosarcoma which metastasized and led to his death in spite of all that I could do. This was shortly after I started practice in Washington and I was not too busy. I was able to make house calls to help care for the little fellow until he died at her home. I became very fond of him and he trusted me. I felt very badly that I could not cure him. It was a terrible blow to Jocelyn but she never blamed me. After he died her marriage broke up in divorce and then her ex-husband died. She remained a friend and was always happy to help me whenever she could. As Agnes started to fail she was a real help to me in looking after her. She was, and is, a very brilliant lady both intellectually and practically. She has all the managerial skills which I lack. After Agnes died I realized that I was in love with her and she agreed to marry me.

We sold my house in Washington and bought a house in Northern Virginia with five acres and a horse barn. She was always interested in horses since she was a little girl and now had an opportunity to rescue some. We acquired a couple of Premarin foals which were the by-product of Wyeth's method of producing the female hormone drug called Premarin. We have two delightful horses that came running whenever she whistled for them. As the foals grew up, our home in Fairfax, Virginia proved to have too little pasture to keep the horses properly. We have been fortunate enough to acquire a farm in Culpeper, Virginia of some 70 acres which is mostly pasture land. We moved our horses to the farm and now have 7 Premarin horses of our own on the farm. We are able, weather permitting, to raise hay on the unfenced portion of the farm. We have sold our house in Fairfax County, Virginia and built a home for ourselves on the farm.

Since I have retired, I have had the chance to live in the country which I have always enjoyed. We are trying to make this a working farm where we can take care of horses and I am starting to understand some of the problems and uncertainties of farming. I have been fortunate in finding that Jocelyn, my second wife has been a pillar of strength. She has interested me in helping her take care of animals. She has been a supporter of a movement to rescue 'Premarin foals'. These are the by-products of the production of the drug Premarin which is a female hormone used to ease the stress of menopause. Mares are bred so that their pregnant urine can be collected to make the hormone. The result of this breeding is a large number of foals (estimated at more than 40,000). They are sent to auction and most go to the meat market. Having acquired a couple of these foals five years ago when we lived in Fairfax, Virginia, we found them delightful loving animals and have become enthusiastic about trying to rescue more. We work with Christina and Steve Follansbee, our friends in Pennsylvania, to find people who will commit to rescuing and taking home the foals that we bring from a Premarin farm in North Dakota. Christina has been able to establish a working agreement with this farmer who works with us to help him find homes for these foals to keep them from going to slaughter. The farmer pays attention to his breading program to produce a quality foal so they will be desirable and not go to slaughter.

I suppose I was always interested in farming and animals so it has become more than a hobby, it is a new life style and a great source of satisfaction.

Chapter 18

CONCLUSIONS

Now that I am retired from active clinical practice, it is interesting to consider some of the changes in the practice of medicine that have occurred over the last 50 or so years since I started to work in the field. The most significant is in the ability of the medical profession to diagnose and effectively treat so many more of the ills that affect mankind. The knowledge of the physiology and the pathology of the human being have grown exponentially. This has led to the increased knowledge of the causes of some diseases and expanded the ability to prevent them and to lessen their effects even when they cannot be cured. These developments have meant that it is not possible for any doctor to know all that is necessary to treat all the problems that may present themselves. As a result the general practitioner often has to call on many ancillary services to make the correct diagnosis and to treat a patient. The professional laboratory has to study the blood and the urine as these substances have been shown to have many components that have a significant influence on the diagnosis and progress of a disease. It is no longer enough to count the blood cells and sniff the urine as I did sometimes when I started out. The use of radiology with its computerization of images and of ultrasound imaging is often necessary. New scopes have been developed, which are flexible and have advanced optical ability. This has led to the development of new specialties and modified the practice of others. There is a learning curve associated with each of these new abilities and the determination of their wise, cost effective, use. As a result the practice of the family or general practitioner has been altered by increasing the necessity for the use of so many specialists. This has had two significant side effects. There has been a serious increase in the cost, both of the diagnosis and treatment of disease. The other is the apparent diminution of the importance of the general practitioner, even though someone needs to guide the patient in deciding how and when all these new innovations should be used to the best advantage. This can only be the patient's own personal physician. Without such input the patient navigates helplessly in uncharted waters. The importance of the personal physician cannot be overemphasized though for a time it tended to be disregarded now there is a move to try to rectify this deficiency.

There seems to have been a change in the attitude of physicians themselves which cannot be attributed solely to the influence of technical advances. Though these may have made the relationship between the physician and the patient more remote and increased costs, they do not account for all that has altered.

Another big change has been a financial one, peripheral to the actual cost of the medical care itself. There have been many factors that have affected this and they are worth discussing. First and foremost is the influence of the third-party payer. Fifty years ago the patient was responsible for paying the doctor and, if he could not pay, the doctor could forgo his fee. Many patients decided to negotiate with insurance companies to help cover these costs, both hospital and medical. Some help was given to the indigent by private or government agencies, but many of the needy were extended charity by the profession. There was a real sense of satisfaction in successfully treating a patient without thought of financial compensation. Now almost all patients are covered by some kind of third-party payer. In fact there is an increasing outcry about the fact that this kind of financial coverage is not universal and has become so expensive that many cannot afford it. The cost of medical services has increased to the point that it is a serious burden for any organization that assumes the responsibility. Since the introduction of Medicare and Medicaid the government has played a big part in covering and setting the fees that may be charged. However Medicare and Medicaid only cover older citizens and some of the poor and disabled. There are several other organizations that cover those not eligible for these plans. They consist of insurance companies, HMOs (Health Maintenance Organizations) and some doctor groups. Each of these has their own sets of coverage's and rules as to where patients can go to obtain the benefits they offer. It is up to the individual patient to choose which plan, if any, to join. Some plans are paid for or subsidized by employers. In this case the patient is tied to the plan selected by the employer. Because of the rising costs of medical care, the premiums for all these plans are continually rising. Consequently employers are becoming more and more reluctant to include this expense as a benefit of employment. The cost of subsidizing the medical care of their employees is a significant burden on industry and increases the cost of their goods and services.

Because the Government, through Medicare, has set allowable fees, other payers have used these figures as guide lines. It is important to reiterate that it is illegal to charge a Medicare patient more than the set fee of which the doctor is only paid 80%. The patient is responsible for the other 20%, an amount that it is illegal for the doctor to waive!

All these payments are based on a fee-for-service figure. This means that someone has to decide exactly what service has been provided to the patient. Since payment is based upon the exact nature of the service rendered, it has become a matter of some importance to define this. As a result it is profitable for the physician to divide each service into as many parts as can be justified legitimately. Courses are now available that explain to physicians the most profitable way to do this. Each service has to be coded so as to facilitate the payer in fixing the correct payment. Unfortunately the number of codes and their modifiers has not only multiplied astronomically but are being changed continuously. Responsibility for accurately coding the service rendered has been allocated to the physician and a criminal penalty for erroneous coding attached. This whole system has two undesirable results. It increases the temptation to pad the services rendered so as to increase the payment and it vastly increases the book work in the doctors' office. It also clarifies the absurdity of the Fee-for-Service concept when applied across the board to the health industry.

The multiplicity of payers is a factor increasing the doctor's work. It is time consuming to sort out which of the many payment systems apply to any specific patient. Furthermore, some of these systems restrict to whom a patient may be referred for consultation or to which laboratory specimens may be sent for analysis. This means that neither the patient nor the doctor has free choice. In fact the doctor may have to consult someone who is not his first choice. Not only does the payer dictate who may be consulted but when and where. An admission to hospital has to be cleared with the third party unless it is an emergency. Once it has been cleared it is cleared only for a specific number of days. To extend this time the doctor has to appeal for an extension. These judgments are made, in the first place, not by doctors but by nurses or other assistants employed by the companies responsible for the payments. There is an appeal process in place but this requires more wasted time by the doctor. Furthermore if the appeal is denied, the patient is required to pay for any extra stay. If the doctor decides to discharge the patient who cannot pay the requested extended stay and the patient gets into trouble, it is the doctor's fault. He can be sued but the company which has denied his extra stay cannot. All these things greatly increase the time and work of the physician and his office staff and thus his overhead expenses. It also tends to diminish his self-respect since he feels that his judgment is being second-guessed by someone who has never seen the patient. All these are things over which the doctor has no control increase the cost of running a practice, while his potential remuneration is limited by fiat. It does not enhance the atmosphere of the practice of medicine nor the basic satisfaction of the physician whose responsibility is undermined.

An aspect of the cost of medical care which is seldom considered is that of the overheads of the third-party-payers. This applies not only to the private parties who undertake this insurance but to the Government plans as well. Each of these entities has voluminous staffs that have to be controlled by administrators. These latter are very well paid, often considerably more than the physicians who deliver the care to the patients. The multiplicity of plans leads to excessive administrative costs which it is impossible to justify on a rational basis.

A problem which inflicts a burden on the physician and causes much stress and unhappiness is the fear of a malpractice suit. We have come to live in an extremely litigious time. The number of cases is increasing and the size of the awards, meted out by the juries, has become astronomical. Wherever there is an untoward happening it seems to justify compensation. Since the doctors carry malpractice insurance the awards are borne by the insurance companies. Because they fear losing increasing amounts of money, they have been increasing the premiums which they demand. These premiums are predicated on the doctor's type of practice and the area in which he works. Some types of practice seem to be more prone than others to results that can produce more malpractice suits. This is particularly true of obstetrics and to a lesser extent to orthopedics. Some of the malpractice premiums have become so high that doctors have modified their practices or retired. In some areas of the country there has become a severe shortage of obstetricians because any abnormal baby is a potential malpractice case for an unscrupulous lawyer. This rise in the number of malpractice cases has been enhanced by the readiness of the legal profession to file suits. Since the lawyers take cases on a contingency basis they have nothing to lose but a little of their time, yet if the case is won they can make a substantial profit. One has to remember that when a jury awards damages to a plaintiff, the lawyer takes at least 30% of the award and sometimes more. If the doctor wins the case he is unable to get compensation for his loss of time, reputation and the expenses of his defense. The result of this inequitable system is that doctors have to have extensive malpractice insurance. Because the awards are determined by the juries hearing the cases, there is no uniformity to them and some of them are outrageously excessive. Often the juries, because they think that the insurance companies are paying, are very generous to the plaintiff, failing to realize how much of the award will go to the lawyers. There is no compensation given to the defendant should he win.

There are three things that could modify the cost of medical care: 1. Abolish fee for service. 2. Have a unified payer (not the Government). 3. Tort reform.

The Fee for Service concept has been a tradition in this country and is supported by the majority of the medical profession. Recently there has been movement among some of the younger practitioners to enroll in salaried work. Physicians have always had this option and many have chosen to work either in the armed services, HMOs which use salaried physicians or the Public Health Service. To expand these opportunities does not seem a very radical change. There are two cogent reasons why Fee for Service, when considered logically, should be abolished. The first is that it is impossible to put a real monetary value on a medical service. The second is that it has had an adverse effect on the way some physicians practice.

The multiplicity of schemes for paying the providers of medical care makes no sense. Each of the providers has overheads. If there was only one payer the overheads connected with this activity would be much less. There are two other advantages. The insurance would be less arbitrary and more certain. As it is now, each of the many schemes has its own rules and is able to exclude those applicants who it deems to be poor health risks. Some of these insurers have been unable to meet the obligations which they have undertaken. This has left their patients and health-care providers with no resource. No one can be paid if there is no money. If there is one plan with a Government guarantee, this unfortunate situation would not be present. This does not mean that the Government has to run the plan any more than it runs banks when it guarantees deposits up to a certain amount. On the other hand the Government could provide a limited service with a salaried staff using the Public Health Service as a foundation. Physicians such as those in the armed services and the public health service are paid on a salaried basis. Their rather lower compensation is balanced, to an extent, by the fact that they retire with a pension. This means that they do not have to put aside a portion of their income to cover their old age.

Part of the physicians' demand for large incomes is because so many are in debt when they qualify. The cost of a medical education has risen so much that only those with substantial resources can qualify without borrowing. If a salaried scheme as outlined above were to be introduced, medical education should be subsidized on the condition that a specific term of service is required. This is currently done by the armed services.

The implementation of the plan to have a universal payer raises some very difficult ethical problems. Such a scheme means that everyone should be covered for all their health needs. This country does not have the resources to do this at this time. It has neither the money, physical equipment nor the personnel to provide everyone with all the health benefits that the medical profession has acquired the knowledge to prescribe. Some of the newer techniques, for example those now available in the field of transplantation, are very expensive and require a lot of personnel. Not only are they expensive at the time of transplantation but the expenses are likely to continue for years. The medications required to lessen the chance, or to prevent rejection, of the transplant in many cases run into thousands of dollars a year. There are many other examples of expensive treatments that the country would be hard-pressed to provide universally. Some form of rationing would be necessary, at least initially. Rationing is an ugly word especially when applied to health care but it occurs now in a totally uncontrolled way. The ultimate health care is not now available to all citizens. It is, de facto, rationed both by the individual's ability to pay and by the geographical resources of different areas. The only way such a universal coverage could be introduced is if it is started in a limited way. That is to say that the coverage would include only certain defined benefits. It would be a good beginning and the extent of the benefits could be extended as circumstances permitted. Individuals who wished to extend their coverage would be able to do so with private payments. This is no different from what is currently happening, except that there would be a bottom line of basic care for all our citizens. The major problem is that of deciding what should or could be included in that bottom line. It raises some ethical questions which everyone is reluctant to face. Should life be prolonged in all circumstances? Is prolonging life and prolonging suffering without hope for ultimate relief a moral choice? Who should decide when this is the case? Too often, in our time, outside individuals try to interfere with decisions made by those most intimately concerned. A plethora of Ethics Committees has sprung up with the idea of helping the individuals concerned make these decisions. It is doubtful whether these committees really do a great deal of good. They can help those in charge of the cases by giving advice when the decision is controversial. These decisions were made in the past by the individual himself, his family and his family doctor. The lack of a family doctor has been a factor in the development of all these problems. If the universal basic coverage that I have advocated were to be introduced it would require the use of a family physician before it could work well. Unfortunately the medical profession is not geared to accept radical change.

The third problem which needs to be addressed is that of Malpractice. It is accepted by all except the Trial Lawyers that the current system is unsatisfactory. Tort reform has been discussed in Congress but the Trial Lawyers have such a powerful and wealthy lobby that it does not get very far. Malpractice must be more realistically defined. The idea that the pursuit of doctors through the legal system will lessen the errors that are reputed to be so prevalent in health-care is actually counterproductive. It inhibits the medical profession from cleaning its own house. If the exposure of an honest mistake through ignorance may lead to a malpractice suit, fellow physicians are reluctant to give evidence or to discipline the erring fellow physician. This is particularly true when the awards in such suits are unpredictably severe. It is certainly true that medical societies and licensing boards are lax in adequately disciplining the bad apples in the profession but the litigious atmosphere does not encourage them to do more.

If the judges who hear malpractice cases used stricter criteria they could throw out many of them. When cases do come to trial, it should be incumbent on the judges to award the costs of the case to the loser. Since most, if not all, of the plaintiffs' lawyers take these cases on a contingency basis they, in effect, make themselves part of the case. If they win they get paid, if they lose they get nothing. The award, if given, is shared by the litigant and the lawyer. If the costs of the case were to be awarded to the defendant and the plaintiff had to pay, his lawyer should be required to pay part of the cost levied by the judge. It is inequitable that a defendant who wins a case should not be compensated for the expenses that he has incurred defending himself.

Looking back over the years that I have been associated with the practice of medicine it is very disappointing that the increase in knowledge has not been coupled with a similar increase in the equitable distribution of patient care. It seems as if physicians' dedication to their patients has diminished. When I think back to my original mentors, first those I worked for in England and then with Dr. Lyons my partner in Washington, I see so few with the dedication that they exemplified. They worked without regard for themselves, solely for the benefit of their patients. They instilled into those who worked with them a standard of personal integrity which represented the highest standards of medical practice. Perhaps I was lucky in those I was associated with. My own partners, when I was in practice, had a similar outlook. Our practice was patient oriented, not money oriented. Current rules and regulations and the litigious atmosphere have made doctors more self-protective. They have been driven to become more money oriented by the increasing costs of practice and the limitations set on their incomes. Many who entered the profession with the highest ideals have seen these eroded. Though the increase in technical ability to treat the sick has been remarkable, this has not been reflected in an equivalent increase in the personal commitment in the well being of the patient as a whole person. The necessity of specialization has made medical practice more impersonal. The public tends to see doctors as incompetent, uncaring money-grabbers. Few are, in fact, incompetent and their apparent money grabbing results from defending themselves from unjustified interference, both financial and legal. One of the most significant aspects of patient care and the treatment of the sick is that of empathy. It is almost a lost art.

The influences affecting the medical profession over the last 50 years seem to have turned what was once a noble calling into an unfeeling business.